MW01141987

VISIBLE MAN

Visible Man

The Life of Henry Dumas

JEFFREY B. LEAK

THE UNIVERSITY OF GEORGIA PRESS
ATHENS AND LONDON

© 2014 by the University of Georgia Press
Athens, Georgia 30602
www.ugapress.org
All rights reserved
Set in Dante MT Std by Graphic Composition, Inc.
Printed and bound by Thomson-Shore
The paper in this book meets the guidelines for
permanence and durability of the Committee on
Production Guidelines for Book Longevity of the
Council on Library Resources.

Printed in the United States of America
18 17 16 15 14 C 5 4 3 2 1

Library of Congress Cataloging-in-Publication Data

Leak, Jeffrey B., 1968–
    Visible man : the life of Henry Dumas / Jeffrey B. Leak.
        pages cm
    Includes bibliographical references and index.
    ISBN 978-0-8203-2870-6 (hardcover : alk. paper) —
    ISBN 0-8203-2870-7 (hardcover : alk. paper)
    1. Dumas, Henry, 1934–1968. 2. Authors, American—20th century—
Biography. 3. African American authors—Biography. I. Title.
    PS3554.U43Z75 2014
    813'.54—dc23
    [B]

                                                                    2013023480
British Library Cataloging-in-Publication Data available

SUBVENTION BY FIGURE FOUNDATION

IN HONOR OF RUDOLPH P. BYRD
1953–2011

Contents

Acknowledgments

The publication of a book, for the writer, is the ultimate affirmation, a time to reflect on the mysterious path that culminates in the rendering of thanks to family, friends, and colleagues. For me, this journey began with a conversation with someone who had already distinguished herself as a biographer. In that exchange, Valerie Boyd suggested that I write a biography of Henry Dumas, and I began a project that would resonate with me in ways that I, at the time, could have never imagined. So I thank you, Valerie, for planting the seed.

I soon contacted Dumas's widow, Loretta Dumas, and Eugene B. Redmond, his literary executor. As a result of the relationship established with them, I have had full access to Henry Dumas's materials. Simply put, this book could not have moved forward if they had not provided me the space and freedom to tell Henry Dumas's story. Loretta Dumas introduced me to the world of Rutgers University and New Brunswick, where Henry Dumas solidified his aspirations as a writer and where they began life as a family after his departure from the air force. Redmond introduced me to the world of East St. Louis, Dumas's final place of residence. Extending their graciousness further, Redmond and Loretta Dumas introduced me to Dumas family members in his birthplace, Sweet Home, Arkansas. Since Dumas's death in 1968, both his widow and friend have led the effort to publish his materials.

The other person without whom a significant portion of this book could not have been written is Lois Wright. Her private papers reveal aspects of Henry Dumas's life that will require many deep breaths. A sleuth herself, she has been both gracious and resourceful. Jay Wright, a close friend of Dumas, husband to Lois, and poet of inimitable vision, has been a steady source of integrity and encouragement.

In addition to Arkansas and New Jersey, I also traveled to New Hampshire and Vermont to view various Dumas materials and conduct interviews. On these occasions I was fortunate to stay with dear friends from graduate school, Mark and Meg Cronin. A special thanks to their daughter and son, Izzie and Byrne, for letting me "hang out" and shoot hoops.

As usual, I have relied on a number of scholars and editors for advice and critique. The anonymous readers for the press provided indispensable insights and questions that enriched this book in countless ways. Arnold Rampersad reminded me that, in the search for evidence, the biographer may have to endure a few unpleasantries and even rejections. My colleague in the History Department at UNC Charlotte, John David Smith, introduced me to Nancy Grayson, a model of patience and integrity, at the University of Georgia Press. Also at the press, Sydney Dupre managed the final phase of publication with effectiveness and assurance. Erika Stevens, formerly of UGA Press, provided critical vision and lucid suggestions apparent throughout the book. To Deborah Oliver and J. Naomi Linzer, thank you for guiding me across the finish line.

To Mark A. Sanders, I still strive to reach the bar that you and Rudolph set way out of reach. A special nod goes to Lawrence P. Jackson. In both your biography of Ralph Ellison and your study of African American writers from 1934 to 1968, you have influenced my understanding of black intellectual and creative activity.

To the reference librarians at UNC Charlotte and Special Collections staff at Rutgers University, thank you for answering every query and request with insight and enthusiasm. I also had an informal librarian in New York, my sister, Julie Leak, who assisted me in the search for public information. Also at UNC Charlotte, the College of Liberal Arts and Sciences, led by Dean Nancy Gutierrez, provided timely research support in both the early and latter stages of this project. As always, my colleagues in the Department of English—Sandra Govan (professor emerita), Malin Pereira, Mark I. West, Janaka B. Lewis, and Peter Blair, in particular—have supported my efforts to balance research and teaching.

During the final stages of completing this book, my mentor, colleague, and dear friend, Rudolph P. Byrd, who over the course of eleven years had been engaged in a resilient battle with a form of cancer called multiple myeloma, left this side of existence in October 2011. In only the way he could do, Rudolph confronted illness with immeasurable beauty and resolve under inconceivable pressure. A scholar of the first order, his intellectual achievement was matched by his endearing humanity. In friendship and scholarship, Professor, I salute you.

I am blessed with family and friends whom I consider to be both. My immediate kinfolk—the Leaks, Franklins, and Anthonys—demonstrate daily what it means to "have someone's back." To Reneé, Jaelyn, and Rylan, thanks for understanding the necessity of my trips to Arkansas, New Jersey, and New England. The best aspect of them was returning to you.

A special tribute to my wife, Reneé: You had your own mountain to climb. And that you did. We are all the better for it.

And finally, to the Creator and Sustainer of the Universe, I bow humbly, with gratitude.

VISIBLE MAN

Prologue

The story of Henry Dumas should start with his surname. The majority of times he Anglicized it (*Doo-muhs*), meaning the *s* was heard, not silent. On a few occasions, in the presence of his wife, he invoked the French form (*Dum-mah*). The question of how to pronounce his surname is a fitting introduction to Dumas's life. Before this book, the personal and literary story on Henry Dumas was like the frame of a house under construction; the outline was clear, but the house was incomplete. The biographical rooms were standard: early childhood years in Arkansas, move to Harlem at age ten, air force after high school, undergraduate course work at Rutgers University, brief period at Hiram College in Ohio, and last year of life in East St. Louis. But each room, each geographical and personal dimension of Dumas, has its own set of untold circumstances, representing his search for the perfect synthesis in personal, creative, and romantic life.

Until now, no one has interviewed people who knew Dumas in these various settings or questioned why his life followed the trajectory that it did and what that meant for his work and for him as a writer; equally important, no one has had access to the privately held Dumas papers or the correspondence between Dumas and Lois Wright (née Silber), from 1963 to 1967 his most significant romantic interest outside of his marriage. My access to these primary sources—enabled by his widow Loretta Dumas, Eugene B. Redmond (executor of the Dumas literary estate), and Lois Wright—has changed altogether what we know about the intriguing, troubled, and visionary life of Henry Dumas.

Thanks in large part to these resources, I have been able to assist in constructing Dumas's biographical house. I am reluctant, however, to call this biography a comprehensive study, as certain primary sources no longer exist. Most notably, Dumas's letters to his soon-to-be wife, Loretta Ponton, written during his time in the Arabian Peninsula in 1954, were destroyed in the 1960s. A source about the circumstances of the shooting that took Dumas's life— documents from the New York City Transit Police—was destroyed in a bureaucratic merger in the 1990s. Other letters are probably scattered across the country in old shoe boxes, hatboxes, file cabinets, or even under mattresses, their recipients long since having departed this world. In short, letters from an important literary voice of the 1960s could be in the possession of persons who know nothing of that voice's story. Someone may simply have taken a box that belonged to a deceased family member to avoid tossing it in the dumpster, unaware of its literary significance. Or worse, significant correspondence may have been destroyed or thrown out.

Nonetheless, the papers and people I gained access to in the course of writing this book enable me to tell a scarcely known story. Through these materials, we have the unprecedented opportunity to trace Dumas's personal, intellectual, and creative development. Letters to at least one publishing house and literary insider bear out his desire to publish his fiction and poetry. In correspondence with Lois Silber, he shared his hopes, fears, and disappointments as a writer, as a citizen, and as an individual who questioned some of his own choices. From these materials, Henry Dumas emerges as a man of wonder and contradiction, a man whose literary legacy finally took shape amid tragedy.

The story of Henry Lee Dumas is a two-part mystery. The first involves his unique yet relatively unknown place in African American literary history and, related to that, his unconventional path to publication. The second focuses on the perplexing and unresolved questions surrounding his death in May 1968. The remembrances and biographical sketches devoted to Dumas have concentrated on his impressive literary accomplishments and the unsettling and dangerous political and social conditions in the United States at the time of his death. He had traveled from his new home of East St. Louis to New York to serve as best man in the wedding of a friend. But for Dumas and those who loved him, May would join April 1968 as the cruelest months.

On May 23, days after the wedding, a white transit patrolman shot Dumas after attempting to intervene in an altercation between Dumas and at least one other person on a Harlem subway platform. Accounts vary about the number of people involved, but it appears that Dumas was involved in a conflict with one person, and given the way in which the conflict evidently escalated, other people who were there felt in peril. The circumstances of the shooting were unclear, and after the passage of nearly five decades, many questions cannot be answered. Just as compelling are questions about Dumas's life before the shooting. How, having participated, at least to an extent, in the fight for black freedom, had Dumas processed the assassination of Martin Luther King Jr. in early April? What were his views on desegregation and the prospects for racial reconciliation? Why had Dumas, a writer whose storytelling talent and imagination were fertilized in the South but who learned his craft in the North, relocated to the Midwest? With such demanding social and political concerns in his life, what kind of husband and father was he? What kind of friend?

Visible Man: The Life of Henry Dumas addresses these questions through the personal, literary, cultural, and social contexts that informed the development of this enigmatic figure in African American literature. Early on, Dumas was interested in stories, myths, and rituals, the cultural marrow of black life. He was steadfast in his belief, consistent with black writers and artists associated with the Black Arts Movement, that black people were not invisible. In the music, language, and emotions of his people, Dumas found the roots of cultural stability and the possibility of individual and collective transformation.

One reason Henry Dumas remains a riddle involves the posthumous publication of his work. He published a handful of spellbinding short stories and poems during his short life, but most of his creative work appeared only after his untimely death. This has contributed to Dumas's being romanticized as an African American literary figure, remembered as a Black Arts Movement devotee with Africa on his mind. Africa was, indeed, crucial to his literary consciousness. But equally significant was his strange journey to personal and creative realization.

In thinking about his life, we inevitably confront the issue of fate. Ralph Ellison, with whom Dumas would have a rather fraught history, mulled the maxim "geography is fate" in *Going to the Territory*. Is a man bound to the physical and psychological landscape of his early years? Ellison would argue emphatically to the contrary, asserting that the individual is endowed with the ability to embrace, refute, or select from both accordingly. Geography need not be fate, although it certainly contributes to a person's cultural genealogy. Paralleling Ellison's feelings about his childhood in the prairie land of Oklahoma, Dumas sought a creative balance between the rural, southern world that produced him and the larger cultural concerns of identity that transcended region.

To access this world, since Dumas didn't leave a journal or much other evidence of his thoughts and feelings, I pool information from Dumas's literary peers, their autobiographies, biographies about them, and literary and social histories to the periods and locales to show what Dumas was likely experiencing. This book situates Dumas in the formative locales of his development: Arkansas, where his cultural roots ran deep; and Harlem, where he would cross into manhood. We follow Dumas through the U.S. Air Force, where he developed intercultural understanding in places like Saudi Arabia; San Antonio, Texas; and Mexico; to Rutgers University, his place of intellectual engagement for seven years; and to IBM, where he would be reminded that he was anything but a company man. The final chapters chart Dumas's way through Hiram College in Ohio, a pivotal place in his post–New York life, and to Southern Illinois University, whose campus in East St. Louis would be Dumas's teaching and creative laboratory during the last year of his life. In these places, the personas of Henry Dumas emerged among a revolving cast of family, friends, acquaintances, and lovers, all of whom knew Dumas in a particular context but rarely in his multiple contexts.

For the first ten years of his life, Dumas was a child of the field, running and riding his way over the six-mile stretch of land that was Sweet Home, Arkansas. This tiny place, located seven miles south of Little Rock, is a constant point of reference in Dumas's body of published work. Three stories set in rural southern communities reminiscent of Sweet Home appeared in *Negro Digest* in his lifetime: "The Crossing" in November 1965, "Will the Circle Be Unbroken?" in November 1966, and "Rain God" in January 1968. Each tale delineates Dumas's connection to this backwoods place that had given birth to his imagination; each piece had been written in an era when many young African Americans were questioning the value of the black experience in the rural South. For Dumas, as for William Faulkner, Eudora Welty, Ernest J. Gaines, and Alice Walker, this region, including his poetic-sounding birthplace, served as cultural core, the mooring for adventures elsewhere.

In the South Dumas developed a modern understanding of women. His mother, Appliance Porter, was unmarried, and in her maternal role she was somewhat unconventional, working as a housekeeper in Little Rock during the week and wanting nothing to do with farm or rural life. On the other hand, Appliance Porter's younger sister, Adella Hale, would take on the daily, traditional role of caring for her nephew. Although it would exact much from her body, she preferred field work over the confinement of the house. She was a country girl and proud of it. Early on, these two women would provide divergent models of womanhood for young Henry.

When he arrived in Harlem in 1944 to live with extended family, Dumas brought his country ways—and more important, his country stories—to the city, blending the black rural and urban experience, as so many black migrants would do in the first third of the twentieth century.

In his adolescent years, Dumas proved to be a good student, and his family in New York adored him. By the time he graduated from the High School of Commerce in 1953, his goal was to parlay his ability to tell stories into the ability to write them, a major endeavor for someone nurtured on the spontaneous and evolving oral traditions of Africa and the black South. College would provide the backdrop for him to develop the skills to become a writer, but in the fall of 1953, while a student at the City College of New York, he experienced a crisis in confidence that, apparently, he divulged to no one at the time. As a result, he left college and joined the air force.

Stationed in the Arabian Peninsula for a year, Dumas would do two things that, to some, would have appeared paradoxical: he became an observer of the Islamic faith, and in the process he developed stronger, more conservative views about his own Christianity. Indeed, he would eventually school himself in other Protestant denominations and other religions. He returned to the States with a newfound sense of religious purpose and in 1955 wedded Loretta Ponton, a demure, brown-skinned Baptist beauty he had met just after registering for the air force in 1953. And for seven years they were quite compatible, while Dumas sublimated his writing ambitions to what he felt was his religious calling.

When Dumas left the air force and the relative stability of military life to return to college, it signaled changes that Dumas's wife and new family could not have anticipated. That change occurred during his first year back on campus. When he arrived at Rutgers in the fall of 1958, students and faculty thought this older black man was headed to seminary or at least to the pulpit.

But as Dumas interacted with the largely white literary crowd on campus, over the next year he transitioned from the Christian conservatism of his recent years and the generally traditional views of his family into the countercultural world then forming on white college campuses. He would develop a deep sense of black consciousness in later years, but his experiences with white students, in the classroom, in various social settings, and especially in his involvement with campus literary publications, was the precursor. His time at Rutgers, from 1958 to 1965, was complicated by financial and family difficulties, providing the context in which he came of age as a writer.

If women had framed a large portion of Dumas's childhood and adolescence, they would form the leitmotif for his adult years. Just as his mother and aunt represented opposite points on the female continuum, so too did Loretta Dumas and Lois Silber. His wife's background seemed to have guaranteed that she would be a dutiful, traditional wife. On the other hand, as a younger Jewish woman in the 1960s, Silber was more willing or able than Loretta Dumas to challenge tradition.

Dumas's struggle with these two women in his life would mirror his struggles with his writing. There was no easy route to success in writing or relationships. In these two relationships—and a few dalliances with other white women—Dumas had not only wife and lover but relationships in which he tried to make sense of his aspirations as a writer. He transposed his literary aspirations onto them, searching perhaps for a level of engagement that was not plausible. Far too often, there was a tension between Dumas's dreams and the larger realities of his life. Further complicating matters in the mid-1960s was Dumas's use of drugs and alcohol.

His classmates and friends, many of whom distinguished themselves as writers, included Alan Cheuse, Robert Pinsky, Jay Wright, Hale Chatfield, Clem Fiori, Earl Thomas, Lois Silber, Jake Bair, and Lennox Raphael. Among the faculty and writers he interacted with were William Wynkoop, Paul Fussell, Ralph Ellison, Maurice Kramer, William Sloane, and John Ciardi. He would also, during this period, informally interview Malcolm X; become a kind of intellectual apprentice to the avant-garde jazz musician Sun Ra; and build a rich friendship with the poet Jay Wright. The would-be preacher who enrolled at Rutgers in 1958 emerged a different person six years later at the end of 1965. His exposure to new personal and creative possibilities would prove a pivotal chapter in his development.

When Dumas left the East Coast in early 1967 for Hiram College in Ohio, he had changed just as much as the unfinished decade. His marriage was threadbare. He was estranged from Lois Silber. Alcohol and drugs were more than fleeting flights of indulgence. He had published poetry and fiction in a number of journals and literary magazines, although a book contract for his novel continued to elude him. After a semester at Hiram College—where he had developed a friendship with a student and future social scientist named Claude Steele—Dumas shifted again, landing in East St. Louis, Illinois. He had returned, demographically and culturally, to a mostly black world. Here he would consider the merits of cultural nationalism and the evolving Black Arts Movement, eschewing the white world for a black cultural home. But even as he spoke about giving up all things white, the walk was far more difficult than the talk. Even as he tried to remove himself from the white world, his complicated life resisted such a separation. In both his life and his writing, Dumas had to acknowledge the contradictions and nuances of the individual, the community, and the region.

East Boogie, as some of the locals call it, would leave its imprint on Dumas, especially in his poetry, but the final drama of his life unfolded in New York. He returned to the East Coast in May 1968. Harlem was, by then, a much different place than the relative haven of his youth, and Dumas was different, as well. The world he created and the world he found himself in were whirling about with unforgiving force. A white transit policeman, thrust into a roiling situation without backup, fired the fatal shots that ended Henry Dumas's life. The circumstances of his death were indeed tragic, but the preceding behaviors, activities, and creative and academic engagement years earlier provide the essential backdrop for understanding both Dumas's life and his death.

This biography seeks to make visible the life of a literary visionary whose work and life offer moments of imaginative brilliance and cultural insight. In the 1988 volume of *Black American Literature Forum* dedicated to the Dumas legacy and edited by Redmond, a cross section of artists, activists, and academics sound what Dumas would refer to as the "Afro horn." Toni Morrison maintains that in his thirty-three years Dumas "had completed work, the quality and quantity of which are almost never achieved in several lifetimes."[1] The poet Quincy Troupe identifies Dumas as poetic ancestor: "Primarily a poet—even in his fiction—Dumas's writing had a profound impact on my own poetry, nearly equaling the influence that Pablo Neruda, Aimé Césaire, and Jean-Joseph Rabearivelo wielded in shaping my own poetic sensibility."[2]

Lest we focus too much on what might have been, the scholar and biographer Arnold Rampersad correctly urges Dumas devotees to focus on Dumas's actual literary record. Both his fiction and poetry "command our attention by their high quality. In addition, there are aspects to his body of work that show conclusively that his talent, far from being a fleeting matter, was as deeply rooted as that of many writers who have become household names in literature."[3] James Baldwin and sociologist Joyce Ladner judged a literary contest in which Dumas's short story, "Thalia," an impressionist tale similar to "The

Lake," won first prize in 1976.[4] From both creative and scholarly standpoints, the power and presence of Dumas's work endures, despite the fact that he has yet to gain widespread renown.

Dumas's personal life was as compelling as his poetry and fiction, imbued with internal conflict and, at times, creative frustration. My approach to telling Dumas's story had to accommodate the facts that his life unfolded in unpredictable fashion and that his life is not fully documented. The interviewees who knew Dumas or were familiar with the period or one of the places he lived were therefore essential to this book. Given their long silence on the subject of Henry Dumas and his life, I am even more indebted to them for breaking their silence now. When possible, I verified personal accounts with additional research and fact checking.

The vagaries of memory aside, the other challenge was the lack of written evidence that Dumas engaged in much self-reflection on the page. There were times when I wanted to hear from Dumas in his own words. More times than not, for lack of a body of materials to sift through, I had to piece together the cultural and social backdrops of Dumas's life. In those moments, I surmise what Dumas would likely have been thinking or doing at that moment in his development.

Aside from his letters to Lois Silber, the ultimate documentation of Dumas's creative and personal preoccupations is his body of work; his fiction and poetry let us know what his concerns and preoccupations were. Whether in verse or narrative, Dumas is focused on how black people made it through the Middle Passage. What skills and sacrifices were required, and how can African Americans of the twentieth century and beyond forge or return to a cultural identity that predates bondage and Jim Crow? His creative legacy rests on these questions. Second, in his stories especially, the sense of place, the southern world from which his characters spring, is a template for understanding his childhood and adolescent years in Arkansas. The tales are not factual, but they provide metaphorical accuracy.

While the poet Countee Cullen had distinguished himself during his life and at a younger age than Dumas, their legacies are similar in this sense: at the time of their deaths there was a sense that their work was not finished. Cullen, seeking to write outside of what he deemed the narrow confines of race, had not regained the acclaim of his Renaissance period. Dumas struggled with personal obstacles and publishing setbacks more than anything else. Both writers, nonetheless, left a record of achievement and creative engagement worthy of note.

In Henry Dumas's life, we have a compelling story of possibilities and pitfalls. His life, by any standard, was full. His life as a writer was chronologically short but creatively deep. Until the end, Dumas was living out the creative challenge for black writers that Cullen so profoundly articulated in arguably his most famous couplet: "Yet Do I marvel at this curious thing: / To make a poet black, and bid him sing!"[5] This biography records Henry Dumas's attempt to do just that: to sing a new song in a key that was attuned to the recent and long-ago past, the psychological and cultural impact of that past, and the imaginative boldness to envision a viable future for generations yet unborn.

Up
From Msippi I grew.
(Bare walk and cane stalk
make a hungry belly talk)

> —HENRY DUMAS,
> from "Son of Msippi"

CHAPTER ONE

Arkansas Boyhood

On July 20, 1934, the mercury rose to ninety-eight degrees in
Sweet Home, Arkansas, as nineteen-year-old Appliance Porter
gave birth to her son Henry Lee Dumas. Typical of fathers in
that era, Big Henry (Henry Dumas Sr.) awaited word that his
child had been born. In the aftermath of the Depression, the
stifling heat of the southern day was an appropriate backdrop,
even an apt metaphor, for the birth of a child who would come
of age in the political and cultural heat of the 1960s.

Blacks in Arkansas were at an egregious disadvantage. In
1900, only 1 percent of the African American population in the
state was considered middle class, and of that group the majority would have lived in Little Rock.[1] But in the 1920s and well into
the Depression-era thirties, Little Rock—while clearly holding
some educational, economic, and cultural advantages for African Americans—reflected on a larger scale the struggles of
places like Sweet Home. By 1925, as historian Gene Vinzant
explains, Little Rock's population was close to 82,000, 24 percent of which was black. There were a few occupations—shoe-
makers, tailors, restaurant owners, and undertakers—in which
black business involvement was proportionate to the presence
of African Americans in the larger population, but generally
"blacks were shut out from the best jobs in the market."[2] They

were not represented proportionally in the business life of Arkansas. Whether in Little Rock or Sweet Home, economic segregation and a withered economy made times hard.

Complicating matters further, although blacks made up roughly a quarter of Little Rock's population, African Americans suffered disproportionate unemployment. They accounted for "54 percent of the unemployed," according to Arkansas historian Michael B. Dougan, and "blacks were over-represented on the rolls, but they were under-represented in benefits. A welfare payment for a white family was $12 a month; for blacks it was $6."[3] The black presence on relief rolls reflected the impossibility of creating a black middle class. Dating back to the northern troop withdrawal from the South after Reconstruction, economic opportunity for most blacks was a distant dream. Their daily life in Arkansas was characterized by negligible economic opportunities and the dangers of breeching known and unknown social conventions and practices.

The 1930 census provides the best picture of black progress and struggle in Sweet Home. Only one black lawyer and two salesmen were listed. "Farmer" was the most prevalent occupation, but others included "carpenter," "mechanic," "maid," and "teacher." With a population consisting primarily of laborers, thirty-eight black families nonetheless were paying home mortgages and nineteen were renters. On the white side of the ledger, the numbers were considerably lower. Seventeen households held mortgages, while thirteen rented.

Only a few households could afford a battery-operated radio in 1930. The lucky few who owned this revolutionary communications tool brought the world to their living room. They could hear President Roosevelt's fireside chats or listen to the latest gospel or blues tunes. Henry's maternal family, the Porters, with whom Henry and his mother and brother lived, owned a radio by the 1940s. Accordingly, their house was a gathering place for family and friends. Not until 1936, when the federal government formed the Rural Electrification Administration, did rural residents in Arkansas begin to have access to electricity. Indeed, it would be well into the 1940s before every residence in Sweet Home was connected to public power.

From 1900 to 1934, the racial demographics of Sweet Home did not change much, but local and national financial and natural disasters disproportionately harmed the state's black residents. The Mississippi flooded in 1927; the stock market crashed in 1929; and the clouds dried up in 1930. By August 1930, Little Rock had gone seventy-one consecutive days without rain, and this drought would continue well into the next year. The economic crisis was devastating. Even "white people bought one-way tickets to anywhere," Henry's aunt, Adella Hale, recalled with a note of irony.[4]

Those whites who were not buying tickets were loading up cars and trucks and heading West. There were simply too few jobs and too many people in Arkansas. Of the white population, notes historian James N. Gregory, "300–400,000 Oklahomans, Texans, Arkansans, and Missourians moved to California and settled there during the 1930s," accounting for "roughly ninety-five percent of those moving."[5] Moreover, with agricultural modernization—tractors doing what people used to do by hand—small Arkansas farm families were becoming more rare. Spurred by the decline of international commodity markets, many white residents in the cities and the countryside saw no choice but to leave. This out-migration was notable as contemporary observers "decided that they were witnessing something unprecedented in the history of white America: a large-scale refugee migration, a flight from privation of the sort America read about elsewhere but hoped never to see in their own land."[6]

This largely white westward migration—captured most poignantly in John Steinbeck's 1939 novel *The Grapes of Wrath* and in the documentary photography of Dorothea Lange—represented the departure of human capital. The drought in 1930 exacerbated matters, sounding the state's economic death knell. In Arkansas "falling cotton prices," according to Dougan, "precluded recovery. Only forty-two percent of the taxes assessed were paid in Arkansas in 1932. The sharecropper had an estimated family income, including the value of home gardens, of $284 by 1934."[7] Black sharecroppers could expect to earn less than that per year, and they also had to contend with increased competition from their out-of-work white counterparts. As the number of poor whites increased, blacks now faced more competition even for menial jobs. And seldom, if ever, were blacks the first recipients of state or federal relief funds. The invisible hand of Jim Crow doled out assistance to poor whites first.

"Remarkably," writes journalist Isabel Wilkerson about the black migration to the North and to the West, "it was the first mass act of independence by a people who were in bondage in this country for far longer than they have been free. . . . It was the first big step the nation's servant class ever took without asking."[8] This is perhaps the best way to explain African Americans' departure from the world they knew: they left because they could.

In the South, over 1.2 million people decided life elsewhere would be better or at least could be no worse. As historian Donald Holley explains the migration data on Arkansas, "the migrants were predominantly white, totaling one in five residents between 1940 and 1960; but black migration was proportionately heavier, consisting of as much as a third of the statewide black population in the 1940s and 1950s." In the 1940s, Arkansas "experienced the third largest population loss among all forty-eight states."[9] Unwittingly, southern states fixated on racial peonage had enabled one of the largest movements of people, talent, and resources to other parts of the country.

For those who lacked the resources to leave or simply chose to remain in the Ozark state, 1934 was one of the most difficult years of the decade. In 1933 the state had received federal relief to the tune of more than eight million dollars, a huge amount at the time, and Henry's birth year looked no better. Between 1929 and 1934, state money allotted to schools had declined by 40 percent, and only a few of Arkansas's teachers had set foot on a college campus or even completed four years of high school.

By any calculation, 1934 was a hardscrabble year for both blacks and whites. These tumultuous times left an impression on young Henry. His people toiled hard, but Henry saw an economic system that required lots of hard work and provided little reward. Money had always been scarce. For the Dumas and Porter families, it was more of the same, though worse. They were schooled in the art of surviving on what the earth yielded. Adella Hale put it this way: "You raised your vegetables and your meat. You got your water out [of] the well, cut your own wood, and you used a septic tank, not a sewage system."[10] The Porters were not well-to-do, but they were self-sufficient. Most of Henry's family remained in the state, but significant numbers of farm workers—black and white alike—fled. "The 1930 census showed 12,165 Arkansans in Chicago and 10,450 in Missouri," writes Dougan. Other Arkansans found work as "porters and servants in the resort of Hot Springs, and a select few in the railroad yards of the Rock Island Railroad and the Missouri Pacific railroad in Little Rock."[11] Some of Henry's people, on both maternal and paternal sides, fled to new territory, but most remained in the only place they had ever called home.

In the farming community of Sweet Home, located just off Arkansas Highway 365, black people worked as day laborers picking cotton, at dairies milking cows and delivering milk to surrounding towns, or underground in the bauxite mines. Most black women who worked outside the home were involved in domestic labor. Henry's mother, Appliance Porter, worked as a housekeeper for a hotel in Little Rock. As a child, Henry sometimes joined his aunts and uncles in the fields. He also played the usual games of childhood, including marbles and hide-and-go-seek. But if young Henry had a favorite activity, it was simply roving through nature. The world of insects, birds, fish, and trees fascinated him.

Henry's engagement with nature occurred within the confines of the black world of Sweet Home. The surrounding majority-white world of Pulaski County tempered the frolics of Henry and other black children. In that world, white power and Jim Crow stood strong. Appliance Porter acknowledged this reality but refused to bow to it.

Henry's mother was charismatic by nature and did not hew to current conventional ideas of family. Unmarried when she gave birth, she worked in Little Rock during the week and, given her druthers, often remained in the city rather than return to Sweet Home on weekends. Even when work was over, Appliance preferred city streets to country roads. Although she certainly would have been aware of the impact of racial discrimination on her life, she nonetheless exuded independence and optimism, traits that did not go unnoticed by her son.

Appliance and her younger sister, Adella, were George and Lynn "Minnie" Porter's only daughters.[12] Their brothers ranged in age from three to twenty-three, the youngest of whom suffered from a mental disability. Their parents had managed to buy their home, no small feat for a couple whose grandparents had been enslaved. When their father died in 1930, the Porter sisters, aged fourteen and nine, assumed a considerable amount of responsibility.

When the eight Porter siblings were growing up, there was no schooling for blacks in Sweet Home after ninth grade. The few families who could afford it sent their children to school in Little Rock, but for most of the black farming community of Sweet Home, including the Porter sisters and their brothers, paying for school was not an option. For the Porter children and most of their peers, life beyond grade school meant work, which most often involved demanding manual labor. Yet there were too few jobs for both black and white young people in rural Arkansas who wanted and needed work. The state was dangerously overpopulated. Arkansas rural economist William H. Metzler delineated this dilemma in basic terms of arable land available to farming families for growing crops: "In 1935," the year after Henry's birth, "there was an average of only 24 acres in crops to support each farm family in the state. Contrast this with the average of 48 acres in crops for each family in the United States."[13] Arkansas farm families had access to only half of the arable land resources available to farmers throughout the country.

The more pressing concern for everyone in the 1930s was the economic collapse of the country; its impact on the state was a sobering reality for young people just entering the workforce. All her life, Henry's aunt Adella had loved the outdoors. But the work she engaged in after the ninth grade was exacting, "movin' quick," as she would say, "to pick strawberries for a penny a box, or pickin' cotton ten hours for thirty-five cents a day." She and the others who could endure the pain of retrieving cotton from its thorny brambles often

found work through the North Little Rock Farm Placement Bureau and the Arkansas Employment Service. Adella Hale remembered "gettin' up before sun-
rise, hoppin' on a cotton-choppin' truck, and by seven o'clock we were doing
back-breakin' work until sunset." The times, however, when Appliance Porter
did make it to the field she was, in her sister's words, "camped out under a tree
for the whole day, claiming she was too sick to work."[14]

Appliance Porter was an "inside girl." Her father had gotten it right by naming her after the word he had seen on a crate containing an icebox: an appliance
belonged inside, and so did George Porter's daughter. Working as a domestic was hard and fraught with other kinds of danger, but she preferred inside
work. "She wasn't no field girl, and she didn't like country life at all. We were
night and day," her sister matter-of-factly explained.[15] Appliance did not look
down on people who worked in the fields, but she preferred work where she
did not have to be in constant contact with nature, and where she could avoid
the bruised hands, calloused feet, and sore limbs that came with picking crops.

Appliance Porter's preference for indoor work also concerned money. She
made eleven dollars every two weeks as a hotel housekeeper, significantly more
than Adella made as a field worker. Both women were wired to be engaged in
activity. Appliance's work provided steady income, unlike field work, and her
location in Little Rock was equal parts necessity, equal parts choice. For Henry's
mother and scores of other black women, there were few opportunities. As
Dougan writes, "More than half of all black females were employed, 86 percent of them as maids for $2 to $5 a week."[16] Options for black women in rural
areas were especially scarce.

Appliance Porter's race and economic status didn't allow her access to a
stimulating job, but she was nonetheless interested in learning about the world
beyond Sweet Home. She had an eye for fashion and an itch for travel. Con-
stantly on the go and an avid picture-taker (Henry inherited both of these ten-
dencies), she exposed her son to a wider range of options than those she had
known as a child.

As a single mother, Appliance was far from the exception. From 1930 to 1934,
of births to young black women in America aged fifteen to nineteen, 48 percent were to single mothers.[17] Like many women of Appliance's generation,
her options were to be celibate before marriage or to pursue romance at the
risk of pregnancy; Appliance was apparently unconcerned with her status as
a single parent, in part perhaps because it was relatively common for single
black women to raise children on their own at the time, and Appliance knew
she could count on the support of her extended family. Indeed, in his early
years, Henry was a child of the village, cared for in turns by an impressive trio

of women who played significant roles in his development. With Appliance at work in Little Rock and Adella working in the fields, Mary Nalls, Big Henry's aunt, kept Henry under her watch during those years before school. Unlike black women of the period, white women had a greater probability of marrying before childbirth. For all women on the lower economic tier, it would be thirty years before women would have widespread access to birth control.

At least in the religiously oriented Porter and Dumas families, there was an awareness or acceptance of different types of family situations. The Porters belonged to Allen Chapel AME and the Dumas family to Greater Zion Hill Baptist. But neither family was interested in forcing their children into marriage. Adella Hale does not remember either family making much fuss over the fact that her nephew's parents were not married or that Big Henry was not the most hands-on father. Big Henry, who was a year Appliance's senior, was for the most part a well-meaning but ineffective father. She and Big Henry were friends, and she seems to have accepted the fact that his ability to be an engaged father was limited.

Although Big Henry was in the army for a period, whether he was far or near, his role in his son's life was nominal. The biggest challenge Henry faced was growing up in the double bind of segregation and the Great Depression. In his family, Henry had a stable cadre of role models, all of whom at one time or another planted and picked crops. Farming was in the family's work DNA, and Henry came to appreciate the bounty of the earth, just as his maternal grandfather had. By the time he was seven, Henry assisted in the fields by picking cotton and rode to truck patches with his uncles to sell produce. If he was not helping one of them, he was outdoors with his cousins, George "Sonny" Porter, Tommy Lee, or later his half-brother Billy, exploring Sweet Home or shooting marbles under the house.[18] He and his playmates had running space in Sweet Home, but even as a child Henry was aware of Sweet Home's limitations.

Not so much a town as a connected rural community, Sweet Home numbered 274 in 1930. The community was mostly black, but whites outnumbered blacks in the nearby township of Big Rock three to one, about 64,000 to 21,000. For black folks there were numerous reminders of the white world that stood adjacent to theirs, and one of the most telling examples of how blacks in Sweet Home were reminded of their subservient place in Arkansas was the presence of the Arkansas Confederate Home. Built in 1890 to address the needs of indigent Confederate veterans, its presence was a monument to the myth of the white promised land that had been lost in the war. Whites who still mourned losing the Civil War had a symbol, a cultural talisman, to signal to them the possibility of a brighter, whiter coming day. White veterans and their widows lived there, and blacks performed the menial tasks essential to its upkeep and to the care of the residents.

Henry's connection to the Confederate Home was more than symbolic. His grandmother, Lynn Porter, worked there as a nurse's aide in the 1930s. She doubtless encountered residents whose views of her and her people dated to the antebellum era. If nothing else, Henry probably heard family members comment on the challenge Lynn Porter faced in working to support her family. In a celebratory book about the home, published in 1920, Zella Hargrove Gaither offered a rosy portrait of a black domestic that resembled Joel Chandler Harris's late-nineteenth-century fictional apologist for slavery and its supposedly benign character, Uncle Remus. A former slave, Uncle Remus laments the passing of the antebellum era, when whites were sympathetic masters over their black chattel.

Writing some forty years after Harris, Gaither continued the myth of white beneficence. Referring to "Aunt Vick (Victoria Davis, descendant of the Barkman slavery estate and domestic worker in the home)," Gaither romanticized how Davis seemed "eager to send the food, well cooked, appetizingly served, steaming hot, to the meal for the veterans and wives and widows."[19] Whites were most comfortable with blacks who appeared eager to serve them. Practically speaking, blacks who wore the mask of civility did so out of necessity— not desire.

Another black personality highlighted in Gaither's homage to the southern cause was one of the home's few black residents, Dan Winsett. "He served through the entire war, as the bodyguard of his master, who was on the military staff of Gen. Joe Shelby." As she did with "Aunt Vick," Gaither called Winsett a true patriot. This "Negro veteran of the Confederate War," she wrote, "never misses a Confederate Reunion. He has been a faithful and efficient servitor in the home."[20] Gaither's portraits of Winsett and Davis, intermingled with the fact of Grandma Lynn Porter's work in the Confederate Home, are reminders of the messy, often imponderable and baffling, history of southern racial practices into which Henry was born.

Henry's family and other black families in Sweet Home had to live in a world in which most whites thought them inferior, content with their subservient status. While the Porter and Dumas families worked to dispel such notions in the minds of their children, they also taught them the pragmatics of surviving in a world of white power. Henry's younger cousin, Minnie Rose Hayes, remembers what the adults in their family practiced and preached with regard to encounters with whites: "You spoke to them and went about your business."[21] This one-way racial deference was almost impossible to practice all the time, and even when exercised perfectly, there still was no guarantee of safety.

Nonetheless, even within the confinements of Jim Crow, there were moments when whites acted with a measure of consideration for blacks. Minnie Rose Hayes remembers distinctly her "Grandma Lynn's relationship with the white family that owned the Jessie Thomas store, one of two white-owned stores in Sweet Home where folks could buy or trade goods. The store was closed on Sunday," Hayes explained, "but the owner would open up if Grandma Lynn needed something to finish Sunday dinner for our family."[22] To be clear, whites en masse were not challenging the legitimacy of Jim Crow, but some individuals treated blacks with decency and respect, acting humanely within a context of racial subjugation.

Blacks understood the power whites held over their lives. Even when individual whites acted kindly, that behavior could not be interpreted as a bellwether for broad social change. For Mary Nalls—Big Henry's aunt and another mother figure for Henry and for other young family members—rural flight was another means of survival. With an older brother living in New York, Nalls moved there herself in the early 1940s. From there she would often write letters home that portrayed New York in all of its color and joie de vivre, and her great-nephew was always excited to hear from his beloved aunt about a world that seemed perfect or at least exciting. For young Henry, New York was a blank canvas for his imagination, the perfect complement to the rural canvas he had become so fond of but whose limitations became more apparent to him as he grew older.

In 1936, about six months before Roosevelt would be elected to a second term, Appliance Porter gave birth to another son, Billy Mack Collins. Not much is known about Billy's father, Joseph A. Collins. He was born in Paris, Arkansas, but he spent most of his early years in Sweet Home. Like Big Henry, he was an absent father. Nonetheless, Billy entered a stable family structure led largely by the Porter family and centered around the boys' Aunt Adella.

In Billy, Henry and his cousins gained another partner in adventure, another buddy to catch lightning bugs with. The brothers were close, but even in their formative years Henry was more studious, and less interested in sports and community activities than Billy. Henry was not a loner, but he was comfortable being by himself. He could spend the whole day marveling at the mystery of creation. Even in childhood, according to Adella Hale, it was clear that Henry was a seeker, the kind of child interested not only in "what" happened but also in "how" and "why." His younger brother would join him on adventures through Sweet Home, especially bike rides. But rarely, based on the recollections of his Aunt Adella, would Billy have chosen to spend the day looking at insects, or plant and animal life by himself. If, for Billy Collins, the natural world was an intriguing place, for his brother it was an obsession.

Henry spent much of his childhood outside observing and sometimes capturing all manner of creatures. Sometimes he would also bring his captives into the house. Undoubtedly, some of his collected species—often grasshoppers and butterflies—found their way loose, but Aunt Adella, while at times inconvenienced by them, was never unnerved. With her own children and a disabled younger brother to care for, and in a few years her own husband and family, she had more pressing domestic matters to address.[23]

Henry would continue his outdoors exploits when the family moved from what is now Sweet Home Park, on Arkansas 365, to a standard, wood-framed structure at 4008 Neely Road. The house, which is still standing, sits on uneven ground with huge chunks of rock jutting out asymmetrically in the backyard, the topography yet another symbol of nature's preference for diversity and what would become a major theme in Henry's writing.

In his new home with Aunt Adella, which had neither television nor radio until the mid-1940s, Henry made his own toys. As he grew older, he created multiple character skits in which he played all the roles.[24] In this place far from Hollywood or Broadway, he had caught the bug for drama and for storytelling.

Minnie Rose Hayes recalled that Aunt Adella would leave the house early on summer days to catch the cotton chopping truck. Hayes remembers the rule her aunt expected her and the other children to follow in her absences: "keep the house clean and eat whatever you want. She always fixed food aplenty for her children and all their cousins, nieces and nephews."[25] On the heels of the Depression, Aunt Adella was certainly not baking pound cakes every day, but she shared whatever she had.

On hot days, the kids would gather underneath the house—it was perched high off the ground—snacking on fruit or simply trying to outmaneuver the sun. As one of the older children, Henry was probably responsible for helping to keep order while his aunt was at work. But Henry was less interested in being in charge and more interested in the outdoors. For him, the natural world was full of negotiations, contradictions, beauty, and brutality. In nature there are no straight lines, and in Henry's work, in which nature is a primary leitmotif, there wouldn't be, either.

           With his considerable skill of observation, Henry impressed his fourth-grade teacher, Geneva Powell, the same loving and demanding teacher his younger cousin Minnie Rose would have. But Henry desired something neither his teacher nor Sweet Home Elementary could provide. He needed a more challenging set of academic and cultural experiences. And he set out to make that happen as he leaned into preadolescence, the most dangerous phase of development in the Jim Crow South for black children.

    By fourth grade, Henry had realized the limitations of his beloved birthplace, and he evidently devised a plan to address this issue. Judging from the family's oral history and Henry's final report card from that year (1943–44), he was a good student.[26] Beyond grades, though, there was something about his intellectual engagement that impressed his immediate and extended family, a level of ability that distinguished itself even in the context of segregated schooling.

    As Henry moved into his preteen years, which would have meant that he was now a target for white abuse, his family would have reiterated the rules of Jim Crow to him and the other children in the extended family. Boys needed to know that interactions with white girls were inherently dangerous, and black girls needed to know that white boys and men could perceive them as lacking in sexual virtue, equating interaction with sexual availability. "Simply put," writes historian Jennifer Ritterhouse, "in the segregated South, the color of a teenager's skin was considerably more important than his or her family's socioeconomic status in determining whether his or her youth would include not only high school coursework but also the football games, after-school clubs, junior-senior banquets, and myriad social activities that were increasingly becoming the hallmarks of American adolescent life."[27] Appliance Porter understood the impact that Jim Crow would have on her son. She knew that his opportunities for educational advancement would be limited, although by now her son would be able to attend a local black high school.

    Henry and his family understood the vice grip of segregation, and this became especially evident as Henry transitioned from childhood to adolescence. As an adult, he never commented specifically about his experiences as a young black male, but his younger cousin by ten years, Minnie Rose Hayes, remembers vividly what it was like to walk to the all-black Sweet Home Elementary in the late 1940s. To reach her school she had to walk through a pasture with ornery bulls and cows, but they were not her primary concern. More difficult was the walk past the all-white Fuller High. Even with her brothers flanking her, they encountered, in her words, "baseball bats and rocks every single day," accompanied by the inevitable racial epithets. "One time some white students took my brother and wedged his head between two trees that had grown too close together. I lit out for the house to get Grandma Lynn, who returned with a saw to cut him out."[28]

If such encounters were part of Minnie Rose Hayes's childhood, her older cousin probably encountered some abuse himself. He would never forsake Sweet Home, but he wanted to see the world, and for him the world was New York. His knowledge of the city had come through his great-aunt Mary's (he simply referred to her as Aunt Mary) letters, and in the summer of 1944 she evidently invited Appliance and Henry to visit. The details of the visit—how they would have traveled and who paid for the trip—are lost to memory.

Mary Nalls had married a man twelve years her senior, John Henry Gillens, known as Uncle Jack to Henry, and they enjoyed a stable life in Harlem. Henry and Appliance visited, and when it was time for them to return, Henry simply did not want to go back home. The city, along with Aunt Mary and Uncle Jack, had won him over.

Appliance must have felt comfortable letting Henry remain with Aunt Mary, and although she returned to Little Rock, within the year she had relocated to New York, while Billy remained in Sweet Home with Adella. A city girl at heart, she could make a relatively good living as a housekeeper, enjoying the action in the black metropolis. In fact, she would work as a hotel housekeeper in New York for most of her adult life. Big Henry, who had long exhibited a nomadic spirit, also made the move, but he struggled with alcoholism and continued to be a transitory figure in his son's life.

It seems that Henry was the impetus for his parents' decision. In their own way, all three joined the millions of other blacks over the first sixty years of the twentieth century who had left the South believing things had to be better elsewhere. Or at least they could be no worse. New York State had only a smattering of black migrants from Arkansas. Overall, from 1930 to 1950, over 466,000 Arkansans had fled the state. As late as 1960, the number of black and white Arkansans living in New York State was a meager 9,867.[29]

The toughest reality in moving to New York, for Henry, was leaving the unspoiled natural world of Sweet Home and the rest of his family. But he wanted to go more than he wanted to stay, and the comfort in knowing he would be with Aunt Mary made a difficult decision easier. Aunt Mary had no biological children, but she raised her husband's four daughters from his previous marriage as well as the children of other family members over the years. For his part, thoroughly familiar with the braiding of pigtails and tea parties, Uncle Jack, whose daughters were now grown, embraced the opportunity to raise a boy.[30]

Although history would prove this period and the great northern and western migration to be complex and ambiguous, to African Americans in the South, with segregation and the specter of lynching ever present, Harlem seemed better and safer.[31] It had to be. Surely it would provide Henry more opportunity to live up to his potential.

Two decades later, Henry would create a young character reminiscent of himself. In his short story "Goodbye, Sweetwater," Layton Bridges contemplates leaving his southern town for the lights of the northern sky. As the narrator explains: "He had heard that in cities up North they were having riots and killing Negroes. . . . He felt himself now ready to cast off the dreams and things people said. He would believe no one, and if he dreamed something, he would not believe it were true until *he* made it come true. . . . If he were going to leave soon it would be because he wanted to. Even if his mother sent a ticket, it would mean nothing unless he wanted to leave."[32]

Young Layton understands that his dreams are tied to his willingness to leave Sweetwater and chase them, to leave home and take on the world. Henry cherished his birthplace, but he sought experiences beyond home in the land of skyscrapers and subways. By the summer of 1944, Harlem was his new home. Appliance and Big Henry soon joined him, though the three did not reside together. But no matter where Henry would go in the future, Sweet Home, the speck of a place off Arkansas Highway 365, would remain with him. Some southern transplants to Harlem would divorce themselves from the world that produced them. But Henry would never absent himself from his rural beginnings. For young Henry, like Layton, it was time to make his dreams "come true."

Looky here, America
What you done done—
Let things drift
Until the riots come

       —LANGSTON HUGHES,
       from "Beaumont to
       Detroit 1943"

[CHAPTER TWO

Skyscrapers, Subways, and Camels

Before Henry ever set foot in Harlem, his new home had been the scene of considerable racial strife since the Depression, with the August riots of 1943 the most recent expression.

An altercation between a black woman named Margie Polite and a white policeman at the Braddock Hotel kindled collective disruption in 1943. A black soldier intervened, wanting to make sure Polite was being treated fairly. Both men misread each other's motives, and the officer fired at the soldier, grazing his shoulder with a bullet. The men reconciled, even riding to the hospital together. But news of the incident—ramped up by a rumor that the soldier had been killed—galvanized the masses, many of whom were southern migrants who still had not tasted the fruits of the Northern Promised Land. Over the next two days, Harlem residents set fires and destroyed property, attacked white police officers and each other. The story of the soldier's alleged death became the reason for collective revolt against the status quo of Jim Crow. In New York, segregation stood strong. As Isabel Wilkerson notes, "the arrival of colored migrants set off remarkable displays of hostility."[1] But in such a densely populated place, whites had to make economic and housing concessions, which they did begrudgingly.

The root causes of the 1943 riots left their mark on black

writers. Harlem, with pockets of blooming black nationalism, was a case study in urban discontent. Not only in the streets but also in books, blacks writers were rejecting the excesses of white liberalism. The 1940 publication of Richard Wright's *Native Son*, a literary and sociological bildungsroman set in Chicago, was a manifesto against white paternalism, signaling this era of black discontent.

In 1944, Edwin Seaver published the inaugural interracial volume of *Cross-Section*, a radical journal known for its appreciation of social realism and ties to the League of American writers and the Communist Party.[2] For blacks looking for acknowledgment of the economic and political oppression they found themselves in, they found it in the Communist Party. Luminaries like Wright ("The Man Who Lived Underground"), Langston Hughes (three poems from the "Alberta K" cycle), and upstarts like Ralph Ellison ("Flying Home") were featured in the volume, along with white writers such as Nancy Wilson Ross, Norman Mailer, and Arthur Miller.

Of the black writers whose work appeared in Seaver's volume of six novelettes, seventeen short stories, two plays, and the work of fifteen poets, Ralph Ellison stood out. Several critics, writes Ellison biographer Arnold Rampersad, praised his contribution to the volume.[3] His modernist voice, defined by attention to narrative detail and cultural symbolism, had won critics over. He could write the black experience with the craftsmanship comparable to the best white writers. Nonetheless, his work and that of other black writers and intellectuals contributed to a chorus of progressive, and in some cases radical, critiques of race in America, to which the writers of Henry's generation fell heir.

By 1944, as Lawrence P. Jackson explains, black writers were creating a literary aesthetic "that did not rely upon white liberals."[4] As Henry was entering his preteen years, black writers were questioning the impact of well-meaning whites on the political and social establishment. The Depression, continued discrimination in the U.S. military and in industry, along with the intransigent hand of Jim Crow, caused these black writers of the 1940s to look at their nation with a scornful eye.

In the meantime, two other publications also signaled the growing discontent of black writers and the Harlem in which Henry found himself in coming years. Rayford Logan's edited collection, *What the Negro Wants*, published in the late fall of 1944 by the University of North Carolina Press (a progressive gesture for a southern university press), spoke to black frustration with the slow march toward equality being trumpeted by the progressive wing of the white political class. In short, progressive blacks were tired of token gestures toward racial equity, and the title of Logan's book reflected that sentiment. The volume featured essays by W. E. B. Du Bois, A. Philip Randolph, Mary McLeod Bethune, George S. Schuyler, Langston Hughes, and Sterling Brown, who "represented," to use Jackson's words, "the unified disgust with segregationist practices and the resolve to transform the nation by the end of the war."[5]

This resolve to end segregation took a hard hit from an unexpected but well-intentioned source. When Swedish economist Gunnar Myrdal's *American Dilemma* was published, also in 1944, the national and literary discourse on blackness shifted. If Logan's volume of essays expressed what blacks demanded, Myrdal's sociological treatise pointed out just how much black citizens, absent of white support, could never have. "The Myrdal matrix of race relations," Jackson notes, "left blacks with few options to change their own condition."[6] Myrdal contended—much to the consternation of someone like Ellison, who believed black culture was a dynamic force in the development of U.S. culture—that black identity and possibility were bound exclusively to the behavior of whites.

The publication of Logan and Myrdal's volumes represented the splintering of race relations.

When Henry arrived in Harlem in the summer of 1944, the bustling center of black culture had lost some of its 1920s Renaissance luster. The Depression had leveled a hard blow, but the wartime economy was helping Harlem bounce back. In the public and intellectual ranks, however, there was still deep frustration with the pace of social and economic change. Nonetheless, blacks were still arriving in droves.

Especially for children, Harlem represented a better opportunity. As Henry and other child migrants dispersed throughout the country, they received, on average, two more years of schooling than their peers who remained in the South. Nevertheless, having spent their formative educational years under Jim Crow, that "middle wave of migrants found themselves, on average, more than two years behind the blacks they encountered in the North."[7]

One way of addressing this educational gap was to require students from the South to repeat a grade—in Henry's case, the fourth. When he entered P.S. 5 in Manhattan, the country boy proved to be a student of solid ability, with room for improvement. Throughout the 1944–45 school year, he received "satisfactory" marks in reading, arithmetic, written language, spelling, nature study, and health education. He received the marks of "not entirely satisfactory" in spoken language, geography, history, and music, all of which he developed serious interest in as he grew older.

Henry's new school may have had more resources than Sweet Home Elementary, but the common denominator was segregation. Even with more resources than black schools in the South, Harlem schools were not equal to white schools in the city. There are contrasting views about the impact of school segregation in Harlem in the 1940s and 1950s. "Harlem," writes Thomas J. Sugrue, was "home to the nation's densest concentration of blacks and Puerto Ricans, its schools were nearly completely segregated by race. By every measure—teacher turnover, physical plant, student test scores—Harlem's schools were among the worst in the city."[8] However, Thomas Sowell—an economist and self-styled libertarian who grew up in Harlem—has not only a different memory but also a different assessment of the schools that he and other Harlem children attended, based on his analysis of school test data from that period. He says, "I went to such schools in Harlem in the 1940s but I do not rely on nostalgia for my information. The test scores in ordinary Harlem schools in the 1940s were quite comparable to the test scores in white working-class neighborhoods on New York's lower east side."[9]

On the whole, Henry's experience in school ran parallel with Sowell's. His relatively smooth adjustment to school was influenced by his home life with Aunt Mary and Uncle Jack, and later Henry's younger cousin Joanne Canales (née Nalls). About a year after Henry arrived to stay, Joanne, aged five, had moved in after her father died.[10] He often shared with his Harlem family stories about Sweet Home, picking Joanne up from school and entertaining her at home with tales of talking animals and days when the sun never went down. "Often after we got home from school," Canales recounted with fondness, "it was story time. That didn't mean reading a book. Henry would tell one of his Sweet Home stories. To set the mood, Henry would play the harmonica, use an old tin washtub to make the sounds of thunder or put the tub over his head—you know, for the echo effect. He would make gunshots by popping cellophane wrap. And slapping his leg, he could sound just like a galloping horse."[11] With his Harlem family, Henry embraced the role of big brother.

As Henry began to explore his new community, Aunt Mary and Uncle Jack Gillens were his source of stability. They treated Henry and Joanne Canales as their own. Joanne's memories of him provide the only firsthand account of Henry's adolescent years in Harlem. Significantly younger, however, she was not privy to the challenges of adolescence or Henry's engagement with the larger Harlem world.

Life for Henry and Joanne at 164 141st Street, between Seventh and Lennox, was close to ideal. For them, their new family was woven with a deep sense of togetherness. "Those years," Canales recalled, "were like a scene out of the artist Norman Rockwell. Only we were black. Uncle Jack was the first black driver at Blanche Motors in lower Manhattan, and Aunt Mary took care of home."[12]

Henry never lived in a traditional home with both of his biological parents, but the Harlem home of Aunt Mary and Uncle Jack was a stable substitute. And Henry accepted both the village approach in Sweet Home and the two-heterosexual-parents approach in Harlem. And if Henry felt anguish over his departure from Sweet Home, he never wrote about it explicitly, nor was Joanne aware of such a concern.

As part of his new, more conventional home life, Henry now had a room of his own, memorable to his younger cousin because he had a fish tank. He played scientist with his chemistry set, at times filling the house with sulfur stink bombs. With his New York family, he had the opportunities and resources of a middle-class life, as Aunt Mary and Uncle Jack implored him to indulge his interests.

Quite apart from material comforts, Aunt Mary was able to convey to Henry a sense of what living in a middle-class family was like. For the first time, Henry lived in a home where the woman didn't work outside the home. On many a night, young Joanne would be called to help set the table between six and seven o'clock, while Henry, "Aunt Mary's pride and joy," was called to the kitchen to assist with making dinner. In these moments with aunt and uncle, Henry and Joanne experienced what Joanne called the "best kind of family life."[13]

In his new urban world, Henry also encountered the multiple, contradictory aspects of black life. On the cusp of adolescence, Henry found a Harlem world in which the New Negro Movement's initiatives in the 1920s, intended to advance the black cause through black cultural achievement, had instead yielded to political frustration and social angst. The celebration of black artistic expression among literary and cultural elites in the 1920s had not alleviated the Jim Crow circumstances in the North. It did not translate or trickle down to the black masses in concrete or material forms. For that reason, Harlem was leaning to the political left. Leftist thinking was nothing new to Harlem, but this leftward tilt, as Jackson argues, had become "indignant," unrelenting in its critique of whites who argued for a more gradual approach to racial redress. In his invaluable narrative history of African American writers and critics spanning from 1934 to 1960, Jackson marks a turning point for black artists and intellectuals that corresponds with Henry's formative years of development.

For blacks who sought immediate racial redress, the communist party pre-

sented a viable option. In Harlem, it "had a strong membership," observed Sondra Kathryn Wilson, "especially among black men. Racism and the low economic fortunes of Harlemites caused a number of blacks to join."[14] One of the
most popular venues for discussions of all things black was Lewis Michaux's
National Memorial African Bookstore on Seventh Avenue. Across the street, at
the Hotel Theresa, the stomping ground for black celebrities and politicians,
the Communist Party regularly held its national convention. In Harlem, there
was a curious mix of political and intellectual forces at work. Blacks who would
not have ordinarily self-identified as communist could appreciate the critique
of economic exploitation and white privilege. In other words, they could consider aspects of the party platform that spoke to their economic and political
realities. This political and cultural backdrop was a major source of information for Henry as he moved through adolescence.

By 1948, the National Council of the Boy Scouts of America
claimed to accept all boys for their program. But the reality was far different.
Local councils were often encouraged to deny African Americans entrance into
the program, and the council offered no meaningful intervention when blacks
challenged the discriminatory act. This practice of racial exclusion would continue until 1974. Nonetheless, fourteen-year-old Henry had distinguished himself in a black Boy Scout troop, having been selected as patrol leader for Troop
No. 165 of Manhattan. He evidently demonstrated these leadership abilities at
the Frederick Douglass Junior High School (139 Manhattan), where he received
a certificate for "having voluntarily rendered faithful and meritorious service"
in 1950. He may have felt some pressure to excel: in the first half of the twentieth century his school had established an impressive record of producing future
black notables, among them artists Romare Bearden and Jacob Lawrence and
writers Claude McKay and James Baldwin, all of whom distinguished themselves in the arts and humanities. Until his death in 1946, Countee Cullen, Harlem's first celebrated poet, was a member of the faculty.

In high school, Henry wrote for the school newspaper at the High School
of Commerce (Lincoln Center is now located on the school's old site in Upper
Manhattan). The goals of the school were to "provide a training which shall
be broad and liberal in its character, and at the same time acquaint students
with the principle and technique of commercial transactions."[15] It would also
provide Henry's first integrated educational experience. Regardless of what racial tensions he may have experienced or observed in public in Harlem, school
and home were havens for Henry. And he was clear about his ultimate goal.

Even at this young age, Henry displayed a serious commitment to becoming a writer who did not shy away from difficult subject matter. The caption under his picture in his senior yearbook proclaims, "creative writing slave." As a member of the newspaper staff, Henry was at least aware of the caption—indeed, it may have been his idea. Either way, it does not appear that he was concerned about its use.

Henry had a sense of purpose rarely found in teenagers. At this point he embraced the concept of sacrifice—the idea that all-out commitment to a person or project required sacrifice of the self. Slavery it was not, but Henry's understanding of commitment involved the voluntary forfeiture of certain freedoms.

Despite his academic-related activities, he still found time to run track, and at home Henry continued his creative endeavors. He was also fond of card games, invented a checker game called Super King, and taught himself how to play chess, which he played with Uncle Jack. Most baffling to his family during his high school years, however, was Henry's interest in classical music. Always curious about and open to new experiences, he may have considered classical music another form of storytelling—albeit through ornate song and music—with the universal appeal of narrative tension and resolution. Classical music, for his family in Sweet Home and New York, was, imaginatively speaking, a world away. Henry's family members were simply of another generation, one in which their people had created blues, jazz, and gospel—art forms indigenous to the United States—to which they felt a specific loyalty.

Henry's family found it difficult to understand his interest in music that was part of a white, elitist tradition. It sprang from a worldview, in their minds, that had defined black people as inferior. Henry's family, like most U.S. families, had not developed an appreciation for an art form largely associated with power and privilege. But Henry, in his mid-to-late teens, could not dichotomize the world in such terms. He divulged to his wife, Loretta, years later that during his high school years "he would listen to classical music late into the night, with the radio volume turned low so his Aunt Mary and Uncle Jack could not hear it." Loretta Dumas later recalled that during the couple's first years of marriage, when they lived in San Antonio, "Henry found a classical radio station out of Austin, Texas. There were many times he would pick up an improvised baton, engrossing himself in the composition."

Henry's immersion in classical music was consistent with his personality. He would dive into an idea or activity to the point of obsession, only later to abandon the object of his attention altogether. It would be some years before he would discard classical music whole cloth. Nonetheless, his interest in the world of Mozart and Vivaldi was probably a result of his move to New York, whose cosmopolitan ethos presented cultural possibilities unavailable in Sweet Home.[16]

Even with his interest in classical music, Henry did not forsake popular culture. Joanne Canales remembers her elder cousin being fleet of foot, "practicing dance moves to the music of Chuck Berry and Bo Didley with friends and brothers Amando, Joe, and Frank Melfin."[17] And Loretta Dumas recalls photographs of Henry at dances with various young ladies. Cultural and social adaptability would become part of Henry's profile as his intellectual interests and network of associates broadened. Henry's life with Aunt Mary, Uncle Jack, and Joanne was interesting and fulfilling and, owing to their encouragement, he was on the path to productive adulthood.

Aunt Mary and Uncle Jack had been successful in sheltering Henry, to the degree possible in New York, from the least desirable paths he could have followed. On his graduation from Commerce in 1953 at age nineteen, with encouragement from his family, his goal, as he vividly expressed in the school yearbook, was to become a writer. As he entered this new phase, however, he was also troubled by developments in his immediate world of Harlem and his nascent sense of inadequacy about his own abilities. That fall, he entered the City College of New York (CCNY), one of the best institutions of higher education in the region, with a history dating back to 1849. Referred to by some as the Harvard of the proletariat, the college, located in upper Manhattan and overlooking Harlem, operated on a radical democratic notion: that the well-heeled should not be the only class with access to the best education. For blacks, Jews, Latinos, and working-class whites denied entrance into the Ivy League or the flagship state schools, CCNY proved that students from different racial and cultural backgrounds could find common intellectual and social ground, and until 1975, New York City residents attending CCNY even benefitted from free tuition.

Henry entered the night school with an undeclared major, taking two general education courses (Introduction to Music and Health Guidance). At one credit hour each, he was not overwhelmed by the part-time course load. He supported himself by working in the packaging unit at the publishing house Allyn and Bacon.

Henry's rationale for attending school part-time may have been partly related to money, but years later he addressed his angst over this entrance into adulthood, framing his dilemma this way: "Entering CCNY in 1953 at night session, I began to experience the first real cycle of depression, for here I was thrust out into the world from the sheltered cradle of high school by forces which I neither understood nor knew existed. The world of men is like a great sea, pounding rhythmic currents of experience upon us. And it seemed the whole sea evaporated and engulfed me in a great fog."[18]

"Engulfed" as he was, Henry remained only a semester at City College. Perhaps he had already lost interest in the loose regimen of college. Grades were not the problem, but Henry felt ill-equipped for the demands of adulthood. Related to Henry's sense of inadequacy at college was the fact that he had no immediate academic role models to follow in his family. His very presence on campus, in fact, was a statistical anomaly. In 1950, blacks comprised 10 percent of the U.S. population, and only 3 percent of that group were college students.[19] And black men, from 1951 to 1955, had a high school graduation rate just over 65 percent, compared to an almost 85 percent rate for white men.[20] A college degree was inevitable neither for Henry nor for his black peers across the nation.

The most credible reason for Henry's departure from CCNY was a crisis in confidence. Removed from what he termed "the sheltered cradle of high school" and home, Henry was quite simply overwhelmed. He had been confident in expressing his desire to write, but now he was woefully unsure about how to go about it. His refuge, for the next four years, would be the United States Air Force, which he signed up for toward the end of 1953.

As he prepared for this new phase of his life, Henry had an experience that he had not anticipated. One snowy evening after work he was walking to the subway station. A young woman, whose arresting beauty and inquisitive expression had garnered his attention even after a long day at her secretarial job at North Atlantic Constructors, was also headed to the subway. She had noticed Henry before, although the two had never exchanged words. But on this evening, as a few snowflakes had begun to fall, she was about to lose her balance on a slippery sidewalk when Henry, who always had a sense of dramatic timing, came to assist. They exchanged names, a conversation ensued, and Loretta Ponton gave Henry her home phone number, completely contrary to her upbringing. Her conservative father, Ashley Ponton, a deacon in a Baptist church and Sunday School superintendent in Westwood, New Jersey, was not pleased.

From this point forward, Henry was locked in on Loretta Ponton. Exceedingly quiet and shy, she nonetheless made an impression on the handsome and slender six-foot-tall young man with a slight gap between his front teeth, whose smile and charm were infectious. From Loretta's perspective, a black man who aspired to become a writer and who introduced her to the beauty of classical music was the ideal potential husband. In looking back on the moment she met Henry, Loretta remembers her natural optimism about the future. "I was impressed with his maturity, the fact that he was going to be a scholar, a writer, someone of great import. On the other hand, I knew nothing about marriage. I was very naive."

Loretta had come from a family with traditional expectations about marriage. Girls were socialized to grow into womanhood and to land a husband with earning potential. Although her father was a church man, church had nothing to do with Loretta's attraction to Henry. She was captivated by Henry's desire to become a writer. But the immediate challenge for the two of them was Henry's impending departure for air force basic training and then subsequent yearlong tour as a water purification specialist in Dharan, Saudi Arabia. For the next year, they knew, their courtship would take place on the page.

At twenty, Henry journeyed to a cultural and religious world of which he knew little. During his tour in Saudi Arabia, Airman Dumas recorded numerous observations about Arab culture, even compiling a glossary of common Arabic terms. In one of the longest pieces he wrote in his early adult years, a handwritten essay on Arab culture reveals Henry's strengths as an interpreter of culture. Henry's ability to see beyond the obvious, to set his own predispositions to the side and explore Arab experience in full confirmed that he had a writer's mind and vision:

> The first time I ever heard of Saudi Arabia was in the "Arabian Nights." Then I saw spectacular movies of Arabian Kings and Princes and beautiful princesses who wore veils over *their* faces. I saw proud Arabian horses by thousands carrying armies of Alibaba's thieves. I saw flourishing palaces fall and Arabian swords stained with blood.
>
> All these things and more I saw and read! (You probably can think of many many more). But that Arabia existed largely in the fancies of dreamers, storytellers and adventures. The real Arabia has a different story to tell. Arabia, I shall divide into two distinct categories: first, the barren land; and second, the proud, religious Arabian people.
>
> The Arabians have called it "Jazirat Al-Arab"—Island of the Arabs. If you look at a map you will see that it is almost an island. But actually it is a peninsula, the largest in the world. The entire country would cover one third of the United States. . . .
>
> As a Moslem is prostrate in prayer so is he in spirit. Whatever happens to him or his loved ones must not be questioned. It is the will of Allah. If he slips and breaks his leg it is not to be questioned. It is the will of Allah. If he suddenly feels that he must take a bath, then he believes it is God commanding him to take a bath.

Therefore, if we make all circumstances convenient for this bath, he will proceed to bathe. If the tub is in the middle of the desert or in the middle of streets of Al-Khobar it matters not because Allah's will is that he bathe. Now you can see the Moslem conception of God.[21]

Just a year out of high school, Henry already demonstrated an awareness of cultural distinctions and an impressive ability to observe Arab culture in its context without judging it by U.S. cultural standards. The sense of spiritual discipline, the Islamic commitment to interpreting all events as manifestations of God's will, impressed on Henry his need to embrace his religion. His exploration of Islam and the Muslim's relationship to Allah marked the beginning of his immersion into Christianity. The Arab commitment to Islam, in his mind, was a model for his thinking about his own Christian development. For the duration of his time there, he would ponder the value of Islam and Christianity. A fervent religious commitment can redirect one's sense of purpose, and it is possible that Henry's religious immersion may have been a way for him to bury his doubts about becoming a writer. His shortcomings, following his new ideas of God-logic, would have been easy to justify as simply a part of the Creator's will or plan for his life.

Creatively, Henry was engaged as well. He conceived a one-time publication called *The Camel*, to which he and his military colleagues contributed stories. Acting as the volume editor, Henry bound them together, giving them out to anyone interested. Beyond that, his effort was a tangible sign of his desire to write, to publish his work, and to reveal to his military colleagues his interest in matters unrelated to the military. The title of the publication reflected his appreciation of the camel in Arab culture. As one of the primary means of transportation across the scathingly hot deserts of the region, the camel is a symbol of patience and endurance, a creature with a deep reserve from which to draw sustenance over a long period of time. Did Henry aspire to have such an intellectual or creative wellspring? Was this his way of reminding himself that he had to await his destiny as a writer with patience and humility? If nothing else, this makeshift publication reveals Henry's need for a creative outlet. Loretta Dumas recalls that, during this period, Henry had carved out a "mini photo lab where he developed pictures and created collages of various subjects in the region."

The experience in the Arabian Peninsula pricked Henry's religious and artistic consciousness, and the evidence of that would emerge in coming years. In the meantime, having completed his yearlong tour, Henry returned stateside in the summer of 1955 to complete his enlistment at Lackland Air Force Base in San Antonio. First on his agenda on return: to finish what he had started with the woman from Westwood.

It did not take long for Henry and Loretta to renew their courtship. He had set the stage for their reunion with his letters.[22] "One of the joys of being with Henry," Loretta Dumas said, recalling the less complicated aspects of their relationship, "was the pleasure of reading his letters, full of sensitivity and expression." These letters confirmed for young Loretta that the author of such thoughts was indeed the man for her.

This was probably the first serious relationship for both of them. Henry had girlfriends in high school, but no relationship had moved beyond youthful attraction. In that sense, Loretta appears to have been his emotional and maybe sexual "first." Either way, Henry was prepared for the next stage of his development: marriage. Upon Henry's return home, Loretta felt that she could see the man behind the letters. Most of what she saw, she liked, or at least understood. The very traditional family structure that Loretta grew up in, including a model of women deferring to men, assured stability, even if it did not allow transformation. Henry seemed to her to possess the same values.

Although Deacon Ponton was skeptical about Henry at first, Henry's immersion into the church on his return to Texas allayed, for a time at least, some of his concerns. Henry may have been making the case for himself as Loretta's future husband, but the other aspect of his personality that Loretta needed to understand was the cost of sharing her life with someone for whom creative expression was "not a choice," as he would say to her more than once over the course of their life together, "but a calling." Loretta knew that her husband, as an artist, was wired differently from the traditional male model she recognized, but in these early days of their relationship, she simply could not have imagined the depth of the differences in their sensibilities.

One incident that proved instructive for her about Henry's psychological and artistic temperament was the gruesome murder of Chicagoan Emmett Till in Mississippi on August 29, 1955. At the time of Till's death, Henry and his beloved were less than a month away from their nuptials. As a northerner, Loretta was only generally aware of the daily assaults black people were subject to in the South. She realized, though, that Henry was almost despondent after learning of Till's murder. "He was distant, detached from me and seemingly everything else for quite a while. The news of Till did something to Henry. I didn't understand it at the time, but I know that the Till murder never left Henry's mind completely."

A child of the South himself, Loretta Ponton's future husband understood that his body could have been in the open casket that contained Till's mutilated corpse. Indeed, for black men, the warning and the danger was clear. Henry's despair at Till's death, however, would be the first event that signified to Ponton that she was marrying a man with a set of deeply rooted preoccupations that were, at times, all-consuming to the detriment of all else.

On September 24, 1955, despite these issues, Henry and Loretta were joined in matrimony in a ceremony at her family home in Westwood. The years that followed were the highlight of their marriage for Loretta. She fell seamlessly into her wifely role, joining Henry during his tour at Lackland Air Force Base. She took a job on the base in the secretarial pool, and on sweltering Texas days during his lunch break, Henry would sometimes bring his new bride home-made lemonade. Their relationship was in full bloom; they even taught the children's Sunday school class together on base. So impressive was Henry in this setting that his military superiors awarded him a certificate of service in "Furtherance of the Spiritual and Moral Program" of the base. But their time in Texas was not without strife. As a couple, they were in fine stride, but the larger world in which blacks were subject to white violence was always there to temper their marital bliss.

In 1956, the couple embarked on a trip to Sweet Home in their first car, a cherished 1949 blue Plymouth four-door sedan. "It had to be four doors," Loretta Dumas explained: "Henry detested two-door cars with a passion because he found them inconvenient." Shortly into their trip, they encountered a serious impediment. On a rainy night in Crockett, a small town in eastern Texas, their car hydroplaned off the road and was flattened, as Loretta Dumas recalled, "like a pancake."

Henry, like a good scout or military man, was prepared, pulling out first-aid supplies, insect repellent, and packaged food. This degree of forethought was necessary for blacks traveling on Jim Crow highways. But he and Loretta confronted a greater potential danger. They were stranded in the deeply segregated and dangerous South at a time of increased Klan activity, when in some communities Klansmen and policemen were one in the same. The arrival of the police shortly after the crash was no guarantee of safety.

Loretta Dumas remembered Henry's response to their situation: "His interaction with the police officers who came to the accident scene was remarkable since this was in East Texas, hostile territory in 1956. He was aware of the social reality, yet was able to maintain confidence and dignity while in a vulnerable position. We were directed to the only black 'hotel' in town, a large run-down house with rooms to rent that were inhospitable, to say the least. He soaked the rim of the mattress with liquid insect repellent to protect us from bugs."

Henry was with his wife in a fraught moment. White men could have exercised absolute power over them if they had chosen to. This experience was yet another example, for Henry, of the tenuous, fraught, and problematic relationship between blacks and whites in the South. Although Henry would not reproduce this exact scenario in his fiction, he would later revisit the emotional and historical tension of black-white relations in the South in *Jonoah and the Green Stone*.

During his enlistment, Henry continued to visit new places and engage new people. As a result of the crash, he and Loretta bought a new 1956 blue Plymouth, which they drove all over Texas and Mexico. In places like Monterrey and Saltillo, Mexico, Henry was completely at ease, interacting freely and even speaking some Spanish with the people there. "It was around this time," Loretta Dumas explained, "that I realized that Henry did not belong to, nor would he ever be content in one place. He was a citizen of the world." That Henry would be a constant journeyman, both literally and figuratively, was probably the most accurate observation she had yet made about her husband.

During one of their trips across the border, Henry revealed to Loretta and her parents a potential chink in his spiritual armor. "My parents, Laura and Ashley Ponton," she recalled, "visited us while we were in Texas. Henry treated them royally. We explored Texas and took a trip to Mexico. On that trip Henry brought back a bottle of tequila. Henry and my father had discussed religion and Christianity many times, so when he discovered the tequila in the trunk of the car he was surprised and displeased. He confronted Henry about it, and Henry managed an explanation that was sufficient enough not to spoil the visit." Henry may have made amends with his teetotalling father-in-law, but the incident anticipated a larger issue that would emerge on two fronts. The tequila symbolized Henry's curiosity about a worldly life and its pleasures and the difficulty in relinquishing certain experiences in the name of Christian discipline. Committed to his faith though he was, ultimately Henry was unable to remove or shelter himself from the world.

Nonetheless, the period after his return from Saudi Arabia was productive for Henry. In addition to marriage and his increased involvement in the church, he had earned a certification in entomology in the air force, affirming that his childhood fascination with bugs, grasshoppers, and all manner of outdoor creatures had not been a passing fancy. This would be his last notable achievement in the air force. With an honorable discharge in 1957 and a solid, two-year-old marriage, Henry seemed to be fulfilling his promise. Making his way as a writer was certainly next on his agenda. But in what context would he pursue his writing? Five years removed from his turbulent time at CCNY, could he now complete his degree? Or was he feeling called to the pulpit? His other option was to move into the straight-laced world of nine to five. Of these options, Loretta Dumas noted that writing and religious purpose held the most important places in her husband's mind. He would pursue both, for a period at least, at Rutgers University.

Of late I have caved into myself
Searching with daydimmed eyes
The musty catacombs of mind
Tunneling finally
Into bone which leads outside

—HENRY DUMAS
"Kef 33"

CHAPTER THREE

Learning to Read, Write, and Think

In 1957, when Henry opted for the early-out program from the
air force, his obligations to the U.S. military ended on October 2. He had performed well during his three-year term, but
he was ready for a change. The life of an artist usually requires
more flexibility than the military is willing to cede. As Henry
made this new transition, he had at least three primary goals:
to become a writer, earn his degree, and begin a family with
Loretta. Pursuing these goals and maintaining a commitment
to a conservative brand of Christianity would prove difficult
for him.

Henry's discharge, then, along with a severance package
that could sustain the young couple for the short term, was
the perfect means for his return to the civilian world. He and
Loretta bid farewell to the air force by doing what they had
been doing for the last two years—taking a road trip to a new
place. With money in their pockets and a 1956 blue Plymouth
revved up to cruise the country, they left the Lone Star State
and headed to California, traveling first to the San Francisco
Bay area and then south to Los Angeles.

The first leg of their trip took them to Chowchilla, California, where they visited Theodore Dumas. How Uncle Ted,
one of Big Henry's brothers, had found his way to the farm

country of central California is no longer known. A nomadic figure who had appeared in Sweet Home periodically in Henry's early years, Uncle Ted had left the land of Jim Crow in the early 1930s in search of a brighter day. By the time Henry and Loretta showed up on his porch, he had been in California for more than twenty years.

Beyond reconnecting with his uncle, Henry was immediately struck by the black workers he met in California farm country. These workers belonged to a steady stream of migrants from the southwestern states dating back to the Dust Bowl of the 1930s. Their struggles reminded Henry of the agrarian toils of his own family. Loretta Dumas remembered that, for their part, the migrants were impressed that a well-traveled black man thought it worth his time to talk with them. They understood, as she put it years later, that "they were part of the invisible masses" of workers that toiled the hardest in the United States but were compensated the least. Henry interviewed farm workers and other people he encountered with his recently purchased reel-to-reel tape recorder, in the 1950s still a high-tech gadget for an individual to own.

Henry was not just interested in these workers' stories, he also wanted to win souls. On this trip, Loretta observed that her husband's "fire for the Lord was getting hotter."[1] Conservative but not evangelical in her own religious expression and belief, Loretta was increasingly concerned about Henry's evangelical zeal, which she felt "was now bordering on religious fanaticism. Henry took every opportunity during the trip to hand out scriptural leaflets to people we met along the way." When he was not interviewing people or passing out gospel pamphlets, he was taping himself, as he acted out character sketches, a creative exercise he had practiced since his days in Sweet Home.[2] To Loretta, this side of Henry was appealing. It drew him back from his intense witnessing efforts.

At this point, Loretta Dumas felt that her husband needed to moderate his zeal for church. She was unnerved by his evangelical stance, and Henry seemed excitable when explaining his religious beliefs to strangers and even to Loretta. He was moving into territory that she simply did not recognize. "If you didn't know Jesus like Henry did, then, according to him, you really didn't know Jesus," she would say years later. This all-or-nothing approach that seemed to be taking over Henry's disposition was proof enough that something had gone askew with her husband.

This change that Loretta observed occurred at the same time that Henry was engaged in figuring out the next phase of his life. Henry could not ride solely on the back of religious zeal. He would need to chart his own course. His goal was to write, but how exactly, he must have wondered, do you become a writer? Other than children, did he and Loretta share other mutual goals or desires? There is no evidence to suggest that Henry imagined beforehand this trip to California as a chance for him to reflect on his life, but it appears that this trip, occasioned by his transition from the air force, served that purpose.

Even with Henry's change in religious sensibility, the couple enjoyed their time on the West Coast. They headed to New Jersey by way of Sweet Home, where Loretta met members of the Porter family: Grandma Lynn, Adella, Billy, Henry's cousin Tommy Lee (son of Adella), and Henry's uncles, among them Walter and George. Henry, a mythic figure for his younger cousins who were awed and inspired by his country-to-city story, impressed his family with his accomplishments since leaving Sweet Home: growing into adulthood in Harlem, becoming a military man, finding a wife, and owning a car. It seemed inevitable that to this list of accomplishments would soon be added "college graduate" and "father." In fact, if the couple had visited a few months later, they could have shared the best news of all: a baby was on the way, due in June. Having reconnected with family, Henry and Loretta set out for New Jersey, with Billy joining them to assist with the driving. At this point, Billy was close to finishing his own enlistment in the army, after which he would relocate to Chicago.

In addition to a bonus that he had received from the air force, Henry would receive a monthly educational stipend from the military as long as he was enrolled full-time in college. Still, he and Loretta needed to save money before he started college in the fall of 1958.

In New Jersey, they stayed with Loretta's parents in Westwood, during which time Henry and Deacon Ponton continued their discussions about religion. On one occasion, Henry wanted to intervene in a dispute at the Pontons' home church. Members were splintering off into factions, and Henry felt they needed to be reminded of the scriptural mandates for Christian believers. His idea, although he did not have a history with the congregation or a context for understanding the current dispute, was to place flyers on church members' cars with specific directives from Scripture. Uneasy about the likely reverberations, Loretta convinced him to refrain from such an intervention. Henry felt it was his responsibility, as a true believer and authority—albeit an unofficial one—on the Lord, to deliver the biblical truth to some of God's wayward people.

Had Henry chosen life as a preacher, his path would already have been set:

attend seminary or go directly to a pulpit, to a life of hallelujahs and amens, baby blessings, and funerals. But the process of becoming a writer was wrapped in ambiguity. There was no prescribed formula, no well-worn path, for becoming a published and full-time writer. Henry had by no means given up on a vocation, but his decision to attend Rutgers indicated his interest in the world outside God's house, with fewer boundaries and precepts. Loretta Dumas does not remember the rationale for Henry's choosing New Jersey's flagship state university, other than their desire to be near her family, and no explanation of his decision appears in his extant papers. But given that Henry had wanted to be a writer at least since high school, and given that the black intellectual activity he witnessed in Harlem during his boyhood and adolescence stirred his imagination, his choice of Rutgers warrants further exploration.

By 1958, the most celebrated African American fiction writers were either from, living in, or had written fiction set in New York. Ralph Ellison had won over the white literary establishment with his modernist interpretation of black masculinity in his 1952 classic, *Invisible Man*. Likewise, in 1954, John Oliver Killens had offered up in *Youngblood* a complex storyline of a strong, proud, black Georgia family impacted but not defeated by segregationists. James Baldwin had mesmerized the literary establishment with a daring and raw form of social realism in his 1955 novel, *Go Tell It on the Mountain*. And in 1959, Paule Marshall's bildungsroman, *Brown Girl, Brownstones*, presented a black female subject wrapped in intellectual and emotional complexity.

A burgeoning cast of promising black writers were part of the Harlem Writers Guild. Ranging in age and artistic vision but united in their desire to affirm black humanity through the pen, members of the left-leaning group included Killens, Rosa Guy, John Henrik Clarke, Marshall, Maya Angelou, and Lorraine Hansberry. In the world beyond the guild, LeRoi Jones (later Amiri Baraka) was part of the bohemian crowd of Greenwich Village, starting the avant-garde *Yugen* magazine with his Jewish wife, Hettie, in 1958. In the 1960s, he would pen two plays (*The Dutchman* and *The Slave*), both of which were critically acclaimed for their experimental explorations of subconscious black male angst. Hansberry, a progressive artist in the vein of Paul Robeson, would become the most celebrated black dramatist of the period with the premier of *A Raisin in the Sun* in 1959.

With family roots in Harlem, Henry could easily have returned to a place effervescent with literary and cultural activity. Had he returned to City College, he would have needed to revive his residency status (which probably would have taken a year) before being eligible for free tuition again. Nevertheless, he chose New Jersey over New York. In that singular act of restarting his literary and academic career in a very different cultural milieu, he took the road less traveled.

One way of understanding Henry's decision to attend Rutgers is to recall his first college effort. Despite his strong academic performance in high school, he acknowledged years later that, having left the cocoon of family and school, he had been in a "fog" at City College. But through all of his experience to this point, Henry had never stopped writing. From the time they met, Loretta Dumas would remember, "Henry had always been writing, it was so evident, so much a part of his consciousness, that I always assumed his end goal was to become a writer."[3] Rutgers represented an opportunity for him to develop absent of overblown expectations. In New York, Henry would have found himself under intense social and creative pressure, a kind of anxiety of influence context in which he found himself trying to match wits with the black literati. That possibility, coupled with Henry's conservative religious beliefs at the time, might have made him reluctant to move back to such a cosmopolitan place. Moreover, CCNY in the 1950s was known as a hotbed for political radicalism. Whatever challenges they presented, Rutgers and New Brunswick were less daunting than either CCNY or New York City.

But the most feasible explanation is that he probably chose Rutgers because it appeared to be the right place for him. He knew New York, he knew of the artists there, but he had never been a follower, and he was not invested in name recognition or institutional cachet. More to the point, in swerving around New York, Henry placed himself on the literary margin that could prove difficult to navigate, but he also could develop his writing with a larger degree of freedom. To be off-center had creative advantages. Henry may have known of Rutgers's reputation and roots dating back to the colonial period. He certainly was aware of the most gifted black man in the arts, letters, and sports in the twentieth century, Paul Robeson, who had left his mark there almost four decades earlier. So Henry, and the smattering of blacks who attended Rutgers, had the luminous legacy of Robeson as their standard bearer. But in the 1950s, as far as Rutgers was concerned, Robeson was persona non grata. His defiance in the face of anticommunist and anti-intellectual forces was disconcerting for conservative America and for his alma mater.

Before Henry walked into his first class at Rutgers, his world had already changed. On June 20, 1958, their son, David Henry, was born. Loretta moved into the role of mother with relative ease, and Henry was enthralled with the child. "Henry," said his wife as she looked back on those early days with their firstborn, "embraced fatherhood." While he seldom spoke about his own father's shortcomings, Henry probably wanted to rise to the occasion more effectively than Big Henry had done. Since he was not working at this point, Henry spent a considerable amount of time with David. "It was like David had given Henry permission to acknowledge his inner child," Loretta Dumas would remember.[4] Early on, it seemed as if Henry would try to replicate the parenting practices of Aunt Mary and Uncle Jack. But after the excitement of having a child had waned, his parenting style fell somewhere between the doting attention of his Harlem family and the intermittent attention of Appliance and the hands-off approach of Big Henry.

Now a father, Henry entered Rutgers University in the fall of 1958 as a full-time freshman. Although it was the flagship in the state university system, Rutgers was always, like the proverbial middle child, in the shadow of Princeton and the Ivy League. Robert Pinsky, a freshman from New Jersey and future poet laureate, was enrolled in an honors section of freshman composition with Henry. He and his classmates were not graduates of high-end public schools or exclusive preparatory academies, as were many of their Ivy League peers. Pinsky, who considered Henry a friend, described himself, Henry, and other talented students in his circle of friends at Rutgers, such as Alan Cheuse, Clem Fiori, Hale Chatfield, and Jay Wright, in this way: "We were diamonds in the rough, definitely not Princeton boys who had gone to good high schools where we were on Student Council, took AP [Advanced Placement] etc."[5] In short order, Pinsky and this group came to understand the difference in social pedigree.

Six years older than Pinsky and others in the first-year class of 1958, Henry brought to campus a set of worldly experiences, framed by adulthood, the air force, and religious immersion that most of his peers had never experienced. Regardless of their ages, Henry and his classmates entered Rutgers at a time when some students were questioning the paternalism and conservatism of the Eisenhower era. But at this time Henry had other things on his mind.

An American Civilization major, five years removed from City College, Henry chiseled out a 2.8 grade point average for the year in a challenging liberal arts curriculum, earning an A in his two composition courses. This would be his best academic performance during his tenure at the university. After this first year, for financial reasons, he dropped to part-time status and enrolled in the evening school program. Also during his first year, Henry's religious sentiments emerged in his assessments of American literature; he was trying to pursue both interests at once.

In a fall essay on Bret Harte's 1868 short story, "The Luck of Roaring Camp,"

Henry based his analysis on the idea of Christian redemption. Set in California's Sierra Foothills, Harte's story catalogs life on the western frontier as white men canvas for gold in the 1850s. The only woman in the community, Cherokee Sal, elicits from men the highest form of hypocrisy; they ridicule her sexual inclinations during the day while coveting them at night. Eventually Cherokee Sal dies while giving birth to a child whose father is unknown. The men in the camp have to then raise the child, aptly named Luck, even nourishing Luck with donkey's milk. Luck and his primary caregiver die in a sudden torrential storm. But not before the men of Roaring Camp, consistent with Harte's literary aesthetic, are redeemed.

Henry's analysis of this story corresponded with his own sense of religious transformation. In commenting on the men's adoption of the baby, he concluded that these men "recognized this new life as something good and wonderful within itself. From then on the moral seed began to sprout upwards in their lives, transforming depravity and violence into virtue and love."[6] Indeed, Harte's literary reputation is based on his nonviolent exploration of good and evil or, as literary scholar J. David Stevens writes, "on the contest of souls rather than a showdown in the street."[7] Henry appreciated the gospel ethos in Harte's story, as human redemption is achieved when the men in Roaring Camp turn from sin to salvation.

In that same composition course, Henry offered a blistering assessment of U.S. capitalism and a religious prescription for healing in F. Scott Fitzgerald's timely and foreboding 1925 classic, *The Great Gatsby*. For Henry, the Tom Buchanans and Jay Gatsbys of the world represented what to him was a "thankless generation which put all faith in the dollar, spent their time at drunken parties and wild escapades and made a mockery of the religious faith that founded America." With the timbre of a patriot and the myopia of a new convert, Henry argued that "America was founded by a small group of men who believed, trusted and obeyed the word of God." These men, he continued, "had a firm faith. They laid the foundation for the wealth of the nation. But the lost generation of the Buchanans and the Gatsbys made a mockery of the religious traditions of their fathers."[8]

These remarks about *Gatsby* demonstrate how Henry viewed the world in absolute, even evangelical, terms at this point in his life. In his mind, the war between sin and salvation had no room for equivocators. Revealing a kind of historical naïveté, he advanced a faith in the Founding Fathers mythology of U.S. history—the notion that these men were dedicated Christians in the truest sense. He articulated the concept of American exceptionalism: the idea that the United States stands as the moral lighthouse to the world, and that its conception and continuation is rooted in the favor of God, not in slavery, imperialism, or the grace of geography (viz., the formidable barriers that two oceans present to would-be enemies or occupiers). This blind faith in a national religious narrative, at best, has always been riddled with contradictions. And it characterized Henry's early thinking about the republic. The writer of this essay was consistent with the Henry who wanted to browbeat the members of Loretta's home church into following Jesus on what he interpreted as the straight and narrow. In other words, Henry believed the answer to all conflicts, greediness, and other forms of sinful behavior was Jesus, and he was willing to aggressively challenge any naysayers.

Despite his early fixation on moral absolutes, Henry's classmates were impressed with his biblical knowledge. Robert Pinsky recalled his contributions to their honors section of freshman composition, taught by Dr. Paul Fussell, who often "appointed experts" for portions of class. Fussell identified "Henry as the expert on Biblical references. He could identify references in John Donne or James Joyce, etc.," with encyclopedic precision.[9] One of the few black women who observed Henry during this period was Gloria Smith. A nursing major, Smith struggled in a philosophy course in which she and Henry were enrolled in the spring of 1960. She remembers how adept Henry was at explaining the material, even if he had missed a class. "Sometimes," remarked Smith, "it was like Henry was the instructor."[10]

With such biblical recall and intellectual authority, Henry thought he could reverse what he perceived to be the inappropriate stylistic and thematic course of the university's literary magazine by shaming the staff into religious submission. Alan Cheuse, a member of the *Anthologist* staff, remembered vividly his first encounter with Henry in the fall of 1958: "It was an early fall meeting of the *Anthologist*, the literary magazine . . . I was second in charge, and Robert Pinsky was an editor also. Henry came to this meeting, with his Bible in hand, and told us he'd read some of the stories in the magazine and that it was clear to him that we were damned because of the material we were printing and that he wanted us to repent and to see the light, and change the kind of material we were printing in the magazine." After listening to this fire-and-brimstone rant, Cheuse and others concluded that "Henry was just kind of loony."[11] But this would not be Henry's last encounter with the *Anthologist*.

Henry's salvo, while aimed at the *Anthologist* staff, was a subconscious response to the cultural and social developments that were challenging the Christian orthodoxy he had embraced. Married and a father at twenty-four, he was looking for a point of constancy as sexual and political mores shifted around him. The Bible, in its simplest interpretation, was his antidote. During his air force days, U.S. society had begun a move toward radical change. The stability, and for some, the conservative zeitgeist of the 1950s, would give way in the 1960s to the countercultural revolution, first symbolized in the Beat Movement. In essence, Henry arrived at Rutgers during a period in which students were being exposed to options for social development that he could not have imagined just five years earlier. Like an older sibling envious of a much younger one who enjoys more freedom and less parental discipline, he witnessed his younger academic peers considering options that, for him, had not been feasible.

The Beat Movement, associated early on with writers Allen Ginsberg and Jack Kerouac, was a cultural lifeline for young, mostly white U.S. writers and artists who resisted what they perceived as the social and political hypocrisy of their parents' generation. The World War II generation may have saved the West from tyranny, but the United States had achieved victory through atomic testing and the nuclear decimation of Japan. The children of this generation, coming of age after the atomic bomb, often found the irreverent poetry, art, and experimental jazz of the day to be tonics for the ills of society. Whether in Greenwich Village, at Columbia, or at Rutgers, they often crossed racial, class, and sexual boundaries in search of like community, often in defiance of what they deemed outdated cultural practices.

Along with Ginsberg and Kerouac, Diane di Prima, Frank O'Hara, Robert Creely, Gregory Corso, and William S. Burroughs were some of the most well-known white writers associated with the Beat Movement. Black writers LeRoi Jones, Bob Kaufman, and Ted Joans were also part of this new phenomenon. "I took up with the Beats," wrote Baraka in his autobiography, "because that's what I saw taking off and flying that somewhat resembled myself. The open and implied rebellion—of form and content. Aesthetic as well as social and political. But I saw most of it as Art, and the social statement as merely our lives as dropouts from the mainstream."[12] Unlike Baraka, Henry initially looked on this movement with disdain, but he adjusted rather quickly to the changing world.

Socially speaking, the introduction of the birth control pill in 1959 challenged ideas about sexuality, the nature of sexual activity, and the formation of family and community. If the 1950s had been about *Leave It to Beaver* and other television shows that focused on the mythical nuclear white suburban family, the 1960s questioned the necessity of marriage and its role in governing sexual behavior.

For Henry, the *Anthologist* represented, accurately or not, this new cultural beat, this strategy of using art to question and even flout authority and convention. Initially he was stung by what he interpreted as brazen rebellion against morality in the pages of the magazine, but those pages ultimately served as a source of stimulation, and he began to reconsider the limitations of his religious and cultural conservatism. A semester later, in the spring of 1959, Henry returned to another staff meeting of the magazine, revealing what would be the second phase of his development. This time he announced to Cheuse and company that he "had completely given up or renounced his Bible-thumping and he was now a philosopher, and wanted to engage us in philosophical discussions."[13] Henry now wanted to engage with, rather than antagonize, his literary peers. To them it looked as if he had made a radical change in temperament, from religious evangelical to critical observer. In fact, this was a return to the more intellectually curious Henry of his high school and early air force years.

As Cheuse makes clear, Henry made a quicksilver shift in his first year at Rutgers, foregoing his march to the cross, embracing instead the idea of philosophy as a source of personal and intellectual fulfillment. His relationship with the *Anthologist* evolved, with him eventually becoming a contributor and a staff member. Indeed, some of his most significant encounters with future well-known white male writers came through the magazine. Henry had solid friendships with Robert Pinsky and Alan Cheuse, but he was probably closer to Hale Chatfield, a graduate student in English and future poet himself, and Clem Fiori, a fellow undergraduate and aspiring photographer whom he would meet in 1960 or 1961. Of the black men on campus, Henry was closest to an education major named Earl Thomas, whom he met in the fall of 1960; and later Jay Wright, a graduate student in comparative literature and future award-winning poet, whose artistic sensibility meshed well with Henry's.

At twenty-five, Henry was becoming more deeply involved in the literary world at Rutgers, but his finances were unraveling at a maddening pace. Never consumed by either money or material acquisition, he found himself sinking into debt. He had celebrated his family's move into University Heights, just outside of New Brunswick in Piscataway, by cultivating a vegetable garden. But during their first year there, the garden became not just a symbol of Henry's love of nature and its bounty; it was also a financial necessity. The couple were not prepared for the precipitous drop-off in their income, coupled with the expenses, even with Loretta at home, of raising a child. Nor had they anticipated Loretta's medical challenges after giving birth to David or the recurring mechanical problems with their Plymouth. Henry's educational stipend from the military helped, but living on that check and taking a full course load was like trying to swim upstream; no matter the intensity of Henry's effort, the current was going to take him where it chose.

At the same time that Henry was confronting money problems, he met someone with similar intellectual interests and financial difficulties. A graduate student in Spanish, Jake Bair also lived in University Heights with his young family. With his experiences visiting Mexico during his air force years, Henry appreciated Bair's intellectual heaviness. Bair's translation of an essay by Spanish socialist and intellectual Ramiro de Maeztu appeared in a 1961 issue of the *Anthologist*.[14] Bair was not part of Henry's immediate literary circle, but he observed and appreciated Henry's disposition in his interactions with whites. He felt no need to defer to his white friends, or to play the role of all-knowing black man, but he was willing to share aspects of the black world to which they were not privy. "For me and other whites Henry befriended," Bair noted, "Henry pulled aside the curtain on black life. We would go to parties. Henry seemed willing to offer up glimpses of black life. In that sense, he was very generous and rather unusual."[15]

Henry and Jake Bair were fast friends, and their similar financial circumstances brought them closer. Together they "raided vegetable plots at the Rutgers Agricultural School at midnight."[16] Henry had never been in legal trouble, but he was willing to breach both religious and ethical boundaries to feed his family, as was Bair. Notwithstanding the symmetry between the two men, there were limits, set, it seems, by Henry, to their friendship.

Bair knew Henry wanted to be a writer, but rarely was that the subject of their conversation. "We did not talk about Henry's writing much," Bair would say decades later. "In fact, Henry's relationships did not overlap. Nor did he invite much interpersonal analysis. He had a lot of confidence in his writing. Henry was mercurial, undisciplined, which was characteristic of young writers." There were other people with whom Henry could discuss writing, and Bair notes that "as a friend, he was so much fun to be with, always wonderfully sharp and funny. I let that be enough. I liked him immensely. The torment came out when he was drinking, but he didn't wear his torment on his sleeve."[17] Even with Henry's considerable skill at partitioning his life, there were moments when the partitions did not hold up. In his friendship with Bair he evidently revealed, on occasion, a sense of torment. It is not clear how much of his backstory Henry had shared with Bair. By the time they became friends, Henry was wrestling with some heavy concerns that had begun at City College and gathered strength in his last years in the air force. In those years, the military and religious structures had enabled Henry to function, thereby pushing this sense of torment momentarily to the side.

Now at Rutgers, in a somewhat less inhibited social context, Henry wrestled with a sense of inadequacy, and he would begin to indulge his taste for alcohol. This side of Henry, Loretta would hardly ever see, but Clem Fiori and Earl Thomas were involved in or observed some of the moments in which alcohol ruled Henry's behavior, some of which occurred in the presence of women with whom Henry may have been intimately involved. However, even when alcohol got the best of him, the good in Henry was never out of reach, and Robert Pinsky spoke for many others when he said he viewed Henry as a "talented, amusing, warm-hearted, somewhat tormented friend."[18]

During this first year, Henry had carved out an important place on campus, mostly among white students. Loretta was not a part of this world. Her husband never stated that she could not participate in these endeavors, but she nonetheless understood that the contours of their marriage were clearly drawn. She and Henry together established relationships with a few black families. With them, Henry was able to stick to the pattern of behavior—holding alcohol at arm's length—that he practiced when he first arrived at Rutgers.

Among the few black families on campus were Laura Lindsey, a homemaker, and James Lindsey, a graduate student in political science. As an undergraduate and graduate student, James had earned scholarships to pay for his education.[19] In the 1960s, he was vice president of Monmouth County CORE (Congress of Racial Equality), an interracial organization committed to nonviolent strategies of human rights protest that Henry would align himself with. He and Henry would often discuss political issues of the day and the ongoing black freedom struggle. During that early period, the two families often ate together, and Henry, putting to practice lessons learned in Aunt Mary's kitchen, occasionally cooked. According to Laura Lindsey, when Henry fired up the stove the result was never a recognizable dish; his cooking, like his literary sensibility, was always something of a deviation from the standard; in Lindsey's words, "quite different, but quite tasty."[20]

When Laura Lindsey looked back on their friendship with Henry, her memory focused on his giving and creative nature. During an especially difficult period when the Lindseys were facing financial hardship, he "showed up at our door with a pile of fish he said he caught. Years later we realized Henry had bought the fish. Had we known, we probably would not have accepted them, because Henry and Loretta were about as bad off as we were." Along with generosity, Henry simply saw things in a different way. "We had dinner one time," Laura Lindsey said, "but not enough chairs for everyone. Henry told us to bring down suitcases. Problem solved. He could make something out of whatever was in reach."[21]

The Dumas and Lindsey families were often joined by Herman and Mattie Robinson. Herman Robinson was a Morehouse man, the only college in the country expressly for black men. Not only did he earn a scholarship to attend, he graduated at age nineteen. Robinson served as president of Monmouth County CORE and was very active in the civil rights movement. He also earned a master's degree in mathematics.[22] He was active in local civil rights initiatives, and in later years he and Henry would travel south with relief supplies for blacks on the front lines of the Freedom Movement.

Both James Lindsey and Herman Robinson were stimulating company for Henry, and discussions with them contributed greatly to Henry's understanding of the ongoing fight for political emancipation in the South. Both men were committed to participating in grassroots efforts to alleviate black suffering in the South. Conservative in temperament and approach, Lindsey and Robinson were both committed members of the National Association for the Advancement of Colored People (NAACP). They were stalwarts in the freedom fight.

These two men provided Henry with an interesting point of departure from his relationships with the mostly white literary vanguard on campus. As black men, they could all speak about certain aspects of their lives in a kind of cultural shorthand. Scholars by any measure, they were good company for Henry, engaging him as if he held the academic credentials they had earned. They recognized Henry's intellectual engagement, despite the fact that he not reached their level of accomplishment. What united this trio were their kindred concerns about black people, their appreciation of the life of the mind, and their experiences as black men. More pointedly, as Henry pursued a life as a writer, these two men, not so much in word but in their deeds, reminded him of the importance of connecting academic and professional success to racial and community uplift. They did not necessarily view themselves as members of W. E. B. Du Bois's Talented Tenth (though in every way they were), but they embraced the concept of lifting others as they climbed. They played larger roles than Henry in the fight for black freedom, and they undoubtedly influenced him in his thinking about the movement.

As he entered his second year at Rutgers, Henry, both politically and culturally, began questioning the religious dogmatism that he had brought to campus. As this process started, he was dealt a startling blow. His only sibling, twenty-three-year-old Billy Mack Collins, was killed on July 11, 1959, in Chicago (nine days before Henry's twenty-fifth birthday). One of two men in a love triangle, Billy was involved with a woman, Alzoria Robinson. She had expressed interest in him, but she wanted to keep her options open with a Leo Patillo. Leo, on the other hand, was not interested in options. He and Billy had fought earlier, and he later shot Billy at the entrance to a restaurant. Billy, who had served in the army during the Korean War, was pronounced dead at Englewood Hospital from a gunshot wound to the right eye.[23]

Although Henry had not lived with Billy since their childhood years in Sweet Home, and Billy had followed the more prevalent migratory pattern for black Arkansans to Chicago, Henry felt this loss acutely. With only two years between them, the two brothers had been partners in adventure for the first seven years of Billy's life. A photograph of them, taken in about 1950, during their teenage years, suggests a tender bond. Seated on the couch, Henry is leaning on his younger brother, his left forearm on Billy's shoulder. With his right hand, Henry is grasping Billy's left hand. Billy is smiling fully, while Henry's is more of a half-smile. They appear to be at home with each other.

The story that most closely explores Henry's feelings about losing Billy and his guilt about having left him in Sweet Home when they were children is "Echo Tree," published in the *Anthologist* in 1961. The story centers on two unnamed black boys. Leaving characters nameless is a recurring motif in Dumas's work, a way of suggesting the universality of black experience. These two boys could be anywhere, any place in the African diaspora where black folks speak English. Their personalities are characterized by their respective belief and skepticism in the power of a particular tree to harbor the spirits and voices of the dead, which is known as the "echo tree." One of the boys, the skeptical one, has a deceased brother named Leo. The other boy, who believes in spirit talk, was Leo's best friend. By naming only the character who is dead, Dumas taps into a naming motif that suggests that African Americans need to learn the names and honor the spirits of their ancestors.

As the story unfolds, the two boys search for the hill that houses this echo tree. The boy who believes in this echo tree chastises Leo's brother for his doubt and for the fact that, like Henry, he left the natural world of the South long ago:

> "Did Leo used to want to come up to New York?"
> "He ain't thinkin bout you whilst you way up yonder."
> "How come you say that? What's wrong with up there?"
> "Leo's grandpa, *your'n too*, well he say up in the city messes you up."[24]

As the boys continue their debate about city and country, or North and South, the believer hears the deceased Leo's voice; in fact, Leo sends a warning through the echo tree to his brother: "He say you his brother, but iffen you don't get that hard city water out your gut, you liable to taint yourself."[25]

Leo's brother cannot understand why Leo, now in the spirit world, dismisses the city and its concrete and skyscrapers. He levels the final blow to his dead brother when he says, "You never stayed down here with us. You always lived up there."[26] In this parable, the city eats away the fruits of the spirit. The impact of this loss of soul amounts to literal and metaphorical death. Mindful of how Leo Patillo took Billy's life, Henry created an alternative Leo who is indeed aware of how the city can siphon one's humanity or how violence can overtake reason.

A year after Billy's death, the Porter family buried two more young men who had been killed just as they were entering manhood. In August 1960, Henry's younger cousins, Lawrence and Warrant Porter (brothers of Minnie Rose Hayes), eighteen and sixteen years of age, respectively, were killed when the car they were riding in careened into a waterhole owned by the bauxite mine company in Sweet Home. The site of the fatal accident was not far from land where the Porters' old house and its neighbors stood before the mine bought out the homeowners years earlier. The cause of the tragedy was never formally determined, but the oral history of the family and others in the community indicates that police with ill intent were chasing the young men, and that the driver of the car was shot in the head.

While Henry was eight years older than his cousin Lawrence, they had shared a similar dream; his younger cousin had imagined a life as a songwriter. With such tragedy pounding the family like hail, Henry seemed to seek some understanding of these inexplicable and surreal events through the prism of philosophy. Central to this discipline is the ability to stand outside of the subject, to analyze it from without. For his own psychological well-being, Henry needed to think in such terms.

Henry's interest in philosophy became especially apparent in a language and literature course that he probably took in the fall of 1960. In this course, taught by Dr. Maurice Kramer, he wrestled with the ideas of two early writers on the U.S. scene: Hector St. John de Crevecoeur, a Frenchman who became a naturalized citizen, and James Fennimore Cooper, a pivotal founding voice in Anglo-American literature. Between De Crevecoeur's *Letters from an American Farmer*, a late-eighteenth-century collection of sketches of Anglo-American life and culture, and Cooper's early-nineteenth-century novel, *The Pioneers*,

Henry had to tackle the question of origins and authenticity—that is, what defines the true American character?

Henry found himself lumbering through these pioneering works, and his writing reflects his difficulty in trying to synthesize their ideas: "Just as Crevecoeur's attempts to describe this 'new' American seem to be an idealistic combination of his observations and experiences interwoven comparatively with his European background, Cooper's attempts of giving significance to the 'pioneer' American seem to result from his actual experiences. He was born and grew up an American. He had a 'feeling' for frontier life."[27]

Like most college students in his era who dared to study pre-twentieth-century literature, Henry labored to make sense of these early landmarks in American philosophy and fiction. He struggled to find language befitting the complexity of the two minds at work. His primary point could have been explained in more direct language, indicating Cooper's supposed advantage of insight as a U.S.-born citizen. Part of the challenge of this exercise was in the genre; Henry was at his best in the worlds of fiction and poetry, not literary criticism.

While Henry was more at home in creative writing, he evidently appreciated Kramer's writing challenge to his critical sensibility and kept this mediocre paper as a reminder of what he, as a writer, had to be open to: constructive criticism. He must have impressed Kramer with his other papers, because his professor's comments written at the end of this comparative essay were cautionary. "I detect some respectable ideas along the way, but this paper is so poorly organized that I really cannot determine what your general conclusions are. In the future, decide what you want to say and say it as clearly and straightforwardly as possible."[28] This paper received a four on a one-to-five grading scale, with one being the highest. Henry nonetheless received an A in the course.

If Henry needed external proof of his talents as a creative writer during this period, he received just that when his first major publication, "A City Game," won first prize for fiction in the 1960–61 volume of the *Anthologist*.[29] It was republished posthumously as "A Harlem Game."

A perceptive exploration of the relationship between human behavior and the environment, the story reflected Henry's interest in detail and character development. Young black boys are at the forefront, looking for something to do, a new activity to engage in or challenge to pursue in the city. As a man, Henry could now reflect on his Harlem experience through his third-person narrator:

Mack and Jayjay stopped at the stoop and while Jayjay bounced the basketball around for practice, Mack slumped down on the concrete steps and fingered an iron spike jutting from the metal rail on the stoop. Up the street the block lights came on and the glow blended with the drugstore's orange-red neons. Mack looked up at the broken lamp in front of his stoop.

"Let's go to the show, Jay."

"I ain't got no money."

"Don't punk out. I can get some."[30]

Convinced that he can finagle more money from his mother while she is engaged in an intense game of cards with his father and some other men, Mack "turned and ran up the stairway. At the top a familiar odor came to him from the darkened hall. Beer cans sprawled near his door and a blood stain streaked the top step where somebody had been cut in a fight."[31] In "A City Game," even the architecture embodies the dangers of urban life. Mack navigates his way upstairs through a "darkened hall" and past a "blood stain" left on the top step. This moment resonates with a fatalism akin to that in the fiction of Richard Wright and Ann Petry in the 1940s and 1950s. In addition to depicting certain eerie aspects of the physical and social landscape of Harlem, Henry reveals a complicated contrast—the ideal and comfortable home life with his Harlem family against a version of Harlem riddled with questionable social circumstances.

Mack coaxes his mother—a woman so comfortable with herself that she can play cards with men absent of pretense and shuttle a beer down her throat— into sharing some of her money with him. As the only one winning any hands, she has enough to share but lets him know she expects repayment. In this case, though, Mack's mother is not the problem. She stands at the refrigerator, keeping watch over the stock of food and drink. His father, whose hand and money are faltering, covertly clamps down on his son, forcing Mack to surrender his money.

Mack lowered his eyes. The big man gently tugged his arm for an answer. He glanced around at the others. They were busy and did not see him, and before he [Mack] knew what he was doing he was putting three of the four quarters in front of the big man.

"Thank you, son. You're a smart punk."[32]

Brimming with anger about the imbalance of power between himself and his father but having no recourse to address it, Mack heads outside, with only a quarter, into the neon lights of Harlem. This story disturbed Aunt Mary and Uncle Jack; they felt the parents in "A Harlem Game" were modeled after them.[33] They were devastated that Henry would render his experience with them in such unflattering terms. Loretta Dumas remembers, "like it was yesterday," the depth of their hurt after they read this story.

In the broadest sense, the story is autobiographical in relation to the emotions Henry re-created, but the characters were not necessarily based on Aunt Mary and Uncle Jack. Henry undoubtedly observed and encountered, in both adolescence and adulthood, situations in Harlem where bullies (either teenagers or adults) took advantage of younger or weaker people. Searching for a way to explore this phenomenon, Henry developed the fictional characters in "A City Game." However, he never expressed to those who knew him well anything but appreciation for having lived with Aunt Mary and Uncle Jack. If the parents in the story resemble any parental figures in Henry's life, they would probably be Appliance and Big Henry, who were not, in some aspects at least, traditional parents. Mack's mother does give him money to attend the show, but, as alert as she is at cards, she is oblivious of her husband's stealthy extortion of Mack. Mack's parents are more focused on the card game than what their son is doing, more focused on the intricacies of their endeavors than their son's activities. The story revealed less about Henry's family and more about his layered view of Harlem, calling into question, in nuanced language and arresting symbolism, the notion of Harlem as economic and cultural haven.

At twenty-six, Henry had his first major publication, a sign of approval from his literary peers and the magazine's faculty advisors, William Sloane and Allan Kaprow. Bringing things full circle, the editor at the time was graduating senior Alan Cheuse, one of the staff members Henry had berated for moral depravity two years earlier.

During this period, Henry had also received encouragement for his talents as a poet. In the fall of 1960, Dr. William Wynkoop, an Emerson scholar who taught at Rutgers for twenty years, commented on Henry's analysis of Emerson's "Self-Reliance." "You are yourself a poet," Wynkoop began. "If you have not done so, find a volume of Emerson's essays and poems and read them in your spare time. You will find it worth your while."[34] Henry earned only a C in the course, but Wynkoop looked beyond Henry's performance in that course to praise his potential, alluding to Henry's talent and the work required to develop as a poet. For this professor to have offered such unmitigated affirmation—speaking in the declarative, "you are a poet"—was certainly encouraging for Henry. Of the faculty he encountered, Wynkoop seems to have taken the most interest in his development as a creative writer. Wynkoop encouraged Henry to read, and so he did, immersing himself more broadly in the American literary canon.

Henry would come to know not only Emerson but the most celebrated poet of the nineteenth century, Walt Whitman, one of the cultural lodestars of the Beat Movement. In fact, reflecting on his days in the Village with the Beat crowd, Amiri Baraka identified Whitman as one of the "prophets" of that moment "who broke away from England with his free verse."[35] The nineteenth-century everyman poet was celebrated for his unfettered delight in celebrating the individual in all of his glory and complexity. Henry was also taken with Whitman.

In an undated essay, written in either 1960 or 1961 of Henry's third year, Henry wrote that he chose to "refrain from an objective analysis of *Leaves of Grass*," Whitman's epic adventure into the American and human spirit via free verse. For Henry, it was too difficult to write about Whitman in the third person, since the poet's reputation was formed by his first person, free-verse flourishes. The poem had registered at such an emotional level for Henry that he could not analyze it objectively. The idea of flouting convention or tradition, of carving out an artistic identity with little concern for artistic ancestors, was a part of the Beat ethos and one Henry identified with as a developing writer. Beat writers had embraced Whitman because he had done what they were trying to do.

In reading Whitman, Henry made one of his first self-acknowledged connections with a fellow artist. "Immediately," he revealed, "I began to think that I would greatly enjoy writing about the effect of the work on me."[36] Through Whitman, Henry recognized that, for him, art had a subjective dimension. As Whitman had sung of himself, celebrating his own creative possibilities rather than genuflecting before the ancients, he boldly called upon himself to portray contemporary realities through a poetic lens. Whitman's confidence in the individual artist to render cultural truth was reflective of the American spirit. Just as the United States had risen against the British crown, Whitman dispensed with social and cultural practices that sought to isolate or place him on the periphery. For Henry, such poetic joie de vivre compelled him to dive into Whitman's free verse epic.

Especially compelling to Henry was Whitman's comfort with nonconformity, his resistance to the constraints of religion. Here we see Henry's turning away from the organized religion about which he had been so zealous. "I have long renounced," Henry wrote in his essay on Whitman, "any orthodox religion. Curiously enough when I came to study *Leaves* my religious ideas practically coincided with the poet's."[37] Henry's previous sense of religious orthodoxy, he suggested in this paper, had more to do with social and familial expectations and less to do with his own sense of spiritual consciousness. This is probably the first time Henry committed to paper his misgivings about religion. His new assertion probably accounts for the way in which he discounted his period as a self-confessed Bible-thumper. What is without question is the fact that, within a two-year period, Henry had moved from Christian evangelist—interpreting scripture through a single lens—to reading scripture and literature from multiple angles and even beginning to refute aspects of religious orthodoxy. For him, the Bible and Christianity were now subject to critique. The religious platitudes he had once embraced now had to stand up to the fire of examination and experience.

Henry not only found common ground with Whitman's religious ideas, he also moved away from the entrenched homophobia associated with mainstream sexual mores, embracing the poet on his terms. "Even Whitman's references to loving the body of men," Henry opined, "(distasteful as it sounds to me) doesn't force me to condemn what I feel an aversion to." "Leaves" was too compelling a work of art to dismiss "because of homosexuality. . . . Maybe I should remind myself here that such a topic seems irrelevant to the experience of poetry, except for scholars and biographers, of which I am neither."[38] As Henry acknowledged the value of Whitman's poetry, he was opening his mind in ways that departed from social and religious dogma to which he had held so tightly.

Henry may have been influenced in this aspect by William Wynkoop. Not only did the professor embrace Henry as a writer, but he was one of the first openly gay men Henry encountered.[39] There is no evidence that the two of them ever discussed Wynkoop's sexual identity, but Wynkoop, from the time he arrived at Rutgers in 1959, became a major figure in Henry's development, serving as advisor for *Untitled*, the evening school's literary magazine for which Henry would later serve as editor. When Wynkoop arrived on campus, he had been with his partner for ten years (a relationship that lasted for over forty years). Because he was not concealing his sexual identity during a rabidly homophobic era when most gays and lesbians were loath to acknowledge their sexuality to family, friends, or colleagues, Wynkoop's example of living true to himself must have left an impression on Henry. In his new world, Henry could no longer cling to certain moral absolutes he had previously embraced. In opening his mind to alternative realities, to nuance and shades of gray, he was becoming more like his mother, a nonconformist.

Whitman's focus on the self resonated well with the zeitgeist on many college campuses. The student scene throughout the country in the late 1950s and throughout the 1960s was one in which pressure points of resistance to the social and intellectual status quo were emerging. This group of students, part of the Beat Generation, viewed the world as a series of changing palettes rather than a static or synthetic template for all to follow, as their parents had practiced. Both literary and political awareness was an essential component of the Beat Generation, and Henry was a part of this peripheral consciousness at Rutgers.

Now Henry was also developing a more profound sense of black consciousness, as the economic and political conditions of life for so many blacks in both the North and South continued to worsen. His commitment—contributing to his neglect of other aspects of his life—was to observe and write about the poor and disenfranchised black masses, to capture in words the story of his people. In this sense, his effort echoed the concerns of Richard Wright set forth in *12 Million Black Voices*. A 1941 collection of photographs taken by photographers who detailed the struggles of blacks in the North and South during the years of the Great Depression, these images depict black life in the crosshairs of Jim Crow.

Henry had long since left the land of Jim Crow, but over the next few years he would return to this haunted place in his fiction and in reality, documenting the fight for black and, ultimately, American freedom.

Hate is also creative:
It creates more hate.

—HENRY DUMAS,
"Thought"

CHAPTER FOUR

Another Conversion

For Henry, the spring of 1961 was both the best and worst of times. He would publish two poems and two short stories. In school he attempted a full course load, but he would, at turns, withdraw from one of his courses, fail one, barely pass another, and, on the brighter side, earn an A in Maurice Kramer's language and literature course. While treading water academically, his money problems persisted. Despite these setbacks, Henry must have been pleased with his literary development. In concert with his publications was his concern about what was happening to blacks down South. Henry was drawn to the ongoing fight for equal rights associated with Martin Luther King Jr. He was less interested in the famous people associated with the movement than in the black tenant farmers and sharecroppers in the nation's black belt. As a result of their efforts to secure political and economic rights, they found themselves evicted from the very land they planted and harvested with no real compensation for their labor.

Through their plight, Henry was reminded of the black migrant workers he had met in California in 1957 and of his own family's struggle as small farmers and plantation workers in a system designed to exact everything from them, giving nothing in return. For Henry, one way of providing some salve for his partial guilt over having left the South—aside from returning there to live, an option he apparently never considered—was to join the NAACP. His friends, Herman Robinson and James Lindsay, both of whom were active in supporting formal and informal efforts advancing the black freedom struggle, were members as well. As publicity chairman of the New Brunswick chapter in January 1961, he led a letter-writing campaign to President Kennedy "protesting the allocation of government funds for use of segregated schools in the South."[1]

At the time, Loretta Dumas was not aware of Henry's position in the local chapter of the premier civil rights organization. With a young toddler and all the attendant responsibilities of taking care of their home, she had enough to do. But her lack of knowledge about Henry's activity speaks to the fact that there were aspects of her husband's life to which she simply was not privy.

The chapter was also likely involved with efforts to assist wrongfully evicted sharecroppers in Tennessee who were making a peaceful case against racial injustice. As publicity chair, Henry probably attended or at least was aware of a meeting organized by the People's Organization on Monday, January 16, in Franklin Township. According to the *New Brunswick Home News*, people had gathered to "lay plans for a campaign to give emergency assistance to 75 Negro sharecropping families evicted from their homes in Tennessee."[2] Amassed in tent cities, or makeshift living quarters with nothing for protection from the elements but large canopies, these black laborers had lost their homes and jobs in retaliation for their two-year campaign to obtain voting rights.

Henry received a fair amount of information from NAACP sources in New Jersey and black newspapers and radio. But needing to bear witness to this tragedy himself, he traveled to Somerville, Tennessee, to interview and deliver much-needed items he had collected from the black community surrounding New Brunswick to black families displaced from their homes. In this effort, it appears that Henry was acting on his own, paying for the trip from his own depleted pockets. Most of the black residents of this western Tennessee town were under siege. Services had been refused to those who had signed voting petitions, insurance policies canceled, applications for bank loans rejected, jobs lost, and store credit—which had long kept black farm workers beholden to white landowners—was suddenly denied, leaving them and their families without the means to purchase commodities or supplies.[3] With everything but at the same time nothing to lose, these sharecroppers risked their paltry earnings, and even their safety, to advance their political rights, to realize more fully, the grand ideals set forth in the nation's founding documents.

In response, the few black business and property owners did all they could to house, clothe, and feed the sharecroppers. Students at black colleges in the

South offered assistance. Blacks from up North also contributed to the cause, as did black and white students from schools in the North and Midwest. Some local whites assisted, for example, by not demanding payment on past-due grocery bills, but there was very little visible support from that population. There were eighty-one people from eleven families housed in the temporary settlement by March 1961. The settlement was officially known as Fayette County Freedom Village, but its residents called it Tent City. Whites evicted their black fellow citizens until 345 families from Fayette and Haywood Counties had been pushed into homelessness. And they remained there well into the next year.

Henry's 1961 short story, "A Boll of Roses," published in Rutgers's literary magazine, *Anthologist*, captures the historical events that unfolded in Tennessee. Henry viewed fiction as a means of processing actual events, as he imagined the fear and courage of the families and communities who dared say "no" to the absurdity of Jim Crow. In the story, black and white students have come to encourage sharecroppers in a southern town to sign a voting petition. Layton Fields, a recurring figure in Henry's stories, is a college-age man with aspirations beyond the cotton field. He discusses with his friend Floyd Moss the viability of talking to these college students who are, in Moss's mind, a class above them. Layton wants to hear their questions, and he also wants to meet a certain black coed who is part of this interracial voting rights effort. The exchange between Layton and Floyd Moss reveals the conversations and tensions expressed among black folks without white folks looking on. The young men can talk without the racial filter. "They can come and talk to me. I ain't scared of a few questions," Layton says with confidence. In response, Floyd Moss explains his understanding of how the world beyond the field works. "They ain't got to do nothin. You ever see any poll takin people come and mess around with us niggers in a cotton patch before?"[4]

In the arc of the story, Floyd Moss raises a valid point. Far too often, the people furthest down the economic pole are rendered invisible. In this story, fiction follows reality, as Dumas presents black "cotton-pickers" who claim their right to freedom, even if the world turns a deaf ear toward them. Henry was interested in what the displaced people in Tennessee had to say. On his journey, as he was joined by his friend Herman Robinson, he took numerous photographs, including one of John McFerren, a local black store owner and World War II veteran who led the initiative to assist displaced residents.

In a photograph that includes Henry, he identifies McFerren, James Frazier, and Frazier's daughter (unnamed). Although he had not lived in the South for almost twenty years, Henry looks as if he never left Ozark country. McFerren's attire—a Stetson, button-down work shirt, work pants, and a three-quarter-length leather coat—are punctuated with a slight smile. Neither Frazier nor his daughter is smiling, but both are standing up straight, looking directly at the camera with confidence that belies their situation. Henry, at six feet, does not look comfortable in his twenty-seven-year-old body. His clothes are suitable for the moment—jacket, casual shirt buttoned all the way up, and a pair of khakis—but unlike the others in the photograph, Henry is slouching. There is ambiguity, not confidence, in his expression. It could be either a smile or a frown. Either way, Henry looks forlorn.

In his temporary return to the South, Henry carried with him a growing sense of religious skepticism. Equally puzzling were his contradictory feelings about his native South and his guilt over having left. *Jonoah and the Green Stone*, his posthumously published 1976 novel that he had started in the 1960s, would place this guilt front and center. Jonoah, the lead character, puts it simply: "But I had fled the South, drifted, played a few songs for college kids, told my story here and there, collected money and wasted it: ran and ran. Fear and terror scrape out the bottom of one's soul. I was almost reduced by the fear of the rope and the terror I had seen my family and friends suffer and die by. I chose the safety of my dreams, and the warmth of ignorance."[5] For Henry, his departure from Sweet Home would be the literary impetus for considering a number of questions and scenarios involving the South. Henry may have left Sweet Home as a child, but from an imaginative standpoint, he never left. The region would animate and bedevil him.

Through Jonoah, he was trying to understand the dogged white resistance to black demands for fairness. Another visitor to Tent City, a tall, lanky, white student named Charlie Butts from Oberlin College in Ohio, had also volunteered to assist the displaced families in Somerville. Shortly thereafter, Butts became the first editor of the *Mississippi Free Press*, which was created to assist in chronicling the black fight for freedom. Butts recalls the period as one in which some whites did help with the movement, but the majority of people on the frontlines were black and from the South.[6] Even Henry, despite his sincere efforts to help, was nonetheless a benevolent interloper; after all, he could leave at any time. He had a world of responsibilities elsewhere, and ultimately blacks who lived in the South, enduring the indignities of Jim Crow, needed to speak for themselves, letting their fellow white citizens know that change was on the way.

Although Butts did not know Henry, Henry had photographed him working at a mimeograph machine. Henry did not identify the context of the photo. But he thought enough of the young Butts to visually document his effort. Butts embodied the possibility, mitigated by the political reality of white resistance, of interracial cooperation and sympathy. Charlie Butts's participation in the movement—not to tell blacks what to do but to assist as they did what was necessary for improving their lives—was a source of hope for Henry.[7]

Henry's experience in Tennessee would likely have pushed him to think deeply about the underlying motivation of white resistance to black demands for equal treatment under the law. Later that year, in the fall of 1961, he found a compelling literary exploration of the psychology of white men. In William Wynkoop's language and literature course, Henry took on the theme of white male violence in Hemingway's 1927 story "The Killers" and in Faulkner's 1931 classic "Dry September."[8] The interpretive lens for this analysis was the moral philosophy of Ralph Waldo Emerson, whose work Henry had come to know well at Wynkoop's suggestion.

In Faulkner's tale, the main character, McLendon, participates in a lynch mob, taking the life of a black man. When he returns home, still fuming and needing to act out his internal rage, he slaps his wife. Referencing Emerson's "Self-Reliance," Henry sought the meaning in McLendon's double assaults: "If you put a chain around the neck of a slave, the other end fastens itself around your own," wrote Emerson.[9] "And the beauty of this law," wrote Henry in full accord, "tragic as it is in our eyes, [it] demands respect."[10] Henry appreciated Emerson's understanding of how slavery had chained white men to sordid and guilt-ridden psychological lives. Their identity was unilaterally tied to bondage. And most scholars on the subject of race in America had only concerned themselves with the condition of the enslaved, not the enslavers who had to deal with certain demons themselves.

Hemingway's "The Killers" revolves around a group of white men behaving like animals. Devoid of morality, they stalk Ole Andreson, whom they say they have to kill for a friend. "They fail as real characters," Henry concluded, "but come alive through the emotion they thrust upon us." Even in their flight from morality, they must reconcile the fact that, as Henry read Emerson, "All things are moral."[11] These men are seeking a world in which they can act with impunity, absent of retribution or consequence. Henry argued that this primal impulse must be tempered with a sense of moral purpose.

As he studied the fiction of these celebrated writers, Henry developed a fuller recognition of how deep the psychology of white supremacy ran. From members of the white literary elite to lynch mobs and Klansmen, white fears of black advancement seemed a kind of rite of passage. Henry elaborated on these concerns in his poem, "Take This River!"[12] True to Henry's concern about nature, its infinite memory, and black folks' yearning to return to their harmonious relationship with nature (i.e., their history and culture) the poem centers on two men following the path of a river in their flight to safety and freedom. The river and all that it touches is nature's memory bank, filled with the sins, burdens, and possibilities of America.

In haunting imagery, Henry explored the intractable sense of white entitlement, as set forth in the fiction of Faulkner and Hemingway, and exercised in the campaign against blacks in the South. Following are lines from the first section of the poem:

> We move up a spine of earth
> That bridges the river and the canal.
> And where a dying white log, finger-like,
> Floating off the bank, claws at the slope,
> We stumble, and we laugh.
> We slow beneath the moon's eye;
> Near the shine of the river's blood face,
> The canal's veil of underbrush sweats frost,
> And this ancient watery scar retains
> The motionless tears of men with troubled spirits.
> For like the whole earth,
> This land of mine is soaked. . . .
>
> Shadows together,
> We fall on the grass without a word.
> We had run this far from the town.
> We had taken the bony course, rocky, and narrow,
> He leading, I following.[13]

The unnamed speaker and a man named Ben are trekking up the "spine" of the earth, following nature's lead. In the process, they observe the "dying white log," as it "claws at the slope." The men laugh, realizing that the time for this log, the age of white supremacy, has past. The history of the United States is symbolized in the "river's blood face," the blood of African descendants. Indeed, the riverbed is "soaked" with the physical and cultural detritus of many thousands gone.

This history of the land, for these two men in flight, is related partially to the fact that they "had run this far from town." For "the hood of night is coming. / Up the river, down the river / The sky and night kiss between the wind."[14] Run out of town by hooded hooligans, also known as the Klan, the speaker notes the mysterious relationship of the sky, the night, and the wind, all of which are infinite and eternal, unable to be held but audacious in their permanence. In other words, not even the Klan can corrupt the beauty and mystery of the natural world or black people. As Henry worked on this poem, he was in the process of clarifying his ideas about the best options for southern and northern blacks to fulfill their collective destiny.

In his understanding, as the condition of the majority of blacks in the country continued to worsen, and whites seemed intent on preserving absolute power, increasing numbers of blacks were fed up with what they perceived to be the shuffle-along pace of black freedom. Among blacks amassed in the nation's cities, and in the South, resentment toward white domination was escalating. In the midst of this social and cultural cauldron, Henry was developing a keen interest in black history, culture, and liberation. He had always appreciated his people, but by now he was searching for literary and cultural answers to political, social, and even economic questions.

With his sojourn to the South and his literary and academic attempts to make sense of what he was witnessing, Henry was finding his literary way. In November 1961, as the Freedom Rides protesting segregated transportation in the South were ending, a new voice of black liberation was emerging in the North. A former petty criminal and hustler, Malcolm X was well on his way to distinction in black political and religious circles. Through the auspices of the Nation of Islam, he was becoming the thorn in the side of black and white leaders who were advocating integration. And he would also become a prominent part of Henry's evolving literary vision.

Buoyed by the fear of black retribution against whites, as laid out in the 1959 documentary *The Hate that Hate Produced*, Malcolm X and the idea of black separatism, though practically untenable, was gaining traction. Produced by black journalist and former convict Louis Lomax and a young CBS news correspondent named Mike Wallace, the film presented the Nation of Islam as a black religious sect spewing white hatred. For white liberals in the United States, it was a warning signal for social chaos if conditions for black folks did not change soon. Malcolm, as his biographer Manning Marable explains, "thought the show had demonized the Nation. . . . But part of Malcolm always believed that even negative publicity was better than none at all."[15] As abreast as Henry was of current events—the inexcusable conditions that blacks were enduring in the South and the assaults on the peaceful Freedom Riders in Alabama and Mississippi—it is safe to assume he was aware of the film. There is ample evidence that he was thinking cautiously but seriously about the merits of the Nation's philosophy of racial uplift and the link between that and racial separation.

Indeed, throughout 1961, Malcolm's agenda was to visit colleges and universities, bringing attention to the Nation and clarifying what he perceived as the distortions or misrepresentations of the organization. Contrary to the leader of the Nation, Elijah Muhammad, Malcolm was more politically driven.[16] Malcolm brought his message to the Newark campus of Rutgers in November 1961, where he debated Dr. William Neal Brown, a social work professor.

Hired in 1956 as Rutgers's first black professor, Brown had served with the celebrated Tuskegee Airmen. He challenged the Black Muslims' proposal for a separate Negro state, arguing, in the vein of King and the NAACP, that integration was the most effective way of creating equality of opportunity for the black masses. Although no evidence confirms Henry's presence at the debate, it was covered extensively in the Rutgers *Daily Targum*, and Henry would certainly have been aware of the event, both as a student at Rutgers and as a member of the NAACP. In fact, following the event, the Rutgers-Douglass NAACP chapter (which comprised the male and female campuses) arranged for Malcolm X to visit the New Brunswick campus.

Even more intriguing is that sometime in September 1961, Henry had received a letter of acceptance into the Nation of Islam. In this form letter, Henry was encouraged to "follow Mr. Muhammad and set yourself in heaven at once! Money, good homes and friendship in all walks of life is the goal that we intend to reach. Heaven and hell are two states of conditions while we live—not after we die. Stop believing the white man's teachings. Get out of his name, even if you just call yourself 'D.'"[17] If Henry ever sought membership in the NOI, no evidence exists that any of his acquaintances knew about it. Although he kept this acceptance letter, he was never a member of the NOI, though he may well have considered joining or even feigned interest in it to find out more about the substance of this black religious sect that seemed attendant to the frustrations and desires of America's urban black working class. Malcolm X and the Nation leadership often vilified organizations such as the NAACP and the Southern Christian Leadership Conference (SCLC) as middle-class entities desirous of integrating with whites at the expense of the majority of blacks. That Henry had—and kept—in his possession an NOI acceptance letter reveals that his curiosity had been piqued. The focus on material well-being and its privileging of this world over the afterlife would have been of particular interest to him, in light of his own shift from conventional Christianity.

Henry was not fascinated by Malcolm X himself, just by the appeal he held for others, and he would soon see the talented, charismatic, new face of the NOI up close. On February 9, 1962, during his visit to the New Brunswick campus, Malcolm repeated his call for a separate Negro state. Earl Thomas, one of the few black students at Rutgers and then one of Henry's closest friends, reflected on Malcolm's visit and Henry's view of the Nation at the time. According to him, "Henry thought the organization was located on the periphery of black life, that the Nation's message was reaching a core group of disenfranchised black citizens," the urban underclass. Henry and Earl Thomas had often debated the merits of Malcolm's logic: "Did he really believe all this stuff he was propagating? Was the myth of Yacub, a black scientist who lived six thousand years ago and created the race of 'white devils,' something Malcolm really believed? Was separatism feasible, and, if it came to pass, what would that mean for black people throughout the country?"[18]

Henry wanted to know the answers to these questions and more. He and Earl Thomas attended the lecture, and afterward, as Thomas would recall years later, they "went out with Malcolm to a diner for three hours (he wouldn't let us tape him) and asked him hard questions about the likelihood of a separate state and other concerns." After spending time with him, they concluded that "Malcolm didn't believe all this stuff. He had leadership skills, and wanted to go somewhere, to do something. It was very clear Malcolm wasn't buying all that, he strongly implied that in the interview."[19] Henry and Earl found themselves reconciling their images of Malcolm the Minister with Malcolm the Man. They concluded that this religious and political figure drew on multiple rhetorical strategies depending on the audience. In their view, he was, at his core, neither a hatemonger nor separatist, but he was comfortable articulating a kind of pragmatic black nationalism and separatism, if that was necessary to secure black folks certain economic opportunities. Indeed, Malcolm had done just that a year earlier, when he secretly met with the Ku Klux Klan to discuss the purchase of parcels of land in Georgia to establish a self-contained black community.[20]

Moreover, as black students at Rutgers, Henry and Earl Thomas were implicitly headed down the path of middle-class respectability, which meant, at least according to Malcolm's excoriation of the black middle class in public, that they would eventually sell out the masses in order to integrate with whites. Following Malcolm's line of thinking, in practice these two friends had already done so, establishing friendships and relationships across racial lines.

Malcolm's bold articulation of black power certainly impressed Henry. But having spent a year in the Arabian Peninsula, learning about orthodox Islam, Henry was privy to the questionable aspects of the Nation that were not consistent with the form of Islam he had observed. Nonetheless, Malcolm X was firing a shot across the bow to America's black and white political class, causing damage to the integrationist ship.

After Malcolm's February visit, the Rutgers *Targum* evidently critiqued the Nation's separatist solution to the race problem, and Henry responded by drafting a letter to the editor. Since it was never published, either the paper rejected it, or Henry didn't submit it, though he kept the draft. He sought to inform the community—some of whose members were astonished at the Muslim position on racial separation—about the deeper proposition at the core of the Nation's argument:

> First of all, the Muslims are nothing new. Not only have they been around for years (unknown to most Americans in all communities), but the idea of separatism has been around since America! . . .

> The question is being asked over and over in different ways: Who are the Black Muslims? One answer is plain. The Muslims are more signs of the Negro in American becoming a VISIBLE MAN. They are signs of black men turning around not to say NOBODY KNOWS MY NAME (although that is an intriguing ambiguity) but rather THIS IS MY NAME! The tragedy of America is that she wants the Negro to echo every aspect of white culture in an attempt at final cultural assimilation. This is our heritage. There is nothing wrong with how Europeans "melted" into a new nation. But the resulting cultural values have systematically screened out the complex of African cultures that once were the "name" of the Negroes. . . . When the Muslims announce their "name," let us hope America will say, Glad to know you, where have you been?

> Mr. H. "Ibin" Dumas[21]

Henry never joined the Nation. He did, however, suggest some kind of association by using the Arabic term Ibin (son of) in his closing, although this term appears nowhere else in his papers.[22]

Henry's *Targum* letter was essentially a minihistory of black separatist thought in the United States. In reality, however, only a relatively small number of blacks had migrated back to Africa. From the founding of the nation of Liberia in 1820 with U.S. blacks to Marcus Garvey's short-lived Black Star shipping enterprise from 1919 to 1922, black separation has been less like a wave and more like an eddy, a relatively contained movement.

Demonstrating his knowledge of the contemporary black literary scene, Henry read the Black Muslim ideology of uplift and separatism as the means by which the black man could achieve visibility. He launched a direct counterpoint to Ralph Ellison's *Invisible Man*, in which the narrator preoccupies himself with becoming VISIBLE in the white world at the expense of his cultural identity. His novel, for all its literary and cultural power, in the end, leaves the Invisible Man underground, literally and symbolically out of sight. For Henry, Malcolm X and the Nation were a collective refutation of the idea that blacks should be fighting for visibility in the world of whites.

By using the phrase "nobody knows my name," he was alluding to James Baldwin's 1961 autobiographical collection of essays, *Nobody Knows My Name*. With Baldwin, Henry's reference seems to be one of convenience, rather than rooted in philosophical difference or counterpoint, for Baldwin's work across genres was sharper, more acidic in its critique of white America than Ellison's. In clear, unromantic terms, Baldwin, one of America's most influential writers of the 1950s and 1960s, articulated the primary frustration among black men: the fact that they were often invisible to society. Even in rare moments of public or social visibility, Baldwin wrote, no one really knows a black man's name, his culture, or his history.

Henry had taken the time to gather his thoughts for a letter that was never published. Nonetheless, his interest in the lives of the black folk who worked the hardest was affirmed in the core philosophy of Malcolm X. Culturally speaking, some black writers were embracing Malcolm's message. In the summer of 1962, an informal band of emerging black radical writers—Joe Johnson, Askia Toure, Charles Patterson, Calvin Hernton, and Tom Dent—invited their black peers in New York to a workshop. Still in New Jersey, Henry was not part of this initial effort, but he would learn about this new black collective that would call itself Umbra, a term denoting the dark area or the blackest part of a shadow. The idea of Umbra, of black writers coming together to discuss race and writing, was appealing, something he had missed in the largely white literary activity at Rutgers.

In the United States, up until this time, blackness in any context was fraught with negative associations. The goal of Umbra, as Tom Dent offered in a retrospective on the period, was to form a creative body to "meet our needs as writers. We felt it imperative that we have a device that could deal with race, that could serve to bring us together, that could be a vehicle for the expression of the bitterness and beauties of being Afro-American."[23]

In the context of Umbra, blackness was an all-encompassing cultural and creative reference, a signifier of universality, the color of the cosmos. For these writers, many of whom had long been exposed to the white tradition, they were interested in turning their imaginative worlds black, in both language and vision. This was indeed the case for Henry. His Rutgers experience had been central to his development, but it had not afforded him access to a community of black writers from which he could draw support and criticism. With exposure, if not formal affiliation with Umbra and Malcolm X's brand of cultural nationalism, Henry was closer to realizing a deeper cultural understanding of his role as artist. He was also beginning to fall prey to some of the same pressures that Malcolm X and scores of other black men would confront: marriage, family, and money.

Those three concerns came together as Henry and Loretta attempted to have a second child. Since the birth of David, Loretta had experienced difficulty conceiving again. As she carried Michael to term, the couple embarked on a grueling austerity program in order to save money to purchase a larger home in the town of Highland Park. Henry cobbled together employment by working odd jobs. Reflecting on the months prior to closing on the house, Loretta Dumas remembers how they saved their money in order to make the purchase. Four weeks before the move, on August 24, 1962, Michael Hassan was born. In naming this second son, Henry gestured toward Malcolm X and the black phenomenon of naming children using African, Arabic, or unique African American names by giving him a middle name with Arabic roots. The prolonged austerity leading up to the move exacted a toll on husband and wife. Their singular focus on the goal of purchasing a house had caused them, understandably, to focus less on each other. They were already growing apart, and this stressful situation did not help.

To be sure, the September 1962 move from University Heights to 408 South Ninth Avenue in Highland Park was fraught with meaning, in some ways symbolizing a point of no return in their marriage. One thing was certain: if Loretta had hoped the couple would revive the blissful period of their early years, the birth of Michael, as she put it, "disabused me of that notion." Loretta sensed, and indeed Henry's behavior confirmed, that the weight of family responsibility was coming into conflict with his artistic imperative. Marriage and family had become an encumbrance as Henry was moving into an invigorating phase as an artist. This move to larger quarters also enabled Henry to invite an exchange student, a Ugandan named Sulemani Sentumbwe, to live with the family for a short period. In a new house with a new baby, Loretta found that the temporary addition of Sentumbwe to the household created further demands on her.

But there was a larger issue associated not so much with Sentumbwe but with where Henry was heading without his wife. Loretta was comfortable as the devoted wife, but as Henry's literary ambitions became manifest, so too did social opportunities that may have been productive for him but not beneficial to his marriage. On a campus with young, white women, at a time when curiosity on either side of the color line was high, Henry immersed himself in the evangelical discipline of his early Rutgers days (recall his moralistic rant against the *Anthologist* staff) in order to avoid succumbing to temptation.

In the meantime, Loretta cared for the boys, eventually getting a job as a secretary herself. Henry continued to work various jobs and to refine his skills as a writer. If Malcolm X represented the idea of speaking truth to power, Ralph Ellison embodied the possibility of black literary distinction. As a writer, Henry was intrigued by the former but wedded to the latter.

During his time at Rutgers, Henry was in close proximity to Ellison, who in 1953 had become the first black American to receive the National Book Award. From 1962 to 1964, as Ellison biographer Arnold Rampersad notes, Ellison was "visiting professor of writing and comparative literature and the first writer in residence at Rutgers University."[24] For Henry and many other writers, Ellison exemplified black literary success, and his Rutgers period could have been the perfect opportunity for them to learn from the master. But Ellison ferociously guarded his hallowed place as *the* black male writer in the white publishing world. This attitude, which the Rutgers writing community got a taste of during Ellison's tenure, was still apparent a decade later. In her work as an editor at Random House, Toni Morrison worked hard to create publishing opportunities for young black writers, "people like Gayl Jones, Henry Dumas, Toni Cade Bambara, Lucille Clifton, June Jordan. Unfortunately, Ralph had no interest in rallying for such writers."[25]

Early during Ellison's tenure on campus in 1962, Henry apparently left the literary standard-bearer a manuscript of short stories and perhaps a draft of his novel-in-progress, but the acclaimed authority on African American culture never responded. Henry's contemporary, Alan Cheuse, who was studying for his doctorate in comparative literature, recalled Ellison complaining to him about material Henry had left for him. Despite his cosmopolitan interests, Ellison could have an acidic tongue, and Cheuse recalls him unleashing the ultimate racial epithet against Henry. Then he derisively compared Henry with the U.S. poet Nicolas Vachel Lindsay (1879–1931): "If that Vachal Lindsay poem-writing nigger shows up at my door," Ellison thundered, "tell him I'm not here. I'll hide in the supply closet if I have to, to get away from him."[26] Lindsay was known for rhyming verse that energized and celebrated the masses. But mass appeal, according to Ellison, was the bogeyman. While much of Lindsay's verse may have been doggerel, Ellison concluded that Henry's work was of a similar nature.

Stung but not stifled by Ellison's dismissal, Henry turned his attention elsewhere, continuing to write steadily. Sometime in 1962, probably on the Rutgers campus, Henry met a fellow aspiring writer who would become a dear friend. Jay Wright, an elegant man-about-town, was studying for his doctorate in comparative literature at Rutgers. Wright would be the first black writer with whom Henry developed a serious friendship. The two had much in common, including modest economic backgrounds, street smarts, a love of music (Wright played bass), corresponding years in the military (Henry in the air force, Wright in the army), and especially their deep appreciation of poetry and literature. Writing years later about their friendship, Wright would join a chorus of Dumas's friends who would agree that "Henry Dumas lived very rapidly, and very slowly. We could never seem to keep up with him, or catch him, or hold him when we did. . . . Dumas had heavy roots, in his people, in the land, that balanced the intensity of his day-to-day push toward a coherent, artistic system that could express and even, in a sense, redeem those values he cared about."[27]

In Wright, Henry now had a black male peer with kindred interests, whose ability to finish projects may well have been a source of both motivation and friendly envy. Wright spent his formative years in his hometown, Albuquerque, New Mexico, and in his late teen years playing minor-league baseball in California. Whether running bases, studying, or playing bass, Wright possessed a level of concentration that enabled him to be both productive and efficient.

Like Henry, Wright entered college (University of California, Berkeley) after the military, but he earned his undergraduate degree in comparative literature in three years, and he eventually completed all but the dissertation in the comparative literature doctoral program at Rutgers. Wright thrived in both academic and artistic milieus. Like Henry, Wright was interested in religion, but he did not experience a phase in which he felt compelled to convert or evangelize. Instead, the future MacArthur Fellow indulged his religious curiosity in a semester at Union Theological Seminary in New York.

Herein lay the difference between two men who were so compatible. As a poet, Wright distinguished himself for his serious study of history, religion, and anthropology. Henry was interested in similar things, but his mind was always racing ahead to the next idea and as a result, he sometimes lacked the ability to develop his ideas in full, finding it difficult to stay focused on one subject. Wright had developed the ability to slow down and dig deeper. He also did not have a family, which offered Henry a ready-made, maybe even justifiable, reason to procrastinate. In so many ways, Wright enjoyed the artistic life Henry came to desire, which was characterized by continual, not just ephemeral, freedom.

Beloved,
I have to adore the earth:
The wind must have heard
Your voice once.
It echoes and sings like you.

—HENRY DUMAS,
from "Love Song"

CHAPTER FIVE

Progress, Setbacks, and Romance

Deeply moved by the Freedom Movement in the South, Henry was considering the merits of the two competing but complementary approaches to black uplift: separation and integration. The merits and problems of both would become part of his evolving literary palette. Surely he and Jay Wright would discuss such issues. By 1963, having shrugged off Ellison's rebuff in the fall of 1962, Henry was searching for ways to feed his cravings for creative expression and for feedback about the quality of his work. In June of that year, he applied to the prestigious Bread Loaf Writers Conference in Middlebury, Vermont.

Begun by New York editor John Farrar in 1926, Bread Loaf had become the premier summer sojourn for the American literati. A list of its fellows and faculty is a veritable roll call in the Euro-American literary tradition. Henry was accepted into the literary retreat, an affirmation of his potential. But the invitation to attend was unaccompanied by assistance with either tuition or travel expenses. With a mortgage and other homeowner expenses now stacking up with the family's other compounding bills, there was no way Henry could travel to the place synonymous with literary excellence. "We should very much like to have you at Bread Loaf," wrote Paul Cubeta, the assistant director of the program, "but our funds are limited and the number of outstanding candidates was particularly large this year."[1] Of the thirteen writers selected for the 1963 summer class, Joan Didion may be the most famous.[2]

The director of the conference was John Ciardi, a major poet and former faculty member at Rutgers from 1953 to 1961, who made his living more from the lecture circuit than the classroom. Also on the Bread Loaf writing staff was none other than William Sloane, the director of Rutgers University Press. The two men, who were good friends, also served as faculty advisors for the *Anthologist*, in which some of Henry's first stories and poems had appeared. They were also good friends with Ralph Ellison. Sloane had led the effort to bring Ellison to Rutgers, as part of a larger initiative to establish Rutgers as a primary player in serious literary studies. It was Sloane to whom Henry would turn for literary advice over the next three years. It is not known whether Henry sought Sloane's help in getting financial support from Bread Loaf. However, Bread Loaf did support writers with hardship cases, in particular those "whose manuscripts," writes Ciardi biographer Edward M. Cifelli, "were clearly superior."[3]

More than likely, Henry had submitted some of his published stories and maybe a draft of his novel-in-progress for his writing sample, some of which Ellison had dismissed about a year earlier. Whatever work he submitted, the selection committee was impressed enough to invite him but not enough to offer funding. What made the difference? What was the line between acceptance and funding? If Sloane and Ciardi had any hand in the selection process, given their connection to Ellison, Henry should have been on the chopping block. But would they have consulted Ellison about a potential fellow in a year when the literary icon would not even be attending? Could they have invited Henry, all the while knowing that he could not come without funding? There are no definitive answers to these questions.

However, it seems likely that the selection committee thought the thirteen other writers, including Joan Didion, held more promise. In any case, apparently the Bread Loaf gatekeepers did not find Henry's literary future to look as immediate or bright.

One student Bread Loaf had supported a few years earlier was Alan Cheuse, whom Henry had met through his involvement with the *Anthologist*, and who earned his way to the conference via the kitchen. Four decades later, in *Listening to the Page*, Cheuse's memoir about his life as a writer, published in 2001, he explained William Sloane's role in his Bread Loaf experience in the summer of 1959: "Came the summer between my junior and senior years and he [Sloane] invited me to Bread Loaf to work as a waiter, one of the great honors an undergraduate writer could then achieve."[4] This experience enabled Cheuse to meet Ralph Ellison, whom Sloane had invited to join the Bread Loaf faculty for that year. Cheuse, who would become a novelist himself, would reconnect with Ellison as a graduate student in just a few years during Ellison's time at Rutgers.

But whatever had compelled Sloane to reach out to Cheuse did not extend to Henry's case. With limited funds at Bread Loaf, neither Sloane nor Ciardi felt Henry a "must." A very good candidate, certainly, but apparently other writers presented more compelling literary cases for financial support. Never one to glad-hand people in positions of power, Henry did not dwell on the role Sloane may have played in his unrealized Bread Loaf efforts. He may not have considered Sloane the enemy, but he probably discerned that Ellison's dismissive opinion of him, which Sloane and Ciardi were probably aware of, could have played a part in his not being offered funding for the conference. He also knew, however, that the conference—aside from substantive discussions of writing and moments of social revelry—could have been a literary game-changer for him in terms of networking.

Bread Loaf's limited invitation to Henry, while clearly a major disappointment for him without the corresponding funding, did not appear to be an issue of racial exclusion. The conference had an impressive list of black attendees. Between 1954 and 1965, Melvin Tolson, Ralph Ellison (as faculty), John A. Williams, Gloria Oden, William Melvin Kelley, Kristin Hunter, and Claude Brown had participated in the elite retreat.[5] For black writers trying to establish themselves in the largely white publishing industry in the 1960s, a couple of weeks spent hobnobbing with industry insiders and published writers certainly did not hurt their chances of seeing their work in print. Ciardi, one of the few Italian Americans from his generation to become a literary star, understood the power of Bread Loaf for fledgling writers.

In missing out on Bread Loaf, Henry continued on the periphery of the literary elite. He could make it to the riverbank but not cross over. Disappointed but not dismayed, Henry continued looking for ways to improve as a writer. Later that year he built on his knowledge of Umbra, the radical black writers collective established in New York in 1962. He was familiar with its efforts, and he interacted with a number of its members, including Ishmael Reed, Steve Cannon, Norman Pritchard, Lennox Raphael, and Maryanne Raphael, all of whom contributed to the short-lived *Umbra Magazine*. Henry appreciated the generation of ideas by black writers, but he was wary of the possibility of falling into creative lockstep with this or any other group, so he never joined the group. All of the aforementioned were listed in Henry's personal phonebook. The group's focus on collective development and consciousness was prelude to the more pronounced political and artistic engagement of the Black Arts Movement that would emerge in just a few years. But such a mandate of conformity was bound to produce dissention, and by the fall of 1963, as a result of internal conflicts, the workshop dissolved; the collective and its publication had already seen their best days. Of all the participants in the collective, Henry would maintain a friendship with Lennox Raphael.

Raphael, a Trinidadian poet and playwright, considered Henry a good friend. "I liked him personally," noted Raphael years later, "and saw tremendous promise in his work. As such, he and I spent lots of time together talking about life and the making of literature."[6] Over the next few years, Henry, in his position as student-editor of *Untitled* in 1965, the evening school literary magazine at Rutgers, would attempt, unsuccessfully, to publish some of Raphael's poetry.

Henry's association with Raphael and other Umbra writers represented Henry's movement into a broader network of black writers. Up through the summer of 1963, with his efforts to attend Bread Loaf and engage the Umbra crowd, Henry was making serious literary strides. This was apparent in the voluminous literary rejection notices he was accruing and in the anemic state of his bank account, both of which were typical for struggling writers. Nevertheless, by 1962, Henry had published three impressive short stories and two visionary poems, and had been a staff member of the *Anthologist* dating back to 1960. But as he was gaining traction as a writer, he was losing ground in his marriage. Money continued to pose problems for the Dumases. Henry had found work as a salesman and clerk at Shelley's Bookstore and also as a building and concrete inspector in 1963. In the latter position, Henry occasionally had access to a concrete truck and drove the truck to campus. "One time," as his college friend Earl Thomas recounted with a hearty chuckle, "Henry pulled up at the library in a cement truck with a six pack of beer."[7] However, Henry needed more than some brew to offset what was happening in his marriage. Loretta was certainly stressed by the lack of money. She still believed in their marriage and in Henry's talent as a writer, but the challenge to their relationship was related less to financial hardship and more to major cultural change and to Henry's evolving sense of what he needed from or desired in his wife. Add to this Henry's now more open stance toward alcohol and the result is a marriage at risk.

For couples married in the 1950s or earlier, the institution of marriage was in the process of dramatic change at the beginning of the 1960s. Reaping the benefits from the post–World War II economic boom, with unprecedented numbers of women having entered the workforce—albeit later in life and at lower wages than most men—the U.S. middle class had expanded and the suburban class was born. As a result, the social understanding of marriage shifted from what historian Stephanie Coontz has identified as a commitment to "obedience" to one of "intimacy."[8]

Men and women began to have greater expectations for personal fulfillment. It was not enough to be a good wife or husband in the traditional sense of managing the household or providing for the family. You had to be a good lover, a companion in tune with your lover's most intimate desires. In essence, younger Americans were introduced to the idea that in marriage they could find not just a helpmate but a soul mate. For the husband or wife who no longer had the giddy or goose-bump feelings of courtship days, the other side of the door was the answer. Life was too short. The spouse left behind had done nothing wrong, but now the concept of commitment entailed larger emotional and psychological expectations. Like an employee forced to deal with an unexpected dismissal, some husbands and wives would now learn that they had been fired. Just a few years earlier, Henry and Loretta would have defined their marriage as solid. In Henry's air force years, they seemed quite the couple, traveling the country and frequently exploring Mexico. But now the romance and adventure had given way to a kind of stasis that creeps, periodically, into all long-term relationships.

That money was scarce posed a major problem for the family, and Henry's interests were increasingly outside the home. Although they had recently purchased a house, he and Loretta were proceeding along different paths. Loretta managed home, children, and a full-time secretarial position. When he was not inspecting batches of concrete, Hank, as his friends at Rutgers sometimes called him, was hanging out with his literary acquaintances or was tucked away in the attic in Highland Park trying to write his way to recognition. The two distinct worlds that Henry inhabited were represented in the "Henry" that Loretta knew and the "Hank" that his friends knew. At home, Henry interacted with Loretta but shared little about his world outside home. On campus and elsewhere, Hank was drinking in the world, and not just figuratively. He had also begun to have more intimate interactions with some of the women on campus. In this sense, Henry was following an inclination that many of the writers in Umbra were familiar with. What was different about this social phenomenon is that the women with whom they were involved—as wives or lovers—were white.

Lois Silber, an attractive Jewish woman at Rutgers's Douglass College for Women (formerly the New Jersey College for Women), had heard about an intriguing, winsome, and occasionally impetuous older black man on campus. Indeed, Henry and Earl Thomas could be spotted regularly socializing with the Douglass women, most of whom were white, many of whom were Jewish, and few of whom were black. So when Lois Silber met Henry during the fall of her junior year in 1963, probably at a party or at the Agora Student Center, the twenty-year-old French major was cautious and standoffish. As Lois Silber (hereafter cited by her current name, Lois Wright) looked back on that period, she remembered one piece of advice a classmate had offered about Henry: "one woman in particular told me to steer clear of Henry. She said he could be volatile."[9] He was not violent, but in his encounters with women, and certainly in his developing relationship with Lois Wright, Henry's passion revealed a potential for excess. He was like jazz—sexy, impulsive, mysterious, and dangerous in an alluring way—the kind of man that women are often attracted to, but not the kind of man they wanted to take home to their father.

The daughter of a local doctor and nine years younger than Henry, Lois impressed him with her beauty, intellectual curiosity, and her sophistication. In turn, he exuded a maturity and artistic focus she found appealing. For both, their mutual attraction and a love of all things literary canceled out the problem that Henry was a married black man with children. It was the 1960s. Romance across the color line did not occur without some level of danger. So-called "miscegenation" was still illegal in some states. In some places, mostly outside the South, there were young men and women who refused to accept what they understood as insane and absurd notions of racial separation. At the most fundamental level, the social sanction against it was often the rationale for doing it. Forbidden fruit tastes better. Another element of drama that heightened their relationship was the fact that Lois lived at home with her family. She could reveal nothing to them about this man in her life. In the most literal sense, this was a perfect setup for Henry. Lois could demand only so much.

These aspects of their relationship would prove difficult for Loretta to challenge. She suspected that Henry was involved with other women, but she knew nothing of Lois. "I saw what I wanted to see," she explained. "I was in deep denial about our marriage, hoping these things would just go away." Loretta was limited to the world of work and home, while Lois, as she neared graduation, embodied youthful possibilities. To a man already struggling with a home life that he had willingly created but now found an encumbrance, the grass not only seemed greener, but with Lois there were no boundaries or fences (the relative obstacles of children, bills, and the monotony of home), as Henry considered the possibilities as he gazed at this new horizon.

That Lois would become smitten with Henry is no surprise to those who knew him. Henry was quite the charmer. "He was a pleasant, charming guy," Earl Thomas remembered. "Not in a slick way. He would walk into a room and the room was his, but not in some deliberate way, and everybody would pay attention to him." Clem Fiori, another Rutgers classmate, offered (with a dash of hyperbole) that "Henry was greatly admired by all women. He loved women."[10]

The Henry of Fiori's recollection would have been the man Lois met. For a young, adventurous woman with modest writing aspirations, coming of age in a decade defined by rebellion and liberation, Henry, despite the warnings she had heard about potential "volatile" behavior, was worth the risk. He was worth being with, even though she could not take him home. At the time, Henry experienced relatively little rejection from white women on campus. Not so with black women. Having done her homework on this man, Lois learned that, in her words, "black women Henry encountered were very class-conscious. They simply were uninterested in him."[11] They were not impressed by his writerly aspirations. They had practical, more material concerns about men they met, and Henry was not focused on the traditional goals of family and homeownership, though he had achieved both. Henry, in fact, explored a variation on black sexual and class politics in his 1962 story "A Boll of Roses."

The story revolves around a farm laborer named Layton Fields. Fed up with his dead-end future in his deep-South hometown, Layton is unnerved by the arrival of black and white college students trying to register blacks to vote in this segregated community. As the students circulate across the plantations to have their petition signed, Layton finally has his chance to interact with a black woman among them, Rosemarie. His response to her is steeped in attraction and fear: "What you think you doin coming down here to mess with niggers? I bet this the first time you ever see a cotton field." In response to this verbal assault, Rosemary signifies that she does not suffer "dirty mouthed" and "mannerless" yokels like Layton.[12]

The class conflict between Layton and Rosemarie certainly could have reflected Henry's experiences with the few black women who were on campus, as well as his experience of trying to be accepted by the literati at Rutgers. But there is no evidence to suggest that Henry harbored deep animosity toward black women who would be considered middle class. There were, of course, black women with whom he could have shared similar interests, but he put his energy into a dark-haired white beauty with an eye for language and literature. With her, Henry seemed able to start anew.

His enthusiasm over Lois was evident in the fifteen letters he wrote to her in the fall semester of 1963. "I received all that you've sent me and I am happy," he noted in one of them, "that Thursday night, Lois, I was thinking of you. I have not called you and I have not tried. I'll see you in the parking lot of the

D Lot at about 8 p.m. Thursday and about 7:30 Friday."[13] With Loretta and the kids at home (in the Highland Park house Henry and Loretta were struggling to pay for) and Lois living at home, Henry and Lois found creative ways—and places—to spend time together.

Some of their friends, as Lois Wright recalls, provided periodic havens or relay points for phone calls. Although Henry was married, few people on the Rutgers campus saw him in that context, which lessened the likelihood of social rebuke. Given his new relationship and his desire to free himself to write, Henry searched for a space outside of the home he shared with his family. "Saturday night," he told Lois with anticipation, "I found a line of connection, a sort of leit motif for a large work and it should go fast and quick once I get a room."[14] But Henry never found enough money for that space. Confined by real or perceived limitations at home, Henry's search for a room, or a place of his own, where he could write and spend time with Lois, was the governing metaphor for his life as a writer.

Both Loretta and Lois were sources of stability, encouraging Henry's literary endeavors, with each typing drafts of his work. Henry could navigate between the more rote home life with Loretta and the more creative and passionate aspects of life with Lois. Nonetheless, managing two relationships must have been stressful, as well. In his marriage, Henry dealt with this stress by more or less disengaging from family life.

In Lois, Henry had found a woman with whom he could discuss literature, politics, and the current state of social unrest. By this point, he and Loretta were far removed from their common days of Sunday school teaching. Loretta was not especially politically engaged, and though she still supported Henry's literary efforts, she was not developing a sense of black consciousness. She was consumed by the quotidian aspects of daily life: work, home, and children. On the other hand, Henry and Lois evidently had spirited debates about the political direction of the country. They had met just weeks after Martin Luther King Jr. made on August 28, 1963, in the shadow of Lincoln's statue, what would become an immortal speech demanding justice and freedom for all Americans. There are no letters documenting Henry's thoughts about that surreal moment, but King's clarion call for the races to meet at the table of brotherhood must have been a source of much discussion.

Deep into autumn, he and Lois would confront another event with deep societal reverberations. After President Kennedy's assassination on November 22, Henry questioned, in a letter, Lois's more hopeful vision of the country. "What do you think of your country now?"[15] If America would kill Kennedy, his question implied in the context of the letter, then what chance did King and black folk have? Henry suggested that Lois's youthful optimism had been nullified. She, in his view, underestimated the social and political obstacles to the social transformation that both of them desired. Henry's assertion, as Lois Wright remembered it, was indicative of Henry's passion and the heightened zeitgeist of the 1960s, which, articulated from various platforms, focused on transformation.

In a subsequent letter to Lois, Henry offered an assessment of the United States that invoked the prophetic rhetoric of both King and Malcolm X: "And I am in Holy rebellion against America. Against its values. Indeed against the very values which it so quickly eulogized in President Kennedy. It is a divine punishment. Yea, a warning to this country that it has no knowledge of itself. . . . It is a land of spiritual maggots. It is a land that gives lip service at high mass and lip service at low mass."[16]

Henry's diatribe against U.S. hypocrisy and spiritual diminution revealed his sense of disillusionment. For Lois, this passionate letter was indicative of what, in her view, "you experienced when you were with Henry. If you were with him, your senses were heightened. He saw things other people had no concept of. His ranting against America, his insistence on the country rising to meet its human promise, revealed how quintessentially American Henry was."[17] This characteristic, in turn, informed Henry's aesthetic sensibilities.

Henry made clear in the letter that he had forfeited his celebratory view of the founding fathers and American exceptionalism that ushered in his arrival at Rutgers. Lois, however, had not. In this exchange with her, Henry missed a key element of their relationship. At age twenty, Lois was more hopeful than Henry about the future. However, as a man about to begin his fourth decade, who, according to his own standards, had underachieved in his twenties, Henry's political ideals brushed up against a world mired in hypocrisy and his own unfulfilled literary ambitions. Just months before meeting Lois, Henry was reminded, by Bread Loaf, of how close and yet how far he was from reaching his singular goal of becoming a published writer.

Even with his distaste for what he identified as U.S. hubris, Henry found partial solace in the fact that what he and Lois shared spoke to the political, personal, and artistic freedoms that lie at the root of the American democratic experiment. "Americans are enslaved, both black and white. . . . For we are all in the same prison. I pray God that mine and yours are cocoons. Why should beautiful things be given this country? . . . We have been a ravenous mad dog since we stumbled upon this land. We have abused it. We have killed to possess it. We have lied, stolen and been everything but honorable."[18]

Henry's reference to the "mad dog" is a central metaphor in his signature autobiographical short story, "Goodbye, Sweetwater," in which the young boy Layton tries to adopt the logic of white exploitation and indifference, only to be rebuffed by his grandmother's biblical mandate to "do unto others." Following the logic of the storyline in "Goodbye," Henry might berate his country and provoke Lois, but both actions were rooted in his deeply held commitment to both.

With Lois, Henry felt he had found not only a woman to vent his political frustrations with, but someone with whom he could explore the sensual and spiritual depths, a woman who could meet his multiple needs as man and artist. By December 1963, or what Henry called "only a few short months" since the start of their relationship, Henry had made Lois an integral part of his helter-skelter emotional life.

Before leaving on a December trip down South, which involved observing the ongoing struggle to obtain black voting rights, Henry sounded like a modern-day Ulysses entreating his beloved Penelope to tend the domestic sphere until his triumphant return:

I must "go away" for a few days, on a long journey into a far country. Thank you for the "coat," the sheaf, the picture of my Beloved. I will carry you with me and when I return I will have many treasures and tales and when you hear that I am coming you must put down the bucket and race the wind and meet me beneath the tree where the fruit falls and there I will tell you how it is that I took my Beloved with me and how the wind is wild in the far country and how I see expectations in your eyes.[19]

As Henry departed for the "far country," he petitioned Lois to be prepared for her gallant knight's return. His persona in this letter could be read as innocuous and playful banter, but many of his letters engendered the tone and shape of this letter. For her part, at this point in their relationship Lois was disconcerted by the swiftness with which Henry could move from romantic overture to perilous self-doubting.

Just six days after his departing tribute, Henry's tone changed, as he assured Lois of her place in his turbulent life:

The real issue facing me now is: Am I ready to face the world in my present condition? The truth is that if I were to cause others unnecessary suffering, the knowledge might stagger me too much. . . .

Lois, Dear Lois, you have made me unspeakably happy in these few short months. Last year this time I was considerably worse off than I am now—I must never hear you say that you might be hindering me. . . . Yes yes yes you give me peace. Remember we have never woke (?) together, never hibernated, wrote, read, planned, plotted and lit each other's bodies and minds like we know we will someday.

I want you to know—that no man can know me like you can . . . you are part of me. It is a divine gift to give. The well you draw from must be very very very deep.[20]

Although it is not known whether Lois's letters to Henry survive, his letters give us some clue about her feelings and thoughts from that period. She had suggested that she might be "hindering" him from writing and taking care of his family. Lois was still capable of feeling insecure about her role in Henry's life to the point that she was concerned about his relationship with Jake Bair. Emotionally, she felt threatened, but Henry assured her that what they shared was the best thing in his life.[21]

Henry made the case for him and Lois to remain together, but theirs was not always an easy relationship to navigate. To be with him was to be in high gear, signs of which we see in his correspondence: "What I broke," he wrote to Lois three days later, on December 12, 1963, "I cannot tell. Forgive me. But I tried to destroy you."[22] Although unable now to recall the context for Henry's apology, Lois Wright does recall that Henry was "highly engaged. Whatever he had done, I'm sure he apologized." Put another way, whatever he had done wrong, he would try to address his mistake with passion and commitment.

While Henry's offense is loss to memory, the striking words in Henry's plea to Lois are "broke" and "destroy." What kind of behavior is associated with these verbs? Was he apologizing for physical abuse, or was he speaking metaphorically? Henry did not hit her, Lois Wright has stated. Clearly, though, whatever Henry was apologizing for, he was deeply remorseful. And she now had an example of the volatility she had been warned about.

Lois still had the opportunity to accomplish what Henry had not. She held the promise of youth, whereas Henry was anchored by marriage, family, and financial responsibility. Lois was mature for her age, a disciplined, goal-oriented student who was closer to graduating than Henry. Henry had not achieved this level of self-discipline. He must have seen in her not only beauty and intellectual vitality but also the clarity of purpose that he would need to cultivate himself in order to become a successful writer. From Henry's vantage point, Lois certainly represented the idealized "other woman." As his wife, Loretta could no longer achieve such status. She now represented the familiar, the monotony of domesticity. By being a good wife and mother, she had lost her luster to Henry. She was unable to compete with the divine persona that he attributed to Lois.

As the holiday season drew near and 1963 came to a close, Henry grew increasingly dissatisfied with his predicament, and gave one of the first hints of the challenges that he and Lois had to confront as an interracial couple. In none of Henry's correspondence to Lois does he explicitly address race, religion, or culture. In no letter, for example, is there an allusion to Lois as a Jewish woman or Henry as a black man, though Henry seemed perpetually amazed at their relationship. "It is awesome for me to think that I have truly met someone as big as you are, awesome because of the future path we must tread. You know how utterly glorious it will be and how utterly tragic and filled with pain, need I even discuss it."[23] Henry appeared to be glorifying in the difficulties, looking for the deeper truth in the struggle he and Lois shared. But he was unable to apply such reasoning to his marriage, an indication that he felt there were no viable chances of renewal there.

In his letters to Lois, there is an absence of language about their particular racial and cultural backgrounds, which suggests that both felt they were following a feeling that transcended racial definitions. Nonetheless, they found themselves in a world where concerns about race and ethnicity were part of the social DNA. As an interracial couple in America, that reality surely had an impact on their relationship.

When Henry referred to their "future path," as "utterly glorious," and "utterly tragic and filled with pain," he was alluding to a future with Lois based on their short time together. The tragedy and pain he spoke of involved both wife and lover. He must have realized Loretta's pain in dealing with the unraveling of their relationship. But rarely does he mention Loretta in his letters to Lois. Had he done so, Lois's feelings may have suffered. More to the point, he would have had to confront the emotional complexity of his life. True to his ability to compartmentalize, he kept his worlds with the primary women in his life separate. By doing so, he may have protected the feelings of both women, but it was also a way of trying to simplify a taxing scenario that, despite his efforts at streamlining, would leave its mark on him.

Although their relationship was filled with what Henry had called "glorious" moments, he could not deny the challenges he and Lois faced as an interracial couple. They could not drive together in the North or South absent of concerns about safety. Lois Wright, looking back on that period, noted that there were only a "select number of public places we could visit together in

New Jersey. Most of them were black bars. Mixed couples were not welcome in working-class white bars."

With such impediments, could they bloom together? Both of them, to use Henry's word, were "extreme" in their love for each other. Could only an extreme form of love keep them together? Henry, rather than asserting that nothing could come between them—which he had done in previous letters—was mindful of the challenge they confronted. Given Henry's growing commitment to a black-oriented artistic consciousness, on the most practical level, a relationship with a white woman might have seemed something of a contradiction. Symbolically, if not substantively, it would have been described by some, in the parlance of the 1960s, as "talking black in the streets and sleeping white under the sheets."

Henry and Lois's relationship, while far from common in U.S. culture at the time, conformed to a larger trend in the 1950s and 1960s that was a significant part of the social development of black men in certain parts of the country. In the North and Midwest, at colleges and in places where black men and white women found themselves engaged in social, political, and artistic interactions, a relatively small number made end runs around social convention for relationships across the color line. Alice Walker, in her 1976 novel *Meridian*, unravels some of the emotional and psychological motivations for such encounters in the 1960s. Malcolm X, Amiri Baraka, and Martin Luther King Jr. also had relationships with white women.

Perhaps the least discussed, but one of the most notable, interracial relationships from this period was that of King and Betty Moitz, a woman of German origin whose mother was a cook at Crozer Seminary, where King studied from 1948 to 1951. They had a serious relationship that King's friends advised him to discontinue. "Finally," writes historian David Garrow, "after a six-month involvement, the couple took the advice of King's friends and ended their relationship on amicable but painful terms."[24] Henry, like King years earlier, held a core optimism about his relationship with Lois, and encouraged her to embrace the possibilities of what they could share together. Race, to Henry, was a factor, though not the most important one.

"You entered my world through a mossy tunnel," Henry wrote, "in the woods where no foot had ever tread. And no matter what we both said, no matter what we think, I have entered yours very greatly also, and I swear before God right now Lois—and you can swear with me—let no man, friend or foe, say that what we began to make together is useless. Let no one ever say that their tree bore no fruit. I swear that we are far more worthy to (be) eaten. We are far more worthy to reproduce, make our art lasting. I respect you and I love your soul."[25]

Convinced they could overcome these formidable obstacles, including Henry's marriage, the difficulties of an interracial relationship, and their differences in age and cultural experience, Henry rejected any suggestion—made by others—that they should dissolve their relationship. Indeed, his use of the term "reproduce" shows that he envisioned a union that would yield much artistic fruit. At times misguided, at times unfaithful to Lois as well as to Loretta, Henry's love for Lois nonetheless seemed authentic, not rooted primarily in a desire to be with a white woman, but in the desire to scale new heights with someone who, in his mind, was more compatible.

Lois's presence highlighted what Henry felt Loretta lacked: the kind of sensibility to accommodate his desires and a lack of interest in racial, political, and literary issues. But in his analysis, Henry never considered that, by making Loretta carry the bulk of child-rearing and household responsibilities, Henry himself made it impossible for her to assume a different role. In relationships with both women, Henry was searching for his own identity in the wrong place.

For her part, Lois was brimming with idealism and less interested in Henry's earning potential than she was in his aspirations as a writer. Floating on the optimism of having witnessed a Roman Catholic elected president, Lois desired a country in which black and white could merge, not just politically but also socially. It seemed not so much Henry's race but his passion that gave Lois reason to remain in the relationship.

Malcolm X is not the most likely source for commentary on romance in black and white. He engaged in exploitative sexual encounters with black and white women during his days as "Detroit Red." And as a Nation of Islam minister he admonished his followers to practice racial separation. But in his autobiography he looked beyond the most carnal reasons for white women to desire black men to explain why some commit themselves to relationships with black men: "The white woman with a Negro man would be with him for two reasons: either extremely insane love, or to satisfy her lust."[26] While invoking the stereotype of the sexually repressed white woman seeking out the hypersexual black man, Malcolm X acknowledged the possibility of what he would term irrational love between black and white. But the insanity involves the willingness on the part of two people to flout social constraints in the name of love. Henry and Lois, for a period, sought to trump the considerable social forces pushing against them.

The couple's idealism, though, ran up against social custom. When Henry and Lois were in social settings with blacks, especially after she graduated from Rutgers in 1965, she dealt with her own form of invisibility. "They always referred to me as 'the white chick,'" she would note with a sense of irony many years later. Often on the social periphery himself, Henry had explored the depths of invisibility in his fiction and poetry, and especially his novel in progress, at the time titled "Visible Man." However, Henry never fully considered Lois's peculiar position as doubly outside, that is, not only as the other woman but as the other woman who was white.

Lois's relegation to the periphery of events outside her and Henry's close-knit circle of Rutgers associates parallels what happened in other interracial relationships in the 1960s between black men and white women. Amiri Baraka, who lived with his first, white wife and family in Greenwich Village, for example, confirms the prevalence of both interracial relationships and the idea that these relationships occurred in separate spheres. He notes in his autobiography that "almost all of us had white wives or lovers. . . . [I]t was an unwritten rule that our wives, lovers, etc. weren't to go uptown with us."[27] Henry's involvement with Lois, his exploration of intimacy with a white woman, is central not only to his personal development but also to his evolving sense of race consciousness.

Baraka acknowledges that many black men were with white women for understandable but ultimately problematic reasons. Certainly racial status was considered a coup for black men wrapped up in the psychosexual implications of being with white women, but Henry's lack of understanding of Lois's struggles cannot only be attributed to dating across the color line; it was far more indicative of the male chauvinism of the day. Women's struggles, no matter the race, were secondary to the concerns of men. Neither Loretta nor Lois would ever receive Henry's full attention. He was caught up in his own entanglements, his own artistic imperatives.

Henry may have found springtime with Lois, but spring was just one season. Challenges from every direction would continue to arise. Henry, in his words to Lois, was "amazed that I have managed to survive the year 1963." The backdrop to that statement certainly included the joy and frustration associated with Bread Loaf, the reality that his marriage was in tatters, the social and political unrest following the death of Kennedy, and his emotionally intense relationship with Lois. The next few years would make 1963 seem like his carefree childhood on the Harlem streets of his early adolescence.[28]

In solidifying his movement away from Loretta, Henry was orchestrating what seemed like a long good-bye to his marriage; he was starting to close the book on the more stable and conventional part of his life. Lois was not the sole motivation for this movement. It had begun before she entered his life, but her presence intensified his intentions. Over the next couple of years, he would pursue the publication of his novel. In the process, fate would intervene, in concert with Henry's own miscues, to reveal the truth about Henry's life: Henry would have to confront the reality that his most daunting challenge was not the women in his life but the man in the mirror.

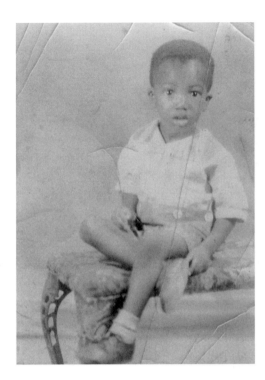

Henry in his birthplace, Sweet Home, Arkansas, circa 1936.
Courtesy of Loretta Dumas.

Henry with his brother Billy Mack Collins and cousin Tommy Lee Stalling in Sweet Home, early 1940s.
Courtesy of Loretta Dumas.

Henry on a bike in
Sweet Home, early 1940s.
Courtesy of Loretta Dumas.

Henry in Harlem with cousin Joanne Canales, late 1940s.
Courtesy of Loretta Dumas.

Henry pitching a tent as a Boy Scout in New York, circa 1950.
Courtesy of Loretta Dumas.

Henry stationed at Lackland Air Force Base in San Antonio, Texas, circa 1954.
Courtesy of Loretta Dumas.

Henry Dumas's passport photo.
Courtesy of Loretta Dumas.

Henry Dumas marries Loretta Ponton on September 24, 1955.
Courtesy of Loretta Dumas.

Henry Dumas visiting what was called Tent City in Somerville, Tennessee, in January or February 1961. African Americans were forced into these makeshift settlements, as a result of their efforts to realize their economic and political rights.

Courtesy of Loretta Dumas.

Standing in front of his tent at Tent City, Somerville, Tennessee, 1961 (left to right): evicted sharecropper James Frazier, his daughter, Henry Dumas, and E. B. Shaw. Frazier holds a bag of seed given him by Dumas.

Courtesy of Loretta Dumas.

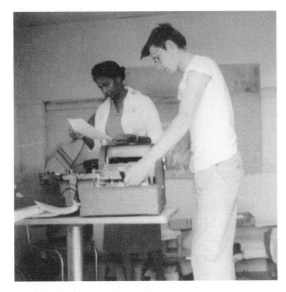

Charlie Butts, a student from Oberlin College and volunteer in the black freedom movement in western Tennessee, runs off copies of circulars and letters to organizations throughout the country. Viola McFerren inspects. Somerville, Tennessee, 1961. *Photo by Henry Dumas.*

Loretta Dumas and friends from Henry's early days at Rutgers, June 2004 (left to right): Loretta Dumas, Herman Robinson, and Laura Lindsay. *Photo by Jeffrey B. Leak.*

Henry Dumas, circa December 1963.
Courtesy of Lois Wright.

Lois Wright, circa December 1963.
Courtesy of Lois Wright.

Henry Dumas with sons David and Michael, circa 1964.
Courtesy of Loretta Dumas.

Henry reading a book,
circa mid-1960s.
Photo by Clem Fiori.

Henry Dumas, William Davis, and Eugene B. Redmond, East St. Louis, circa fall 1967.
Courtesy of Eugene B. Redmond.

Eugene B. Redmond,
East St. Louis, 1968.
Courtesy of Eugene B. Redmond.

Toni Morrison, 1970s. Photo by Eugene B. Redmond.
Courtesy of Eugene B. Redmond.

You shouldn't have to
Re create
You shouldn't have to
Recreate what you create
Create
Beeeee!

—HENRY DUMAS,
"Kef 35"

[CHAPTER SIX

Chasing Change

True to New Year's tradition, Henry ushered in 1964 with at least, in his words, "one resolution. You know what it is," he reminded Lois in a letter. "For I made it four days ago, and I told you."[1] Forty years later, Lois Wright did not remember the circumstances informing Henry's comment. That unknown resolution mirrors certain gaps in our knowledge about Henry's life. The decision could have involved advancing their relationship, which would have in turn meant separating from his family, if not legally, then at least physically. Or it could have centered on Henry having that elusive literary breakthrough. If Henry had been thinking about financial stability, the resolution could have also involved finding a viable job.

What we do know is that Henry found full-time work, landing a position as a Multilith operator at IBM in Dayton, New Jersey, ten miles south of New Brunswick. He would oversee the running of a rapid offset printing press, not the most appealing job for a man dominated by creative impulses. But artists have always struggled with the desire to create and the need to survive. Some African American writers, Ralph Ellison, Ishmael Reed, Nikki Giovanni, and Paule Marshall, to name a few, have held academic positions that offered them the chance to address both imperatives. Finding an academic position, while not impossible, was not likely at this point in Henry's life. He still did not have a college degree, nor could he boast a major publishing record. For him, IBM represented an uncreative, even mundane, opportunity to have access to a modest but consistent level of income.

Henry would work for Big Blue, as IBM would come to be known, dealing with what he perceived to be the drawbacks of corporate culture, for about a year. Even with this job, Henry remained as connected as possible to the literary life at Rutgers, where he still attended evening classes. Serving on the staff of the *Anthologist* and editing the evening school magazine *Untitled*, he was working hard to refine his skills and expand his knowledge. He was even enrolled in an intermediate French course. But with his other responsibilities, studying the language of love proved too much. At the end of 1964, Henry barely passed the last course he would take at Rutgers.

With IBM, college, and the Rutgers literary publications, Henry's goals for the year undoubtedly revolved around the theme of time and space: finding the time to work on "Visible Man," and a place where he could do it. This secondary spot would also serve as a refuge for both him and Lois; with a year to go before her graduation, she was still living at home, making it difficult for them to see each other. A room or modest apartment elsewhere would also enable Henry to dichotomize in more concrete terms his life with Loretta and the boys and his life with Lois. But even with his steady income, an alternative space remained out of reach.

In Lois, Henry had found someone with whom he could mull over the questions that preoccupied him. One of the best and most suggestive examples of the nature of their relationship, and the ways Henry processed his artistic struggle, is their exchange regarding Nobel Prize–winner Herman Hesse's 1922 novel *Siddhartha*, considered one of the finest fictional explorations of Eastern philosophy and spirituality in twentieth-century Western literature. The first English translation wasn't published until the 1950s, and especially for the college-age generation, it became a creative anthem for resisting social conformity.

In the novel, spiritual discipline and carnal desire converge in the life of an Indian boy named Siddhartha, who struggles to find his way forward. Henry could certainly appreciate the spiritual journey of this protagonist. His life had moved along a similar continuum. Lois had read the novel, mindful of the timeliness of its themes in the 1960s United States. After Henry finished it, he wrote to her in the affirmative: "Yes, I too thought much of *Sidd[h]artha*."[2] Henry did not explain further, but the novel undoubtedly struck a chord with him. He had kept a handwritten excerpt from the novel in his notebook of inspirational passages, along with other selections from Nobel Peace Prize–winner Albert Schweitzer and British bibliophile Richard de Bury.

In the passage Henry kept, Siddhartha speaks to his love-interest Kamala about the importance of focusing on one's goals, ignoring the distractions and transitory aspects of life. "Listen, Kamala, when you throw a stone into the water, it finds the quickest way to the bottom of the water."[3] In this philosophical parable, Henry is the stone. He desires to have a similar kind of focus, an ability to separate himself from the clutter of his life, to dive deep into himself, leaving the surface reality of his life to a higher level of consciousness, realizing his ambition as a writer.

Other elements in Hesse's novel would have resonated with both Henry and Lois. Siddhartha, a member of the elite Brahmin caste, initially devotes his life to asceticism, a practice that—whether religious or philosophical in nature—requires the rejection of all desire. The narrator puts it this way: "Siddhartha had one single goal—to become empty, to become empty of thirst, desire, dreams, pleasure and sorrow, to let the Self die."[4] Henry would likely have remembered the time when he was a would-be Baptist preacher, exhorting the unsaved to march toward the cross. But now, for him and Lois—indeed, for many students in the 1960s—Siddhartha's temporary rejection of the ascetic life for one of sensual pleasure resonated. Many of them resisted the postwar mores of their parents, rebelling against social restraints, sexual conservatism, and what they perceived as the overall hypocrisy of American society. Henry was a late convert to this kind of thinking, but his study of *Siddhartha* would build on his understanding of himself and the relationship he shared with Lois.

One of the moments in the novel that surely captured Henry and Lois's attention, paralleling their own relationship, is when Siddhartha meets Kamala, the beautiful courtesan. Her intelligence and beauty call him out of his ascetic shell, compelling him to answer the call of the flesh. From Kamala, Siddhartha learns about the need for emotional and erotic reciprocity, "that one cannot have pleasure without giving it, and that every gesture, every caress, every touch, every glance, every single part of the body has its secret which can give pleasure to one who can understand."[5] Henry and Loretta had not engaged in this level of intimate awareness, and Loretta, given the more tradition-bound parameters of their marriage, probably would have viewed such overtures with skepticism. For Henry and Lois, Hesse's novel stood as a variation on their experience together. Even if Henry had not been involved with Lois, the subject matter was not something he could have discussed with Loretta, nor was it the kind of material he would have discussed when he arrived at Rutgers in 1958.

Literary and social emblems of the period, Siddhartha and Kamala spoke to the reciprocity that Henry and Lois experienced with each other, simultaneously confirming for Henry what was missing in his marriage.

For Lois and women of her generation, Kamala, a liberated woman unapologetic in her desire for erotic intimacy, was a fresh, invigorating model of womanhood. Women who graduated from college in the 1960s—coming of age just after Gloria Steinem and with Angela Davis—could pursue unprecedented levels of self-awareness and professional advancement. These women could appreciate Kamala's confidence in expressing her emotional and erotic needs to Siddhartha.[6] This novel, written forty-two years earlier by a German man, signified to women that men had the capacity—if not the will—to engage in mutually satisfying relationships, provided men could move beyond social practices designed to placate their fragile egos and to maintain patriarchy.

Those with a more Victorian sensibility, like Loretta, would have found the encounters between Siddhartha and Kamala prurient, but even they could acknowledge the value of lovers caring about each other's erotic and emotional needs. Ultimately, the novel presents a man who embarks on a spiritual journey with one set of objectives, only for them to be interrupted and recalibrated by his own imperfections. The novel ends with Siddhartha coming to terms with himself despite his troubles, achieving a fuller understanding of his relationship to the Spirit.

Like Siddhartha, Henry confronted his propensity for gravitating toward unstable or somewhat precarious behaviors. Even when achieving more balance in his life, he found ways to undercut his efforts. As Henry conducted an overview of the last ten years of his life, dating back to his enlistment in the air force in 1954, his letters to Lois served a therapeutic function. He reached, as the following excerpt to her suggests, the most difficult stretch in his journey and, like Siddhartha, found himself somewhere unexpected, in a situation from which there was no simple exit.

"It was ten years ago today," Henry wrote to Lois, "that I went off from the city to begin three months of training in a regimented group of men (and a few women) called the Air Force. Ten years. How I would like to know ten years hence. . . . Making sense out of experience is like trying to get the last drop of wine from an earthen jug and wiping the sides with the finger. The smell is always there." Henry was looking for keys in his past to explain a contemporary reality that was somewhat disappointing. Perplexed by the past decade in which he felt he had too often run in place, Henry envisioned a major transition: "I know that I have not heard music in my soul in many many years. Maybe not years, but months. . . . It wants to sing now. I am ready. That is why

I know this thing. That is why I write this for you now. . . . I am sure that there is to come change soon."[7]

In this frank assessment of himself, Henry acknowledged a longstanding feeling of disappointment in both his marriage and writing. Though undated, the letter from which these excerpts are taken was probably written in the spring of 1964. Contemplating a past that he could not adequately explain and a future filled with tenuous questions, Henry held on to hope, to the idea that "change" was on the way.

Henry was disappointed with what he felt was nominal progress as a writer. His actual progress was better than he thought, however. He had published three poems ("Take This River!," "Listen to the Sound of My Horn," and "Oceanic") and three short stories ("A City Game," "A Boll of Roses," and "Echo Tree") in the *Anthologist* between 1960 and 1964. The themes in these stories, and in his larger body of work, present the North and South in terms of spiritual defeat and spiritual renewal. Blacks in the North, seemingly better off than their southern counterparts, have weary spirits. The city has had its way with them. In the South, blacks find themselves in the crosshairs of violence and Jim Crow, but they maintain a connection to the natural and thereby spiritual world. Like most people looking back on the inflated expectations of their youth, Henry knew what it felt like to have his dreams tempered by hard doses of reality.

Six years removed from the air force, Henry had progressed as a writer, but slowly in comparison with some of his peers who, by now, had published books. While he was not one to keep score with his literary contemporaries, Henry would have been cognizant of their accomplishments, especially those associated with the Harlem Writers Guild, the Umbra collective, and the nascent Black Arts Movement. By 1964, most of the Rutgers crew had graduated and moved on to academic, creative, or professional pursuits.

Of Henry's black contemporaries, LeRoi Jones (later Amiri Baraka) had already established his credibility in the mainstream publishing world. By 1964, Baraka had published *Blues People: Negro Music in White America*; the Obie-winning play, *Dutchman*; and an impressive volume of beat poetry, *Preface to a Twenty Volume Suicide Note*. He had also founded an avant-garde journal (*Yugen*) with his wife Hettie Jones, and coedited a journal (*Floating Bear*) with his lover Diane di Prima.

Other black contemporaries were productive, as well. William Melvin Kelley, born in the Bronx three years after Henry, published his novel *A Different Drummer* in 1962, and a short-story collection, *Dancers on the Shore*, in 1964. Older black writers were also making their mark. Georgia-born John Oliver Killens had published his second novel, *And We Heard the Thunder*, in 1963. John A. Williams, born in 1925 in Mississippi, had published his novel *Sissie* in 1963 and a collection of essays, *This Is My Country Too*, in 1965. Henry could not help but know that black male contemporaries were finding ways to publish their work.

Honest with himself about his sense of underachievement, Henry found it difficult to view his own accomplishments independent from the expectations of his youth. Since 1958, he had been productive, but he clearly had not made the inroads into the publishing world that had led Baraka, for their generation, to be crowned as leader of the pack. In so many ways, Henry's literary and personal activity would echo, on a smaller scale, that of Baraka.

Still plodding his way through his novel, Henry resolved to publish a literary magazine with Lois's assistance. He was not necessarily following in Baraka's footsteps, but he was interested in alternative publishing venues for some of his work. The impetus for the magazine emerged from Henry's experience with the *Anthologist* and *Untitled*. Henry had enjoyed the opportunity of working with fellow writers at Rutgers, learning more about the craft of writing from publishing insider William Sloane and English professor William Wynkoop.

Moreover, in 1964, the small literary magazine was in vogue. "It was one of our grandiose ideas," Lois Wright explained. "We could have a good little magazine, distribute it ourselves to the little bookstores in New Brunswick." Eventually, Henry and Lois concluded, a publisher would notice the quality of the publication and they would rise to the top of the list for New York publishing houses. Lois was more smitten by the world of books and ideas than with becoming a writer. The literary venture with Henry was both a reflection of her commitment to him and the outcome of her study of literature. As plans go, theirs was neither the best nor the worst plan. It did, however, accurately represent the respective stages of their lives. Henry was exasperated with his struggle to enter the New York publishing world, whereas Lois was more youthful and idealistic in her thinking about his publishing prospects. In discussing the magazine's prospects with Lois, Henry appeared upbeat and enthusiastic: "Maybe we can get some ideas talked over concerning the venture, the magazine. . . . . Have you done any thinking about titles and names. . . . [J]ust before I took to writing you, I was hashing out titles and names, just a few, not many at all, and maybe I was doing more thinking than anything."[8] More to the point, this effort enabled Henry to imagine a critical reception for his work. Neither fame nor money was his focus; he was in search of something more elusive: recognition as a writer with serious ideas.

Although Henry framed this project as a joint venture, he made clear his role in this enterprise. "You and your characters can vote on a cover title, and naturally . . . I've just got a great idea. Why don't we use the name [*Hidden Word*] for the title but situate it strategically on the title page very small but neat, and feature one poem with a title."[9] The prospects of publishing the magazine were invigorating for Henry. It represented, as well, the connection he and Lois shared. She, too, found the process enlivening, although her role in the creation and planning of the magazine was secondary to Henry's. Their effort, though, spoke to a kind of intellectual yearning in the 1960s for alternative outlets for literary and cultural expression. "Few magazines," as Hettie Jones explained the origins of *Yugen* in her memoir, "out of New York, to that date, had promised the new consciousness that everyone downtown agreed was just what the world needed."[10]

Consciously or not, Henry and Lois sought with *Hidden Word* to build on the examples of *Yugen*, *Floating Bear*, and *Umbra*. A major obstacle, however, was that he and Lois had no contributors other than themselves. The masthead listed as editors Craig McDonald, Marla Roth, Fred Thies, Juanita Johnson, and William Conley, all *noms de guerre*. Fiction and poetry filled the magazine's pages, yes, but Henry and Lois were the only authors. The plan was to print copies—in this regard IBM unknowingly contributed the photocopying and stapling of materials—plant them in bookstores and coffee shops, and wait for publishers to come calling posthaste.

With his campus connections, Henry could have secured real-life contributors, but by this point he wanted to establish his own literary credentials. His work with the *Anthologist* and *Untitled* had given him the confidence to trust his abilities, but both of these publications were subsidized by the university. Henry's was not. Henry and Lois followed a simple, if foolhardy, formula: publish it and they will read it. A bold effort that turned out to be a dud.

Beyond Henry and Lois, few people took notice of their modest creation. This sophomoric effort offered an appealing distraction from quotidian challenges, at least for Henry. But the real world beckoned forth. Just as he had shared with Lois thoughts about their magazine, in another note to her he acknowledged the strain of meeting his financial responsibilities. "Some kind of depression is also upon me," he wrote with withered spirit. "I know what it is, I guess, because I have to do so many idiotic things. The car goes in the shop tonite. I hope to get it by Friday. I'll have to write bad checks to get it and it will come close to 60 dollars maybe more. Plus I have to get to a driving clinic tomorrow or lose my license. I have been fussing about overtime with my wife. No work here. No revisions or insertions. No nothing."[11]

In this list of things gone awry we catch a glimpse of Henry's dissatisfaction. Money continued to avoid his pockets. His car had its own personality, starting when it wanted to, with Henry parking atop hills to jump-start it. And then there was the time, as Earl Thomas and Clem Fiori recalled, "that the brakes failed and Henry plowed into the family house."[12] Add to that a usually demure wife now pressing him to work more overtime to bring more money into the household. With such legitimate but nonliterary distractions and the dissatisfaction with being a glorified errand boy and button-pusher at IBM, Henry revealed to Lois a cascade of emotions that had been on the rise for the last few years.

Lois was aware of these challenges. She understood the pressure Henry confronted regarding the welfare of his family. Even if Henry left them, Lois understood that the move would be fine in theory but messy in practice. To his credit, Henry appeared not to have defamed or ridiculed Loretta to Lois. But Lois, and ultimately his family, were caught up in the messiness of his life. He was becoming battle-worn. During this period, he wrote to Lois that "he would not stop writing, but really," he had to ask himself, "when do I write?" Exasperated, Henry wanted to flee everything. "Somehow I feel that I need to pray a while . . . Lois I must get away from the machines. . . . The job was hectic today. I'm rather sick and need a time of relaxation and productive thought. Also I'm very pissed off at things, specific things that happened here. But one of these days! One day!"[13] Working in a blue-collar capacity in a white-collar world, Henry felt the work sapping the creative force out of him.

In 1964, he wrote "Machines Can Do It Too (IBM Blues)," which captured his angst over a world that was giving itself over to the machine. The final stanza is a blues refrain, an affirmation of the human spirit rather than technological innovation:

> Let me tell you, tell you what I have to do
> Let me tell it like it is people,
>   tell you what I have to do
> If I find a machine in bed with me
>   that's the time I'm through[14]

His marriage essentially in tatters, his family steeped in debt, a stimulating but at times stressful extramarital relationship, a botched literary magazine, and a stable but unfulfilling job were plenty reason for Henry to be singing the blues day and night. He did not discuss his frustration with Loretta, but "I could see this disappointment in his face," she would say years later. "By that point, he was hardly ever home. And when he was, he was often distant, even despondent. I think also at this time Henry was experimenting with drugs and alcohol. This man was far different from the man I married."

Because Henry had sectioned off his relationships rather skillfully, none of his friends, family, or colleagues had a firm handle on what Henry was experiencing. He divulged relatively little about his writing aspirations or the women in his life to Earl Thomas and Clem Fiori. In that sense he was a private man. The woman to whom he revealed his deepest frustrations was Lois. Whether it was about love, work, literature, or, eventually, even his family, she was often the confidant who had won his trust.

Henry was frustrated with family life, although by now he often wasn't at home, but he nonetheless appreciated, at least in certain moments, the goings-on of their children. An example of this emerged in a letter he wrote to Lois while at home with his family in Highland Park. Written on an icy March day, the letter is a microcosm of Henry's life: "The Five Blind Boys [of Alabama] are singing very softly in the background. They're singing: 'Wherever There's a Will There's a Way.' Mikie is screaming downstairs. David is driving his little car loudly over the floor. The wind is beating against the sides of this old house. The day has not settled in my mind yet. I would be good to Lois."[15]

This scene of domestic beauty and chaos, with one of Henry's favorite gospel groups lifting up the Lord in the background, offers a glimpse into the Dumas family. Mikie and David are doing what children do best: making noise and playing with toys. In response to the chaos, Henry flees:

> (I just went down stairs because the screaming grew so loud—and turning the record up did no good—that I wanted to cry . . . or something. While down there I couldn't get mad at Mikie . . . and he kept on screaming. So guess who I have in my arms as I am typing this and guess what kind of cute look is in his eyes as I type right now. His tears are hanging and his eyes are droopy and he seems ready to grin if I choose to make him. . . . He just wiggled his feet. Now he's winking at me. We have a little private game with winking and Mikie knows. . . . he is quiet now and awed by the attic and the new environment. . . . Soon I guess someone will come with news that Mikie is missing. . . .)
>
> (And my wife just came and got him.) Long live Mikie![16]

He typed the letter to Lois—a brazen, insensitive move—with Mikie on his lap. Henry appeared to want Loretta to catch him, and then grant him the pass out of the marriage.

This moment spoke to Henry's dilemma: disengaged though he was, he loved his family and he loved Lois. But it also represented a prevailing pattern in Henry's life: a few moments with his son and then off to find the writing muse and seek his pleasure. Despite Henry's disappointment with his marriage, he actually had, as he inadvertently pointed out to Lois, a sweet deal in his home life with Loretta. Life with children is inherently chaotic, but Loretta did her best to make Henry's time as conducive to writing as possible. When Loretta swoops in, she carries off Mikie without paying attention to what Henry is typing, leaving Henry to attend to his work. This moment also reveals just how naive Loretta was about Henry's activities. She assumes her husband is working and not typing a letter to his lover.

Loretta's efforts reflected her support of Henry, but the larger problem involved options. She knew their marriage was in trouble, but she did not feel comfortable confiding in family, and she had been raised to believe in "'til death do us part." In time, she would adjust her thinking, but for now she would make the best of a troubling situation. For Lois, as the other woman, there was an equally troubling reality. Most of Henry's time, outside of work, was spent with her. From the attention and sheer time Henry gave her, she knew she was not a footnote in his life, but as the secondary woman, in fact if not in form, she would in time expect to be acknowledged for her place in his life. She, too, exercised considerable patience, especially in light of the few dalliances Henry would have during their time together.

With two women loving him—one providing a home life and children, the other intellectual and romantic stimulation, and both women typing his manuscripts—Henry had quite a support team. In their experiences with Henry, both Loretta and Lois had seen tremendous good in him, so much so that their love for him would continue, even as he adopted more troubling social practices that would impact both of them.

As he began his fourth decade, Henry could no longer attribute his shortcomings to youthful caprice. Well into adulthood, he had to look at himself and decisions he had made. In that vein, Loretta Dumas sensed that Henry had begun questioning whether he had made the right decision in creating a family. It was apparent to Loretta by his behavior in this period: "I knew Henry loved us," she said with certainty, "but I sensed that in his mind we were burdens to him." In a marriage that required steady, rather than creative, work, in a world where the artistic expressions of black men and women were still undervalued, Henry was a kind of alienated artist.

In most of his fiction and poetry, especially the former, the male protagonist is out on his own, in search of some lucid moment of recognition, removed or distant from family and community. The main exception is *Jonoah and the Green Stone*, in which the character Jonoah does flee family and the segregated South, returning years later with a desire to reconnect those severed ties. But Henry did not reach that point. Even when home with Loretta and the boys, by 1965 a rare occurrence, he often read at the dinner table. Henry was rarely fully present with them. Loretta remembers a phrase he often used to describe himself: "He always said he was an in-and-out person."[17]

Emotionally and even intellectually, Henry had a short attention span. When he was intrigued by a social or political situation, an artistic, intellectual, or spiritual question, he would dive into that world but just as quickly emerge, ready to pursue another question or subject. He might have made a good journalist in that respect, with his ability to navigate from subject to subject. But the pragmatic question, not involving the nature of marriage or the difficulties of becoming a writer, at this point, for Henry was, "How do I pay my bills?"

By late June 1964, he and Loretta were facing bankruptcy. He submitted a letter to his creditors that laid bare his financial predicament:

> Over the past five years my attempts to try to further my education at Rutgers, support of family, the buying of a home, an unusual amount of costly illnesses, misfortunes and trouble with automobile transportation, all have sunk my wife and I so far in debt that we don't know whether we are coming or going and this whole business drives us both to the doctors all the time. Something has to give to preserve my sanity.
>
> At the present if I don't straighten things out before this winter I will be literally forced to declare bankruptcy, a thing I am not anxious to do.
>
> Therefore following a line away from the necessity of ruining my credit, we are asking your credit office to allow us an extension for 6 months OR until we can get on our feet and resume payments. At present my wife, only recently released from Perth Amboy Hosp., where she had a major operation, cannot work, but by the end of this period she hopes to be working, and between us we hope to be able to honor all our debts in the agreement.[18]

Henry was acutely aware of his precarious position at this point. On the brink of bankruptcy, he acknowledged that he was also skating close to a breakdown. "Something has to give," he had declared, "to preserve my sanity." He knew enough about himself to understand he was edging closer to an emotional breaking point. Loretta rebounded from the surgery, but in order to make a full recovery she had needed to take her time in returning to work, and during that period the family's stack of bills grew higher.

Henry acknowledged Loretta's efforts in this bankruptcy letter. Although the marriage was fading, Henry credited Loretta for her financial contribution to the family and clearly depended on her. At the last hour, Henry and Loretta did receive a reprieve from creditors, but they never recovered from their debt. Nor could they re-create a period comparable to those first years of marital comfort. That time was long gone. Debt was not the cause of their marital collapse, but it certainly precipitated its unraveling. And, as July approached, Henry found himself beset with bills and writing commitments, neither of which he could fulfill. He must have expended a lot of mental energy oscillating between creative and economic concerns.

By the fall of 1964, Henry seemed resigned to his economic and artistic fates. "Time mocks me," he wrote to Lois with a festering pessimism. "I do not care, but time laughs at me."[19] Nevertheless, he kept clawing away, working on his novel, poems, and short stories. He also continued to explore, through his editorship of Untitled, the role of the black artist in America and the Diaspora. In the process, he made significant strides in honing his craft, due in part to his informal sessions with Rutgers University Press editor William Sloane. Frustrated but encouraged by his progress, Henry would continue his search for a publisher.

Along with this effort, Henry deepened his cultural understanding of black writers and artists. This growth became most apparent when he met the experimental jazz artist Sun Ra who, as mentor, would push him to consider the cosmic possibilities of blackness.

All the glory of the world would be buried
in oblivion unless God had provided
mortals with the remedy of books.

—RICHARD DE BURY,
British bibliophile, 1345 A.D.

CHAPTER SEVEN

Pages without a Publisher

The epigraph to this chapter joined selections from theologian
and medical practitioner Albert Schweitzer and novelist Herman Hesse as a handful of handwritten inspirational passages
Henry kept in his notebook. These passages spoke to Henry's
evolving sense of aesthetics and of the importance of books
and ideas across time and space.

De Bury's observation is featured on an exterior wall of
the Archibald S. Alexander Library at Rutgers. It served as a reminder, for Henry, of the ennobling potential of books. He
may well have envisioned his own words someday gracing the
wall of a public place. That did not happen. But his major moment of acknowledgment would occur posthumously, in 1974,
when selections of his poetry appeared in *The Black Book*, a collection of African Americana.[1] This sense of black consciousness had taken significant form in Henry's thinking by 1965. A
key moment in his development, though he never captured it
explicitly in his work, was the assassination of Malcolm X that
year. While his nationalist approach and fiery rhetoric were
cause for concern, Malcolm's commitment to the uplift of the
black masses made him a cultural icon. Henry had conversed
with him in 1962. And in both life and death, Malcolm's sense

of race consciousness left its mark on Henry. Stories like "Harlem" and "Riot or Revolt" would bear the minister's imprint.

In a March 1965 letter to William M. Sloane, then director of Rutgers University Press, whom Henry considered a literary mentor, Henry expounded on his interest in matters of art and the African diaspora:

> I have invited Lennox Raphael from Trinidad to have an informal evening with me and the Book Room audience [at Rutgers University] on Friday March 19th at 8 pm. This will be a part of a larger idea in which I hope to have some more people, namely poets and writers, to discuss the topic of the development of the Negro artist, which is really—I would say—the discussion of the creative process.
>
> I am still hoping to finish my manuscript by July.
>
> Somewhere along the way I have learned a lot from the consultations with you. I cannot put my finger on one thing, but if I did it would be—perhaps—a feeling for the essence of what a piece is trying to say, a vague feeling at that but it has enabled me to approach the manuscript with a keener eye. Perhaps I will feel a bit more confident in selecting clothes for my own characters and in eventually putting them on my characters. Thank you.[2]

Henry understood, as he pointed out to Sloane, that regardless of racial sensibility, to call himself a writer he would need to master the craft. His consultations with Sloane had evidently brought this point home. The former publishing executive had stressed to Henry the importance of character development, emphasizing an age-old literary truth: a story is only as good as its characters. These lessons are especially evident in some of Henry's most spellbinding stories, among them "Ark of Bones," "Boll of Roses," "Will the Circle Be Unbroken?," and moments in *Jonoah and the Green Stone*. In "Ark," the characters are clothed with historical questions. In "Boll," the concerns are political in nature. In "Circle," the characters must figure out what racial identity means in the South. And *Jonoah* is a meditation on the concepts of home, family, region, and place.

Henry credited Sloane with his growing confidence in "selecting clothes" for his own characters and, while he never said so directly, it is clear that Henry's Rutgers experience enabled him to learn the critical skills associated with writing. Indeed, he was learning to layer his writing with issues that mattered most to him. Of course he had arrived at Rutgers with a keen interest in writing, but the fact that so much of his published work was completed or took shape during this period is not coincidental. For the first time, perhaps, his letter suggested he had figured out how to merge his commitment to exploring the diaspora with the skill set necessary to pull it off. Simply put, he was becoming more comfortable with the challenges inherent to the craft of writing.

Like most relatively young writers, Henry had not developed the ability to disengage from his writing, to remove himself emotionally from the creation and to view it on its own terms. He credited Sloane with highlighting the importance of character development. A story may contain an overarching issue or theme, but the expression of such is tied to character and storyline. This concept was not new to Henry; he was quite the griot in Sweet Home and during his Harlem adolescence. But he clearly had difficulty moving from the oral to the written tradition. Sloane had provided concrete guidance; moreover, Henry's run as editor of *Untitled* and staff position on the *Anthologist* taught him to engage his own work in a more self-critical manner. This involvement with Sloane and the literary enterprises on campus simply furthered Henry's interest in storytelling and in writing as a way of life.

After his update to Sloane on his critical and creative progress, Henry had achieved a good literary rhythm, and in this period he arrived at a moment of further resolve: in early April 1965 he relinquished his editorship of *Untitled*. In his letter to Dean Helen Hurd, Henry cited the reasons behind his decision: "(1) a difference of opinion as to the purposes and goals of *Untitled* and (2) The adherence to traditions."[3] At the moment, this decision appeared to bring Henry to a point of creative clarity.

Henry had sought to expand the scope of the magazine, changing it from a fairly parochial and white publication with only student contributors to one in which diverse writers from outside of the campus community, such as Lennox Raphael, with whom Henry had developed a friendship through a 1963 Umbra workshop, could also be featured. These new voices would have challenged the literary status quo of the conservative, high-buttoned literary crowd at Rutgers. Henry's attempt to broaden the intellectual scope of the campus literary community was met with resistance. "When I invited several poets to contribute to *Untitled*," Henry explained in his letter to the dean, "I knew it was against tradition (which had been broken only in thin-line cases) but it was for the purpose of creating a broad literary horizon for the magazine and its future."[4] For Henry, this was part of the magazine's natural evolution. Henry viewed his effort as a moment of instruction for the white literary establishment at Rutgers. Expanding the scope of *Untitled* was certainly in tune with the political and cultural transformation of the 1960s. But Henry reasoned, in a letter to Lois the day after he met with the magazine staff for the last time, that he was "depressed" about the atmosphere at the magazine. He didn't even stay for the staff photo. "They bore me," Henry wrote. "I do them an injustice by going. So I left and never plan to return, for with this issue I am too much an outsider and not connected with school anymore."[5]

In trying to bring new voices into literary and cultural discussions, Henry, in the minds of some whites on campus, had moved from being an individual black man to a race man, one who was symbolically colluding with other black writers unaffiliated with Rutgers. Henry was surely aware of the tension his presence stoked, especially regarding the possibility of liaisons with white women, but he seemed not fully prepared for dealing with this level of creative recalcitrance. To bring Raphael and others into the fold, such engagement would have presented a threat to white literary dominance. Nonetheless, by trying to engage more with other writers and diverse voices, Henry had clarified for himself the meaning of art and activism, the need to understand the world from a black perspective. This concept has not been a central tenet in the development of white writers and audiences. Whites have never been expected or had to lift up their race, or felt compelled en masse to contemplate a white perspective. The white view was, for them, the only view, at least the only one that mattered. As Henry tried to usher *Untitled* into the conversation about race, he realized that too many people at Rutgers were ready for individual but not institutional transformation.

In both his life and his writing, Henry had experienced the benefit of crossing certain boundaries. He knew he could not solve all the world's problems, but his vision of the future called for boundary-crossing overtures. By inviting Raphael and others to contribute to the magazine, writers whose politics and aesthetics may have challenged white conventions, Henry kindled some resentment on campus. He finished up his stint with *Untitled* after the spring publication of the yearly magazine. Although his time ended on troubling terms, Henry's exposure to the world of literary ideas and intellectual engagement was essential in his ongoing exploration of black cultural and intellectual expression.

Moving beyond his campus publishing organs in 1965, Henry sought to place his fiction and poetry in small arts journals and magazines like *Negro Digest* and *American Weave*. He wanted his work to be taken seriously, and small, independent publishing organs open to avant-garde or different kinds of writing were appealing. Given his experience with *Untitled*, he especially appreciated the work of Hoyt Fuller at *Negro Digest*. Fuller's work at the magazine was a model for Henry, one in which art and activism could coexist. *Negro Digest* was one of the relatively few venues where blacks could engage across disciplines, professions, and social classes through creative expression and opinion. During Fuller's time as editor, the *Digest*, which was renamed *Black World* in

1970, became one of the leading publications for writers who identified with black cultural nationalism and the idea that black art went hand in hand with political engagement.

This aspect of Fuller's profile was crucial for Henry. No matter how much he honed his craft, Henry could not divorce himself from the quotidian realities of black people. How could he simply write, contemplating the beauty of a sunset, when black people's rights were not acknowledged in the United States? In fact, one of Henry's last gestures as editor of *Untitled* was to send Fuller a copy of the magazine. In some sense, Henry considered himself part of this burgeoning Black Arts Movement. The relationship of art to activism, as a concept, was appealing to him, and he considered his artistic activism with *Untitled* an extension of Fuller's work. In publishing Henry's stories and demonstrating a socially relevant editorial vision, Fuller proved what Henry had suspected: that art and activism need not be antagonistic.

In that vein, Henry was able to articulate his vision as a writer in a query letter to Viking. This letter, quoted here in full, is the best available account of Henry's publishing aspirations and aesthetic point of view as a novelist:

> Henry Dumas
> 408 So. 9th Ave
> Highland Park, NJ
> April 14, 1965

> The Viking Press
> 6521 Madison Avenue
> New York 22, NY

> Dear Sirs:

> I have decided to query the editorial board of the Viking Press concerning the possible consideration of my first novel.

> On Friday, April 23, I hope to be in New York, and at that time I would like to know if it would be advisable to make an appointment with you in order to deliver an outline and first chapter of my novel.

> A little bit about myself and my writing: Many of my short stories and poems have appeared in the undergraduate publications of Rutgers University. At present, I am the Editor-in-Chief of one of these publications, *Untitled*. Poetry of mine is to appear in *Negro Digest*, *American Weave*, and *The Rotarian*. I have recently finished a book of poems and have started another. My novel has undergone extensive

changes after consultations with Mr. William Sloane (formerly of William Sloane and Associates), who is now Director of the Rutgers University Press. Therefore, at present, it is my novel-in-progress. Over the years Mr. Sloane has been especially helpful to me, and I would say that he has become quite familiar with my work.

Briefly, my novel covers about a thirty year period, from 1930 to the present, the span of the major character's age. It begins in the South where I was born, weaves northward, and returns to the South. I attempt (through the major character's eyes) to throw a vivid spotlight upon the curious mosaic of race in America, and the terrible maladies afflicting Americans—not because of race—but because of their inability to deal with mistakes of the past and their inability to handle the changes of the present. However, this is not the major theme! The major theme is primarily man in search of himself; it is an odyssey of the Negro, but a psycho-social odyssey, in which man is confronted with the problem of good and evil, or, if you will, Christ and Satan, since Christianity and its effects (both historical and psychological) on the Negro will be one of the anchors of the book.

I would be interested in knowing if I can deliver my manuscript to the Viking Press on Friday, April 23, since on that date I will be in the city to attend the Writer's Conference at the New School.

As I have said, this is my first novel and it is still in progress. I would like to know if you might like to read what I have so far, accompanied with an outline of the entire work.

Thank you for your cooperation and interest.

Very truly yours,
Mr. Henry Dumas[6]

In this letter, typed by Lois and without the knowledge of Loretta, Henry highlighted his relationship, "over the years," with William Sloane but stopped short of encouraging Viking to contact his mentor. Henry struck a balance between name-dropping and standing on his own ability. His work—his poetry and the unfinished manuscript and outline—rather than his relationship with Sloane, were the jewels he offered to advance his cause at Viking. This may have been a noble but imprudent move.

Thematically, his manuscript and the final posthumous version titled *Jonoah and the Green Stone*, anticipated Alice Walker's *Meridian*, published in 1976. Both stories re-created the social tensions of interracial encounters in the South of the 1960s. *Jonoah* also recalls Twain's *Adventures of Huckleberry Finn*. Much of Twain's epic treatment of slavery occurs as Huck and the enslaved Jim journey in a raft down the Mississippi, in and out of free territory, much to Jim's despair. *Jonoah* also occurs in or along the river, as blacks and whites try to survive its deadly floods. Even as they confront nature's wrath, people also confront the equally devastating racial tensions that threaten their community.

These points of natural and human-made friction consume southern life. Blacks and whites struggle to deal with natural phenomena, as they struggle to deal with each other. Henry had witnessed the poor white response to his efforts at diversity with *Untitled*. In both his life and his fiction Henry identified what he concluded was his country's primary problem: America's "inability" to confront its past and, in turn, imagine a more socially just future.

Jonoah, the lead character, is orphaned in childhood when the mighty Mississippi crests to dangerous heights in 1937, taking Jonoah's family with it. A sharecropping family, the Mastersons, with only a boat to their name, snatch Jonoah from imminent death. Their boat is not big, but they look beyond the limitations of space and see the possibilities in this child's life. "I was protected," says Jonoah, "because of Mama Masterson, Papa Masterson, Jubal, Aunt Lili, Uncle Bean, and Lance. And just as much as the river gave *them* to me, it gave *me* to them."⁷ This act of love sustains Jonoah, but it also becomes a source of guilt.

As Jonoah grows older, he decides, as Henry did as a youngster, to leave the South, to leave his family as the freedom fight is reaching, in some places, a violent crescendo. Vexed by what he knows his people are facing, Jonoah finally returns. Here is how he sums up his life to this point: "I had fled the South, drifted, played a few songs for college kids, told my story here and there, collected money and wasted it: ran and ran. Fear and terror scrape out the bottom of one's soul. I was almost reduced by the fear of the rope and the terror I had seen my family and friends suffer and die by. I chose the safety of my dreams, and the warmth of ignorance. But it was always Jubal's [Jonoah's brother] voice in the songs that came ringing back into my mind like an arrow shot out of the sky."⁸

Often a writer's first novel is largely autobiographical. In Henry's case, the novel evokes the emotions Henry felt over his beloved South, but not so much the actual blueprint of his life. Jonoah's reference to his adopted brother Jubal and the "song" that he cannot get out of his head speaks to the folkways, to the cultural practices of the black South from which he had migrated, that he tried to run away from. The South, in all of its beauty and ugliness, is home. And Jonoah's return, while not signaling an end to black plight, expresses his desire to reclaim the home of his youth as it undergoes a forced transformation.

Henry would never return to the South to live, but in Jonoah he created a character who does. In this story and in much of his poetry, Henry pays tribute to the rural black world that sustains him in a distant land. In this letter to Viking and presumably in correspondence to other publishers that has not been found, Henry offered a lucid argument for his vision as a writer. And his intention to attend the Negro Writers Conference at the New School lined up perfectly with his deepening commitment to writing and to the exploration of black culture. But in none of the historical accounts of the event is there any mention of Henry Dumas.

Harold Cruse's firsthand account of the conference mentioned several people, many of whom were associated with the Harlem Writers Guild or what Cruse termed the "leftwing literary elite." Ralph Ellison was noticeably absent. James Baldwin was the biggest name in the house, and the gathering also honored the late Lorraine Hansberry, who had died from cancer at the age of thirty-four earlier that year. But "Henry Dumas" did not make Cruse's roll call. Nonetheless, the trajectory of his writing and his life embody the central tension that Cruse identified with the black writers of that period: "Thus these conference writers want to join the prevailing cultural superstructure of America while protesting its standards and values, under the misapprehension that the injection of *their* values (whatever they are alleged to be) can change that superstructure."[9]

At the heart of Cruse's critique was this question: "how much does the black writer or intellectual have to give up or sacrifice for white acknowledgment?" And Cruse did not think the old guard of writers and intellectuals who were wedded to the left by default had formulated the right answers to this question. The white superstructure would have to be dismantled, Cruse argued. In the meantime, as part of that superstructure, Viking declined the opportunity to even meet with Henry. They were not impressed.

Henry's difficulty in finding a publisher was linked to a number of factors. By 1965, Lois had been with Henry for two years, observing his personal and creative setbacks firsthand. As one of Henry's confidants, and as someone who would enter the publishing world right after her graduation in 1965, she could support and advise him as he pursued publishers. She concluded that Henry's publishing difficulties were not tied to one source. But there was a recurring theme. "No matter the publisher," she recalled, "no mainstream editor would look at him. Henry also had a meeting with Farrar Straus, and they sent the manuscript back. The editor thought Henry was a con man."[10]

From her vantage point, Lois thought Henry's challenges had more to do with his personality when he met with potential publishers. In these encounters, he kept to himself, maintaining what she would remember as an aspect of "mystery and unpredictability, and an obsessive level of intensity."[11] This kind of intensity in a black man would have made potential (white) editors uneasy. In other words, Henry appeared to be an unknown quantity. As for those he did meet with to discuss the publication of his work, they had no better sense of Henry even after meeting him. In person, Henry needed not only to make the case for his work but also to create a level of comfort, establish a certain rapport with potential editors. In the most fundamental sense, an editor has to want to collaborate with a writer or at least believe in a writer's work. For all the charm and pleasantry Henry could call up when he approached women, Lois concluded that he really could not parlay those talents in the publishing sphere. Henry's struggle with New York publishing houses was the result of a strange confluence of his intensity, his race, and his experimental writing, all of which pushed publishers away.

Beyond Henry's rather puzzling personality in these settings with publishers, he nonetheless was part of a larger publishing context in which trade presses tended to have allegiances to only a few black writers. "Most of the major publishing houses," writes Lawrence P. Jackson, "enlisted the work of at least one black novelist . . . Harper touted Richard Wright, who in two works sold nearly one million hardcover copies; Random House claimed the erudite Ralph Ellison but shored itself up commercially with the blockbuster sensation Willard Motley; Farrar Straus published all four of William Gardner Smith's books; Houghton Mifflin supported Ann Petry; James Baldwin started out with Knopf and then settled in at Dial; and even the poet Gwendolyn Brooks tested the waters of seminarrative fiction at Harper."[12]

The pattern Jackson delineates continued in the 1960s. Trident Press and Knopf published John Oliver Killens. John A. Williams, with his connections in journalism, published with Farrar Straus; Chatham Bookseller; Little, Brown; and American Library. And Doubleday was the place for William Melvin Kelley. These publishers, however, seemed predisposed not to load up on black writers. One, maybe two, was enough.

For its part, Viking had not published any up-and-coming or major black literary figures in the 1950s and 1960s. Its list of writers was an impressive collection of modern, postmodern, white, and Jewish writers—Saul Bellow, Jack Kerouac, Ken Kesey, and Barbara Tuchman among them—but the press was slow in adding black writers to its roster. Strategically speaking, Henry could have chosen a better candidate than Viking for a pitch letter; of the mainstream houses, it was the least likely to bring him aboard. Henry's decision to pursue Viking, in the end, was a calculated gamble that did not pay off. Henry left no record of his thoughts on this subject, but he apparently reasoned that he would have more success with Viking, since it did not already have the obligatory one or two black writers on its roll. In other words, since the press had no black writers, this was the perfect chance for it to catch up with some its publishing counterparts.

For her part, Lois's understanding of Henry's challenges would come from positions she landed in publishing. When she graduated from Rutgers in 1965, she secured her first professional job at Western Publishing. Her brief tenure was long enough for her to receive a brisk reminder of the conservative culture prevalent in the United States and the precarious nature of interracial relationships. One day she met Henry in the lobby of her office building. Nothing occurred that would have caused people to take notice, except that it was clear that she and Henry knew each other. A few days later, one of Lois's male colleagues told her that her behavior was scandalous and that if she was going to continue at Western, her interaction with blacks could only follow the Booker T. Washington model—for business or civic purposes only.[13] In all things social, she was to stay white.

Although she and Henry dealt with legitimate problems—his marriage, his debt, his literary challenges—Lois may have resented being rebuked by society for exercising her free will by being with a black man. The surest way to stoke someone's interest in what is considered the taboo is to forbid them to do it. After all, it would be another two years, in 1967, before the nation's highest court would affirm in *Loving v. Virginia* the right of couples like Henry and Lois to marry.

After being admonished by her colleague at Western, Lois soon found work elsewhere. By the early summer of 1966, she had become an administrative assistant at *Harper's Magazine*. In addition to their secretarial tasks, Lois and other assistants were often the first people to review manuscripts. They would offer brief comments on submissions—"liked it" or "hated it," as she characterized it—and send them on to the editor. Lois remembers being the first one to read the manuscript of Phillip Roth's *Portnoy's Complaint*. Encountering some of the major writers of the period (Norman Mailer and David Halberstam, for example), she developed an informed understanding of the publishing world. She certainly shared information with Henry, and there is reason to assume he followed her advice, since she typed and helped Henry compose the letter to Viking.

Henry's search for a publisher was at least twofold. He was in search of literary affirmation and financial stability. He and Loretta were chin-deep in the red, as Henry explained in a 1965 application to the Carnegie Fund for "emergency aid under your clause for writers." Henry applied to the organization hoping to receive some small amount of assistance and relief. "Up until yester-day," he wrote to W. L. Rothenberg, the fund administrator, "things were bad enough but then today my wife had an accident with her car. I am working only part-time at Shelley's bookstore, and we are two months behind in our mortgage, plus our front steps fell through and with this and other debts I not only cannot continue writing, I have to withdraw from school."[14]

Henry's most dependable but stultifying job had been at IBM, but the weight of feeling like an automaton was overwhelming, and Henry quit in the latter part of 1964. The racial environment was unpleasant, and despite the title of Multilith operator, Henry's daily activities were limited to copying and run-ning errands for management. As financially strapped as he and Loretta were, Henry ceased course work after fall 1964, although he had maintained an un-official presence at Rutgers through his positions on *Untitled* and *The Antholo-gist*. Unfortunately, bill collectors were not impressed with his literary efforts. Financial matters in the Dumas home were fragile, and Henry had to make a change to put his family on firmer ground.

Henry found work as a substitute teacher in New Brunswick and as a tutor-counselor in a youth program at the Harlem All Dimension Youth Cen-ter, then located on 217 West 125th Street. In this latter position, Henry ben-efitted from some of Lois's success. Her job at Western and then at *Harper's* had enabled her to secure an apartment at 324 West 76th Street soon after her graduation in 1965. That Upper West Side apartment became Henry's new home, as well. With Lois now working in the city, Henry's relationship deal got sweeter. On the social scene, he took full advantage of Lois's new spot. He could now, as Lois Wright quipped, "stay out late and run the streets. Since I had a steady job, I could also put a few dollars in Henry's pocket." At the same time, Loretta resigned herself to continuing on in a one-sided marriage. With her traditional view of marriage, she knew there would be some turbulent pe-riods. In time, she thought, "this too will pass." Even when the circumstances of their relationship did not give her reason to think positively, she held on to hope anyway, believing that at some point Henry would step off the emotional high wire and work to renew their marriage.

Lois's base in the city was also key in Henry's decision, in 1966, to work as a tutor and later as a social worker. In the latter position he was not well-organized, and it was outside his evolving area of expertise. But it did provide him with a firsthand look into the social underclass in the city. Henry undoubt-edly absorbed some of the major psychological aspects of the roiling Harlem scene, to which he devoted serious narrative space in stories like "Harlem,"

"Strike and Fade" (an urban tale with allusions to Vietnam), and "Riot or Revolt"—all of which riff on the fate of the black masses gathered in U.S. cities.

In his poetry, speakers comment on a Harlem life that is jagged, and where, if blacks are not careful, they will lose their soul to the harshness, to the acidity, of the modern city. In "Knees of a Natural Man," a father and son of limited means head out to hunt for food:

> my ole man took me to fulton fish market
> we walk around in the guts and scales
>
> my ole man show me a dead fish, eyes like throat spit
> he say "you hongry boy?" i say "naw, not yet"[15]

This journey through guts and scales in downtown Manhattan depicts a father looking out for his son as best he can. In this and other poems, Henry portrays Harlem in all of its cultural wonder and social contradiction, as a place where tragedy and beauty often dance hand-in-hand. In "The Playground Is My Home," the speaker sums up the city this way:

> a lot of garbage in the alley
> we climb over the bed mattress and
> I grab me a fist full of cotton
> and throw it up in the sky
> rainin cotton, rainin cotton.[16]

Compared with his southern tales, these northern stories are shrouded in ambiguity. There is more doubt as to whether an authentic, fulfilling black life can be had in the city. Henry posed this question in his fiction and poetry, but he remained in the North. The North was far from perfect, but there he had an opportunity to appreciate the South.

Beyond practical considerations, Henry's presence on the Upper West Side put him in the center of cultural activity. And two friendships would prove important as he continued to find his way as a writer. He would reconnect with Jay Wright, his literary compadre from his Rutgers years. And he would develop a friendship with Sun Ra, one of the most accomplished experimental jazz musicians of the period.

It had been over a year since Henry had last seen Jay Wright, during which time Wright had been teaching English and medieval history at the Butler Institute in Guadalajara, Mexico. Having had a year of inculcating himself in another culture, Wright was now fully living the life often associated with artists, one of adventure and intellectual exploration.

Upon Wright's return to the area in October 1965, Henry brought him home to Lois's apartment for dinner. Wright was a reserved fellow with a citizen-of-the-world sensibility. Somewhat shy herself, Lois had invited a woman named Bonnie Thornton from the apartment upstairs to even out the impromptu dinner party. Thornton's roommate, Joanna, would soon marry Clem Fiori. But for the moment, Lois found Wright merely intriguing.

The integrated social dynamics of this evening highlighted the way in which Henry navigated between black and white worlds. In 1966, he was best man in Clem Fiori's wedding. Fiori and his fiancée had been concerned about how their families would respond to Henry's presence at the wedding. Fiori had grown up in rural New Jersey, where his family and hometown were not progressive on the race issue. The same was true for Joanna, so they wanted certain family members to meet Henry prior to the service. In this way, they thought that they could get it over and done with before the ceremony with any sting Henry's black presence might cause. Fiori introduced Henry to his Sicilian grandmother who, in his words, "had suspect opinions about everything. It wasn't just blacks but Jews, it was a whole lot of things." He need not have worried, however: "Henry walked in with his tuxedo and charmed the shit out of her. She wanted to go with him, she was ready to jump on him, such a funny scene. Henry had that effect on people, he charmed everybody."[17]

Socially and artistically, both Henry and Jay Wright would establish relationships beyond the black world, while remaining connected to it. Over the next two years, the two would solidify their friendship, and part of that involved their outsider status on the black literary scene in New York. Both men were just as comfortable in the library or local drinking haunts, and neither was interested in ingratiating themselves when they rubbed elbows with the literary well-to-do. Often, the two aspiring writers would chase down jazz spots and blues basements for the unfettered expressions of black culture they found there. Also during this time, Henry would reconnect with a talented white jazz drummer, William Seiboth, a man he met in the early 1960s. Henry and Jay would also form a loose association with the Harlem Writers Guild, which counted John Oliver Killens and Paule Marshall among its members.

On the literary scene, as Lois recalls, Henry and Jay were not on the mailing list of John Henrik Clarke, the legendary self-taught black nationalist historian, but the Harlem man of letters would often extend informal invitations to them for social gatherings at his apartment. Lois has a clear memory of those opportunities arising, because she never attended these parties. For that matter, it was understood that she could not go, but she remembers the stories Henry, and later Jay, would tell about the black literati who attended. While Henry and Jay seized the opportunity to attend some of these black cultural events, they concluded that their presence did not denote full inclusion into the circle of published and up-and-coming writers. They could attend events associated with the black literary well-to-do but never have their own place in that group.[18]

In their view, there was a bourgeois affect in these gatherings exemplified in cultural nationalist figures like Clarke. According to Lois Wright, Henry and Jay Wright knew they would never be accepted into what they considered a highbrow club. In Henry's case, the lack of a formal connection to this net-work was indicative of his challenge of succeeding in a publishing world whose understanding or appreciation of black writers was limited to just a few no-table names. For their part, Henry nor Wright was wedded to a singular idea about cultural expressions of blackness. To the contrary, they were probably more engaged by the aspects of black culture that were, in their view, untar-nished by pretense and artifice.

It was this idea of an organic black culture, springing forth from black trag-edy and triumph, whose roots stretched across the Atlantic, that took them to places like Slug's in the East Village. This was where Henry and Jay would en-counter the electrifying sounds of jazz pianist, numerologist, and self-proclaimed prophet Sun Ra. Born in 1914 as Herman Poole Blount in Birmingham, Al-abama, and later renaming himself after the earth's energy source, Sun Ra would have an inimitable impact on Henry. As a writer, Henry was trying to synthesize the past and present to create a fertile future. And Sun Ra was the kindred spirit of that synthesis. Henry came to know Sun Ra through his in-teractions with Tam Fiofori, who, according to Lois, "took the money at Slug's when Sun Ra was playing."[19]

Fiofori, notes Sun Ra biographer John Szwed, was "a Nigerian poet-writer who had come to New York in 1965 by way of London, where he had been the London editor for the journal *Change.*"[20] As a Nigerian, Fiofori was, for Henry, a direct connection to Africa. In both his fiction and poetry, Henry was inter-ested in African themes and language, and the chance to interact with a fellow creative writer from the continent was stimulating and informative.

Lois, on the other hand, was not impressed with Fiofori. In her estimation, Fiofori was more hustler than artist, and Henry contributed to her negative as-sessment. Henry invited Fiofori, without consulting Lois, to live in her apart-ment in the summer of 1966. Lois found out after she returned home from a short vacation: "I had taken a short trip to Martha's Vineyard. When I came home, I found Henry and Fiofori had been treating my place like a bachelor's pad," a still-incredulous Wright recalled years later. "Henry had just let him move in. Without consulting me! I was livid and told Fiofori he had to go."

Henry knew he should have cleared Fiofori's move-in with Lois, but this gesture was consistent with his generous spirit and his openness toward new people and experiences. It also sprang from Henry's growing interest in African culture and its manifestations in America. In this Nigerian, he had the diaspora right in Lois's apartment, a need that first found expression in 1962, when he invited Sulemani Sentumbwe, a Ugandan student, to move into the family's new Highland Park home. The problem in these scenarios was that Henry failed (twice) to consider the opinions and feelings of the women sharing his life—Loretta and now Lois. His gestures toward both these men demonstrated his willingness to share what he had, even if it was not entirely his to give, and despite his own money problems.

Although Tam Fiofori was a good friend, Henry revealed his writerly aspirations instead to Sun Ra, a fellow seeker or traveler on the black way. Twenty years Henry's senior, Sun Ra was one of the most intellectually curious artists of the 1950s and 1960s. A jazz pianist who eventually assembled his own band in Chicago, called Sun Ra's Intergalactic Arkestra, Sun Ra built a cosmic caravan of avant-garde musicians whose composition was ever-changing; they never kept the same core group of musicians.

Vertamae Smart-Grosvenor, who was part of the Arkestra in her role of reading or dramatizing poetry, remarked that "Sun Ra didn't hire or fire you. If the spirit led him to invite you to participate with the Arkestra, that superseded any notion of a contract stipulating terms of employment. I was only with the band a few years, but years later, if we were in a public gathering Sun Ra always introduced me as a member of the Arkestra."[21] Such a unique and free-flowing vision was certainly appealing and intriguing to Henry. Sun Ra's conception of music as a means of cosmic revelation—not merely ephemeral entertainment—was the corollary to what Henry sought to achieve as a writer. Fiction and poetry could entertain, certainly, but Henry felt writing and art had a more lasting purpose.

"To young black poets," writes Szwed, Sun Ra "provided a means for releasing the words from the page, and for relocating them in the conventions of black instrumental and ritual performance."[22] Henry was not the only writer to identify with Sun Ra. Amiri Baraka and Ishmael Reed also spent time listening to the Arkestra at Slug's, which became the gathering place in lower Manhattan where black artists met to partake of a different cultural milieu. During this time, Henry was embracing the cultural thesis of the Black Power Movement, continuing a steady gravitation toward a sensibility that was more overtly invested in the cultivation of black cultural consciousness. Just as Sun Ra had built a sacred cultural ark, Henry was working to forge a similar trajectory in his fiction, which Sun Ra may have helped Henry explore.

The notion of a sacred cultural ark was the impetus for Henry's story "Ark of Bones," a metaphysical exploration of black life published posthumously in 1970, and there is no evidence to suggest it was composed before 1965, the year he met Sun Ra. A prototype for black fiction in the post-civil-rights era, it features a "soul boat" that journeys down the Mississippi collecting the bones of African ancestors. Two adolescents on the cusp of manhood, Headeye and Fish-hound, are the main characters. Headeye has been called into this spirit world, and he introduces the narrator Fish-hound to this unknown realm. They learn about American bondage through this mythical vessel that carries sacred cargo: ancestral bones. The bones mesmerize Fish-hound. He becomes part of the chosen few who witness this black inversion of the biblical flood story. In this tale, a select group of people and animals are not saved from the flood, but human bones are recovered from the iconic American river that ushered blacks into both slavery and freedom. Fish-hound saw "Bones. I saw bones. . . . I looked and I saw crews of black men handling in them bones. There was a crew of two or three under every cabin around that ark."[23] As metaphor, this story, in haunting narrative vision, delineates the ultimate cost of the middle passage: the black sacrifice for America has cut to the bone.

Fish-hound continues observing this ritual. As sacred bones are recovered, a man sings in a strange yet familiar language. That much Fish-hound can discern, but he says he "never was good at foreign talk." Nonetheless, Fish-hound remembers the sounds though he cannot translate these utterances:

> Aba, aba, al ham dilaba
> Aba aba, mtu brotha
> Aba aba, al ham dilaba
> Aba aba, bretha brotha
> Aba aba, djuka brotha
> Aba, aba, al ham dilaba.[24]

In this moment where past and present are conflated, Henry explores the challenge for blacks of learning about their African past and returning to their first, as in original, language.

It is not clear what these lines mean. Aba, depending on context, is associated with camel's hair. "Al ham dilaba" is Arabic, meaning "praise God." Djuka refers to black people of Dutch Guiana. These two southern black youths do not know their place of origin, the original language of their ancestors. The "foreign talk" that Fish-hound describes is actually a way to acknowledge the history, language, culture, and traditions destroyed by the Middle Passage. Like Henry, Fish-hound pieces together the African words as best he can, knowing they represent another world. Most black Americans know little of their African ancestors. Headeye and Fish-hound certainly are oblivious. The sacred bones serve as conduit to their history, as Henry's literary companion to the Arkestra of Sun Ra.

"Of all the young black writers of the time," writes Szwed, "Henry was closest to Sun Ra." They shared an artistic kinship around the belief in the power of art to transform worlds. Sun Ra's ability to "draw on Egyptian and West African mythological material, as well as Deep South folksay and science fiction," was affirmation of Henry's own literary quest.[25] In Sun Ra, Henry had an older mentor who had found a way to merge the African—its rituals and history—with the modern black American world. Henry's closeness to Sun Ra is evident not only in "Ark of Bones" but also in his poem "Outer Space Blues." He embraced Sun Ra's notion that humans are part of a vast cosmic universe: "Yeah, a spaceship is comin / guess I wait and see / All I know they might look just like me."[26] The coming of this spaceship also represents the dawning of black power in Henry's work. In other words, Sun Ra helped Henry arrive at the idea that black may well be the color of the cosmos. Or, equally important, the cosmos certainly was not white.

In his short story, "The Metagenesis of Sun Ra," Henry crafted a rather obtuse allegory on the cosmic origins of Sun Ra, who in fact claimed that his origins were fundamentally different. As Szwed explains, "at the heart of everything Sun Ra said or did was the claim that he was not born, that he was not from earth, that he was not a man, that he had no family, that his name was not what others said it was. For almost fifty years he evaded questions, forgot details, left false trails, and talked in allegories and parables."[27] He resisted the concept of viewing himself in strictly linear terms, of defining himself by chronology.

This kind of approach conforms with the African traditional worldview of understanding human experience in cyclical, rather than linear, terms. Sun Ra's insistence on reformulating his history and his desire to link himself with a higher order of creative perfection was certainly a compelling idea to a struggling black writer. Unlike most people who may have made similar otherworldly claims, Sun Ra had demonstrated, through his music and the work of the Ark-estra, that a higher plane of artistic consciousness was possible.

So enamored was Henry with Sun Ra's approach to exploring the cosmic dimensions of jazz that he recorded dialogues with his artistic compatriot in 1966 at Slug's, when both Dumas and Sun Ra resided in New York. In this exchange Sun Ra spoke with Henry about how his music was the medium for reaching the next level of universal consciousness:

> For the Blackman the first step will be toward discipline. Music is a force of nature. I am a force of nature. I am in the role of Ra because the Creator has left it up to me to give some order and harmony to this planet. Not everyone is in need of it. Many people are well developed spiritually and growing. But most are not. So a force of nature gets them all. It's just like when it rains, it rains on everything and everybody. You might say that I represent everything and everybody. You might say that I represent all the force of nature. People don't all know about this mind-cept, but in the Yoruba culture it is understood.[28]

Impressed with Sun Ra's fusion of blackness with cosmic identity while invoking Yoruba culture as a point of reference, Henry continued his move toward a more radical form of black identity. Intrigued by the notion of a "mind-cept," Henry delved further into the contemporary conversation on experimental jazz.

Henry had saved an article by Nat Hentoff, published in December 1966, on what some aficionados were calling "the new jazz." Hentoff attempted to explain the avant-garde jazz ethos that was, for some, revolutionary and for others simply self-indulgent. The article presented this new genre as the pure expression of the avant-garde. Hentoff explained how this "new jazz erupts in speechlike cries, squawks, moans, and cackles. And in that sense, it resembles the sounds of the early jazz of 60 and 70 years ago, played by southern Negroes who had no lesson books and accordingly turned horns into extensions of the human voice—slurring, burring, braying, crying."[29]

For the practitioners of this new jazz, these primordial sounds were equivalent to the shouts in black churches, the emotional manifestation of the desire to view themselves outside of the lens of white America. Henry was developing a deeper understanding of black historical consciousness and he found intriguing the idea that black people could move beyond Du Bois's idea of double consciousness, which was framed around the idea of African Americans seeing themselves only through the lens of whites. For their identity, ultimately the history and culture that produced them, predated whites and American bondage. And the two places that were associated with this more authentic state of consciousness, as Henry was coming to understand in his fiction and poetry, were the rural South and Africa.

Artists like Sun Ra represented for Henry a means of understanding the nature of his people. He felt that African Americans, in the context of adjusting to American cultural norms, had lost their natural, pre-American selves. Slavery and Jim Crow had caused a rupture, for most, with Africa. Henry parlayed Hentoff's essay into a provocative exploration of the essence of race and black power in "Will the Circle Be Unbroken?" The story appeared in the November 1966 issue of *Negro Digest*. That edition was focused on the "meaning and measure of black power." It featured a number of contributors (among them Julian Bond, John Oliver Killens, and Anita Cornwell), and Henry's story provided a different entry point into the discussion. Indeed, one of his most puzzling stories, it explores through the prism of jazz the notion of racial and cultural authenticity. In it, the Sound Barrier Club is where experimental jazz artists with names like Probe and Magwa search for authentic approaches to sounding the Afro horn.

Three white enthusiasts, one of whom is good friends with Probe, seek entrance. All three possess intimate knowledge of black music, and they assume that they are in sync—emotionally, musically, and culturally—with these musicians and, by extension, black people in general. The guards inform them that this session is for "Brothers and Sisters only."[30] After much protest, Jan, Ron, and Tasha are allowed to enter. Upon hearing the music, their hearts literally stop; the mysterious vibe in the club overcomes them.

The narrator does not explain the deaths of this trio. He leaves it to the reader to make sense of this surreal scene, this moment where music both gives and takes life. To begin with, this white trio insists on entering a sacred cultural space. The result proves fatal, as this alien sound overwhelms their sensory experience.

On the surface, this is a tremendous price to pay for not being black. However, in their effort to enter the Sound Barrier Club, the trio is an example of white hubris. They think that because of their engagement with black musicians they transcend the race barrier, that they can be—at least in cultural terms—black. They know and appreciate the music but equate that with knowing or experiencing blackness. However, they fail to perceive that there are moments in which a marginalized group needs to gather together, not necessarily to plot against the group in power, but to remember and affirm the collective experience, to honor what Dumas called the sacred "ark of bones." They also fail to realize that they can never experience blackness; it is an existential impossibility.

Larry Neal, a major figure in the Black Arts Movement, offers a prescient observation of "Circle" and the cultural context undergirding the story: "It was time, some of us thought, to be in certain contexts socially, unashamedly on our own, and to define ourselves on our own terms without someone else intervening in our definition."[31]

In this sense, Henry was signifying on Norman Mailer's essay "The White Negro," published in 1957. "So there was a new breed of adventurers, urban adventurers who drifted out at night looking for action with a black man's code to fit their facts. The hipster had absorbed the existentialist synapses of the Negro, and for practical purposes could be considered a white Negro."[32] In his exercise of provocative and, for some, sensationalized cultural criticism, Mailer made the case for the Negro man as the ultimate symbol of the hipster or the jazz man in American culture. For white men who dared pursue a masculine identity rooted in being cool or hip, they had to, in Mailer's parlance, become a Negro. Following Mailer's thesis, the black man could rarely, if ever, afford the sophisticated inhibitions of western civilization. He therefore maintained the art of the primitive, living fully in the present. There was an element of cultural truth to Mailer's idea that the black experience was born out of the ultimate existential dilemma: succumb to oppression or develop forms of cultural resistance. But Mailer came dangerously close to defining blackness in crudely reductive terms.

In their more progressive iterations, the Black Arts and Black Power movements attempted to galvanize communities through recognizing the history of African American struggle in America and throughout the Diaspora. Henry's vision, far from exclusionary, called for conversation between the races, but part of the lesson, for whites at least, was that even in the context of creating interracial discussion, whites should not assume unlimited access to black communities.

But complicating the way in which Henry was working through questions of identity, Americanness, and belonging was his deep involvement with Lois. Was he signaling to Lois in "Will the Circle Be Unbroken?" that there would always be a barrier between him and her, between black and white? Was he moving toward an understanding of blackness that required separation from whites, especially white lovers? There was, in the dawn of the Black Power Movement, a precedent for shedding white girlfriends and wives.

After Malcolm X's murder in 1965, the de facto face of the Black Arts Movement, Amiri Baraka, literally said good-bye to his first wife, Hettie, who was

white, and their two daughters. "In a few days," writes Baraka in his autobiography, "I had gotten my stuff and gone uptown. . . . My little girl, the older
one, Kellie, picked up instinctively a sense of my departure. . . . I was gone. A
bunch of us, really, had gone, up to Harlem. Seeking revolution."[33] Baraka's
experience echoes that of the fictional Truman Held, a black revolutionary in
Alice Walker's second novel, *Meridian*. He leaves his black lover for a Jewish
woman named Lynne, but he sees too many contradictions in talking black
and sleeping white.

Even loosely reading Henry's life through "Will the Circle Be Unbroken?"
raises the question of whether Lois had now become a problem for Henry. Or
had their relationship reached its natural endpoint? Lois was aware that Henry
had strayed from their relationship a time or two. In her professional life, she
was learning the ins and outs of the publishing world, perhaps concluding that
Henry may not have been quite the writer or person she thought him to be.
Out in the world herself, Lois had more to measure Henry and their relationship against. Whatever the root causes of their problems, both "Circle" and the
substance of Henry's relationship with Sun Ra suggest that, by 1965, he and
Lois may have both viewed their relationship with ambivalence.

In the midst of such personal and social activity, it is hard to imagine Henry
focusing primarily on either his family or Lois. The all-encompassing political
and cultural movements were addictive to him. In fact, Henry was probably
most at home in the middle of such flux. A life built on such turbulence will,
of course, yield compelling stories, narratives about survival, and eventual as-
cent to higher ground or a peaceful place. On the other hand, it can bottom
out. In Henry's case, as he continued in the muck and mire of his life and the
world, he would test the range of all these boundaries.

(Up from the Ghetto)

RECALL!

They shall come to you one day

and they shall laugh and say,

Tell us again the place you come from.

—HENRY DUMAS,
from "East Saint Hell"

[CHAPTER EIGHT

Headed to East Boogie

In August 1966, Henry was still living with Lois in the city. He had stopped tutoring at the Harlem All Dimension Youth Center and had begun working as a social investigator for the New York City Department of Welfare. On his résumé, he claimed an eighty-person caseload. The irony is that Henry's life at the time of this productive employment was becoming increasingly unstable, though his literary fever never abated. But at this point, drugs and alcohol were establishing a more prominent place in his life.

Too occupied coping with Henry's absence and with being, essentially, a single parent, Loretta Dumas never saw him imbibe firsthand. When he was around, though, she observed his emotional fluctuations, attributing them to his experimentation with amphetamines. "He was more sullen," she would remember years later, "antagonized by the least little thing." Lois Wright, who probably witnessed more of Henry's drug-induced moments, remembered that his primary struggle was with alcohol. "When he went on a binge," she matter-of-factly recalled, "he could say or do just about anything."

From classical music to evangelizing for the Lord, Henry demonstrated the capacity to become overabsorbed with a subject. Exhibiting the signs of an addictive personality, Henry was crossing, at times, the line separating free spirit from rogue personality. To Loretta and the boys, when they did see him, Henry was "moody and erratic." But more often than not, Henry was just gone. Although he was in the process of disengaging from his family, he may have stayed away from home to protect Loretta, David, and Michael from his substance abuses. Even if his absence could be partly attributed to his not wanting to hurt his family, his absence itself hurt them. It could not have been easy for Loretta to explain Henry's absence to their sons or to herself.

Whatever the source of Henry's erratic behavior, he was now ceding power of his mind and body more regularly to potentially harmful substances, a practice in which he was certainly not alone. Experimentation with mind-altering substances was part of the social landscape of the 1960s, especially in the New York arts scene. In his autobiography, Amiri Baraka notes the casual way he came upon drugs during his Greenwich Village days in the late fifties and early sixties.[1] His former wife, Hettie Jones, concedes the same in her memoir.[2]

Henry became part of this scene of wild experimentation and recklessness. His involvement with drugs and alcohol seemed to have been intermittent at first. But it was part of a larger transition for him into the realm of experimentation. It began with shifts in his thinking about Christianity and later his marriage. These changes certainly contributed to his evolving worldview and creative sensibility, but drugs now presented a different set of challenges for him as writer, husband, father, and lover. And when he indulged in drugs he became, according to Clem Fiori, a "different person. The times when Henry would be high it would look like he was in another persona. . . . He could get pretty stoned."[3] Much of the drug use during this period in the arts community seems to have been predicated on the search for a deeper relationship to the universe. Artists are hardwired for that search. But for the person like Henry, who might be described as having a feverish or addictive personality, the results of such behavior could prove debilitating.

As 1966 came to a close, both Henry's marriage with Loretta and his relationship with Lois were going to pieces. His increased drug use made him less capable of repairing the multiple breaches. With the new year approaching, Henry may have made a resolution to correct course. He had at least one publishing opportunity on the horizon. In November, his short story, "The Lake," had been accepted by *Trace*, a small, ambitious literary magazine whose editor was based in Hollywood, California, and that was published in London. James Boyer May ran the magazine. Part of its unique place in the

literary world involved its wide-ranging list of contributors and subject matter, as well as its commitment to publishing news about the goings-on of other
small literary enterprises. On a smaller scale, but quite effective nonetheless, it
served as a literary version of the Cannes Film Festival in France.

One of Henry's shortest and most provocative fictional vignettes, about a
man and woman who meet at the lake for an enchanting encounter, the story
is a surreal, expressionistic piece, more evocative than narrative in form. The
editor, Milton Van Sickle, was impressed and wrote to tell Henry so. But Henry,
consumed by other matters, did not respond immediately to the good news.

One of the reasons for this lapse probably involved the state of his relationship with Lois. On New Year's Eve, she and Henry had a heated argument
that lasted into the morning hours. Lois Wright's memory of that moment is
informed by one violent and terrible thing: "In a drunken fury," she recalled,
"Henry landed a blow across my head." Through that act, Henry erected a
wall between himself and Lois that would never come down. She realized that
while Henry still looked like the man she had fallen in love with, the substance
of that man had dissipated. If Lois had previously been slow to call off the relationship, she was now determined to do so. "If you don't leave me alone," she
warned, "I'll call the police." Ending his relationship on such an ominous note,
Henry had entered a perilous zone. He would continue to attempt reconciliation over the next six weeks, even as he half-heartedly pursued other women.
For Lois, however, there would be no turning back.

Henry's behavior leading up to and culminating on that New Year's Eve
revealed what Lois called the "maniacal" side of Henry. In correspondence
a year later with Jay Wright (with whom she had become friends), she confided that he did not know this side of Henry. In her estimation, only she and
Earl Thomas had seen his drunken "maniacal violence."[4] At his worst, Henry
would act out or say whatever took form in his mind. And it had been a long
time since Lois had seen Henry at his best.

In a letter to Wright, who was in Mexico, Lois explained her former relationship with Henry: "Part of my love . . . was based on a man who very simply
did not exist—that ideal Henry, a person he helped create but could never
be."[5] Lois concluded that her love for Henry had been rooted in a kind of emotional blindness, a refusal to see Henry in full form. She expected writing to be
a major distraction in their relationship, but drugs had overtaken it as a more
powerful and destructive obstacle.

At this point, Henry had placed himself in a corner. Headed out of control, he knew a change was imperative. Loretta and Lois would never converse
with each other about their experiences with him, but both were disillusioned.

They had envisioned much different scripts in their respective lives with Henry. Nine years younger, Lois had been naive in some of her expectations. And Loretta, contrary to the emotional reality, had long clung to the idea that she and Henry would eventually craft an updated sequel to their early years together.

After the breakup with Lois, Henry probably needed to return to his home and family, which he did, if only nominally. He had never officially left in the first place. This would give Loretta a measure of optimism, but Henry never really did anything to suggest he was willing to try to rebuild their marriage. He also needed to complete his studies at Rutgers, but it did not resemble the place he entered nine years earlier. Most of the people with whom he had attended Rutgers had moved on to productive lives and careers, neither of which Henry could boast. As Earl Thomas explained it, "all the white people Henry knew at Rutgers had moved from being students to fairly successful earners. These guys went on to at least entry-level faculty positions at colleges."[6] Henry was working welfare cases. Noble work, indeed, but far from the literary world from which he sought recognition.

Thomas himself was married and finding his way in the fields of education and social work. Alan Cheuse and Robert Pinsky were earning further academic credentials and forging ahead in their respective pursuits in fiction and poetry. Jay Wright had left Rutgers in 1967 with a master's in comparative literature, publishing his first chapbook that year. Another such person who had already left Rutgers, but who proved a major resource for Henry, was Hale Chatfield. He and Henry did not talk frequently, but through the grapevine word had spread quickly to Chatfield in Ohio about the altercation and breakup with Lois.

Chatfield lobbied for Henry to come to Hiram, a private college founded in the mid-nineteenth century as the Western Reserve Eclectic Institute, which had produced the country's twentieth president, James A. Garfield. Beyond that fact, however, the college had a history of experimental and innovative educational practices for which Chatfield thought Henry would be a good fit. For her part, Loretta hoped that the somewhat isolated, bucolic setting in the hills of northeastern Ohio would offer fewer social temptations. Henry would work as assistant director in the Upward Bound Program, part of President Lyndon B. Johnson's War on Poverty, which identified students from disadvantaged backgrounds and provided various forms of support to encourage them to earn college degrees. With his experience as a tutor and social worker, Henry would be able to appreciate the challenges confronting many underserved students. An additional perk for Henry: he could serve as one of the editors of the school's journal of poetry, *Hiram Poetry Review*.

Henry arrived at Hiram alone, with Loretta and the boys remaining in New Jersey, in late February 1967. In a short period, he managed to impress a number of people, and it was easier to do so in a new place. One person whom Henry befriended was Claude Steele, a black student involved with Upward Bound and on his way to a distinguished career as a social psychologist.[7] Claude Steele's memory of Henry aligns with the recollections of many who knew him. "Henry was a vessel of pure energy. He wrote his butt off during that period of time, I mean he wrote a lot of stuff," Steele would say years later.[8] During this period Henry's creative life was focused on poetry. Steele was unaware of Henry's inability to find a publisher for his novel. A scholar-in-training, Steele simply welcomed the opportunity to have, finally, a relatively young black man nearby with whom he could discuss a range of intellectual issues.

In Steele's case, Henry's arrival on campus could not have come at a better time. His previous mentor at Hiram had been Dr. Edward Crosby, a renaissance man who had also served on the editorial staff of the *Hiram Poetry Review*. Crosby, a scholar of medieval German languages and literature and of medieval history (also fluent in Spanish) was, during the mid-1960s, in the process of reinventing himself as a Pan-Africanist. Specifically, he committed himself to creating programs to educate young African Americans. To that end, he had resigned from Hiram in 1965, moving in 1966 to East St. Louis to direct the Experiment in Higher Education at Southern Illinois University.

Claude Steele had certainly valued Crosby's guidance and encouragement, and now he appreciated Henry's. At a time when young black men were often dissuaded from pursuing lives of intellectual exploration, Steele appreciated the seriousness with which Henry approached his writing. "He was amazing with the intensity with which he worked, and his expressiveness. I was a young guy, I was twenty-one, and I wanted to be an intellectual and really admired Henry and reveled in the opportunity to see someone like that. I can remember riding around with Henry and saying, 'I'd like to be a writer too, someday.'"[9] Henry was certainly not a picture of perfection for the young Steele, but he confirmed for him a powerful concept: that black manhood and a life of the mind could occur simultaneously.

Steele admired Henry's creative gusto. But he also realized the difference between himself, a budding social scientist interested in reality as understood through objective data, and Henry, who was interested in the same phenomena through the exploration of narrative. Steele framed their relationship in this way:

We had some emotional similarities and connections, but we thought very differ-ently and I just thought so much like a social scientist—and he thought so much like a poet, an expressionist. He was just absolutely, dazzlingly, brilliant. Some of the poems just knocked me sideways. He could get something going in there that would just be amazing. Some of those poems were like the *Rime of the Ancient Mari-ner* to me—they just went on and on. I can just remember knowing that was some-thing I couldn't do. I thought I was good at social science stuff and political analysis and so on, and Henry had very little interest in that, but he just had such a connec-tion to human experience it was amazing.[10]

Henry's artistic engagement and his commitment to finding in art a means of understanding social conditions provided a model for Steele as he devel-oped his understanding of the role of the social scientist. He could appreciate Henry's ability to tease out the meaning of experience at the micro or indi-vidual level, but Steele felt compelled to do the same at the macro or collec-tive level through the use of quantifiable data. Steele valued the way Henry pushed him to develop his own critical sensibility. For his part, Henry saw an opportunity to mentor Steele. Although he had benefitted from his interac-tions with William Wynkoop, William Sloane, and the literary set at Rutgers, he had never had a seasoned black male writer lay out the rules of the game for him. Now presented with the opportunity to do that for Steele, Henry em-braced it.

Henry's ability to engage black experience was nowhere more apparent, for Steele, than in July 1967. Harkening to his visits back south, Henry, Claude Steele, and some other men headed to Detroit to observe the race riots that occurred over a five-day period. Detroit police had intended to raid an after-hours drinking spot located in a mostly black neighborhood at Twelfth Street and Clairmont Avenue, instead crashing a party for two Vietnam veterans. The patrons and gathering crowd were enraged by the intrusion. And the po-lice overreacted to their frustration. The end result was five days of death and destruction.

"Just to be there in Detroit on the scene," Steele emphasized, "was crucial to understanding the racial and social tumult of the 1960s."[11] And Henry ab-sorbed that moment, processing the larger cultural forces at work, as fed-up black folks responded with a fury that was certainly understandable, even jus-tified, but their response was ultimately counterproductive. Henry understood that the rioters were expressing a kind of urban angst regarding the overall con-ditions in which they were forced to live. To Steele, as he was preparing to cut his own path in academia, Henry imparted a major lesson: there are multiple ways of arriving at truth.

The trip to Detroit also brought Henry's own formative experience in New York full circle. From adolescence to adulthood, he had witnessed the changes in Harlem, his second home. And it was clear that the conditions blacks labored under in Harlem were akin to those in Detroit, Watts, and other urban centers to which blacks had migrated. The Detroit riots were a reminder, for Henry, of the diverse, but nonetheless culturally coherent, diaspora or community of aggrieved black citizens. As Claude Steele settled into manhood, having Henry as a resource to model black consciousness was crucial. Despite his own challenges, Henry imparted to Steele the idea that blacks did indeed constitute a diaspora. And while race would be one of many factors impacting black lives in the United States, Steele's future scholarship would echo this thinking relative to the psychology of nonwhite and nonmale populations in the country.

Despite the favorable impression that Henry made on Steele and others in the Hiram community, he had been unable to shake off certain troubling behaviors he had engaged in back East. Claude Steele witnessed how Henry's creative capacity and his strong drive for intense political and cultural engagement could emerge even in the midst of unstable behavior. Steele remembers, in his words, "very distinctly, a drive that we made from Ohio to East St. Louis, Illinois. Henry gave me and another friend amphetamines. And it was one of those experiences where you didn't want the trip to end. The conversation was so intense. And we, Barry and Henry and I, talked a huge amount about the black power movement—which had just emerged."[12] Both the pharmaceutical and the verbal stimulants made for an intriguing journey, and Claude Steele, in the course of this trip, would introduce Henry to his former mentor, Edward Crosby, adding to the heightened intellectual discussion that had characterized their trip.

Later that year, Henry's penchant for the dramatic had not lessened. Steele was to be married on August 27 in Chicago. For the occasion, he had asked Henry to compose a poem to read at the ceremony. On top of that, as Steele noted, "it was a huge wedding (four hundred guests), and I was marrying a white woman. Her father was a pastor, and the whole church was invited, so it was like a black and a white thing."[13] As Steele tells it, this scenario was a real-life version of the 1967 film *Guess Who's Coming to Dinner*, in which a white woman (played by Katharine Houghton) brings home her black fiancé (played by Sidney Poitier).

But the night before the wedding, the real drama unfolded. Henry and other friends had come to Chicago for the couple's prewedding party, "where," as Steele put it, "everybody got drunk." A white woman with whom Henry had been involved in Ohio was in attendance. She had already ended whatever relationship they had explored, but Henry did not accept that her good-bye meant that she was truly gone. So when he spotted her having more than a conversation with a male acquaintance of his, Henry's ego shifted into overdrive.[14]

From that point, as Steele recounted, a surreal sequence of events unfolded. "Henry and this man got into a real argument. The apartment was on the second floor. Henry went out to the balcony and jumped off into the street. And he was not injured. Do you hear me? He was not injured. Can you believe that?"[15] Henry could have hurt himself, but he had anaesthetized himself through alcohol and probably amphetamines, as well. More to the point, his ploy to convince the woman that her decision had driven him to such desperate action had shifted all the attention to himself. This rant was more about him than her. He still called Lois on occasion, and his family remained in a holding pattern in New Jersey. What is clear is that Henry's acting out had taken the party to a whole new level.

The party then moved to the street, where the guests flocked to see how Henry was doing. The police arrived, and Shelby Steele, Claude's twin, who would follow a similar but divergent track in academia, decided to convert this event into a protest. "This was when," explained Claude Steele about his brother, "Shelby was on the other end of the political contingency of where he is now. But he got into a real fight, a physical fight, with the police. They tried to subdue him; he kicked in the side of the police car; he was thrown in the police car. And then five of us all go down to the jail. They tell us if we can get him—my brother—out of jail, we can have him. So we go in. He doesn't want to leave the jail. He wants to make a political thing out of this."[16]

A white woman had rejected Henry, and Shelby Steele built on the momentum Henry created by turning Henry's public spectacle into a moment to antagonize the police. Both were struggling to make sense of a world in flux, a world in which the problem of race was bound to all their endeavors. Shelby Steele, future black conservative icon—author *The Content of Our Character: A New Vision of Race in America, A Bound Man: Why We Are Excited about Obama and Why He Can't Win*, and other books—used Henry's moment of theatrics to protest the institutional bigotry of the police. But on this night, Henry and Shelby were simply out of control. Henry's ego was smarting because a woman he had pursued had moved on. His response was immature, and Steele's impetuous. Neither the woman nor the police was guilty of anything that night. In the end, Claude Steele's wedding was what it should have been: an age-old ritual commemorating the joining of two lives. Henry, notwithstanding the drama of the night before, presented his poem, and no major racial animosity was expressed on either side.

The Henry of Claude Steele's memory, consistent with the Hank of New Jersey and New York, was drawn to the rush of things. Some people flee from chaos; others crave it. What Steele noticed was that even with drugs altering Henry's consciousness, his cultural awareness and creativity were his two constants. Indeed, Henry's sense of creative edginess was attractive and also dangerous. This relationship between creativity and higher states of consciousness had already been well-plumbed in the twentieth century. Ralph Ellison's *Invisible Man* opens with the narrator smoking a joint and listening to jazzman Louis Armstrong, on his way to a kind of hallucinogenic clarity. From the Beatles to the O'Jays, Ernest Hemingway to Ntozake Shange, artists have often extended or blended their search for artistic perfection with narcotics. Of course, creative energy, whether narcotically induced or not, can lead to personal and social complications. Now in his post-Lois, post–New York period, Henry was fairly productive (primarily with his poetry), but his use of amphetamines made him more prone to bouts of volatility. With moments of unparalleled insight came comparable moments of stagnation or self-destructive behavior.

In this new, riskier phase of his development, Henry was presented with the opportunity to relocate once again, less than six months into his Hiram position. Edward Crosby invited Henry to join the Experiment in Higher Education (EHE) at Southern Illinois University as writer in residence. This program, with its emphasis on urban, mostly black students, was housed in East St. Louis. The EHE seemed the perfect place for such work. Crosby also invited Shelby Steele and some of Crosby's classmates from his undergraduate and graduate years at Kent State to join him in the struggle to transform black lives. Henry was actually headed to a hub of the diaspora, a place that many black Arkansans had fled to earlier in the century. Along with Chicago and Milwaukee, East St. Louis was a main receiving station for blacks wanting to plant their feet on ground not governed by Jim Crow.

In New Jersey, New York, and Ohio, Henry had friendships and sexual encounters that crossed the color line, and he would interact with white colleagues who were involved in the EHE. But East St. Louis, in cultural and physical terms, was altogether different, and Henry embraced his return to a largely black world. Like many places, it was a city with a sordid racial history. Black migrants, fed up with southern limitations and dangers, had taken the chance to flee north during World War I. Their arrival was a boon to white industrialists. To white workers seeking fair wages and safe work environments, these barons of industry could call their bluff with black labor. In July 1917, blacks replaced striking white workers from the iron ore plant. When some whites responded with violence, some blacks fought back.

By the 1950s, East St. Louis was on the decline. Chemical companies like Monsanto, maker of the laundary detergent All and the organic insecticide DDT, had over the decades created company towns on the periphery of the city. By doing so, they no longer paid city taxes, and white workers followed these companies to these unincorporated areas. Other industries packed up and left, as well. But with no tax base, the now mostly black city faced the problems of urbanization absent of substantial city revenues. Vulnerable to exploitation, the city became a literal dumping ground for some of the chemical companies.

Despite white flight and the struggles of both black and white leadership over the twentieth century, the black cultural imprint of East St. Louis on the nation—largely the result of the black exodus from the South—is undeniable. East St. Louis was an incubator for the trinity of black secular music: jazz, blues, and rhythm and blues, and as such certainly one of the reasons for Henry's embrace of the place. The city boasts an impressive list of important performance artists—Ike Turner, Tina Turner, Miles Davis, dancer-choreographer Katherine Dunham, and of course Eugene B. Redmond—whose lives began there or whose careers were influenced by the place.

Its impressive artistic imprint notwithstanding, East St. Louis also had a rougher, seedier side that mitigated its cultural vitality. Henry called Earl Thomas a couple of times with stories that gave his friend pause, telling tales of "high stakes card games with guns piled up on the table, where the gang subculture was an economic force unto itself. It sounded like a place," Thomas sighed years later, "I would never want to go to."[17]

Henry was now living in this stimulating and dangerous place, in an apartment that was decent but unsuitable for his family. Although no progress had been made in solidifying his marriage, Henry moved his family to Illinois. Just after Christmas in 1967, with trailer in tow, he, Loretta, and the boys eased onto the Pennsylvania Turnpike, confronting as they headed west what had become the governing metaphor of their marriage: a snowstorm. Frigid temperatures met them in Illinois, as well; they stayed briefly at a spot called the Star Motel, outside the city. Loretta was taken aback by East St. Louis. To her, it looked "poor and run-down." She did, though, find the people "friendly, not cold and distant like New Yorkers." But that is not where she wanted her family to live. In short order, she found a reasonably priced house for them to rent in Edwardsville, twenty-five miles northeast of East St. Louis. Henry would live with them, but he maintained his apartment in the city.

Loretta was thinking positively about the move. Henry had been living a rather adventurous life that included Lois and other women. She suspected infidelity but knew of no specifics. Impacted by the strain of a stressful marriage and naive about how Henry now thought about their relationship, Loretta attributed Henry's extramarital activity to his increased dependence on drugs, but their challenges existed long before Henry's extended involvement with drugs. Although there was no tangible proof that their marriage was improving, the time away from Henry gave Loretta the appearance of a fresh start. With Henry several states away, she could justify his absence in a way not plausible had he been back in New Jersey or New York. At least now her family was back together. She was willing to do almost anything to renew her marriage, which had been in a coma-like state since 1962. She thought that if Henry caught a couple of breaks—published a book, landed a good academic job— that they could put the pieces back together. She understood Henry's sense of angst, but she did not grasp his desire for a different kind of woman. Or she knew the truth but simply did not want to face it. She thought these moves to Ohio and Illinois would help stabilize him, but in this equation Henry was the unknown variable. She knew him as well as she could or as much as he would allow. But sometimes the husband or wife is the last to know or acknowledge realities that to others seem so apparent.

So, Loretta would hang her hopes on 321 Liberty Street. It was, she remembered, "a beautiful house. The backyard ran right into the woods, so the boys could venture out as far as they pleased." And Henry fashioned himself a study area in the basement. To signal to himself and anyone else the creative purpose behind this space, he draped the door frame with beads. With his family in place and a space of his own, Henry, in theory, was on the right track. Indeed, he may have held an earnest desire for things to work out. That is, he probably wanted to feel the desire to return to his family, but even with their recent arrival, he was still searching for another form or level of fulfillment.

Absent from his family for most of 1967, Henry continued the same pattern of inattention to his family. In the meantime, he had immersed himself in the social and cultural life of East St. Louis. He established meaningful relationships with a cadre of black men, many of whom were involved in creating a black studies template of instruction for future generations. One of the first people he met, a fellow poet, literary scholar, and instructor at the EHE, was Eugene B. Redmond. Born in East Boogie (as some of the residents called it), Redmond is the East St. Louis poet laureate in perpetuity. His career as an artist, teacher, and civic leader is rooted in a progressive, community-based expression of Black Nationalism that spans fifty years. He has taken poetry to the people in schools, prisons, wherever there are ears to hear. His verse, characterized by riffs, multiple entendres, and perspectives, is rooted in the "we" or shared experience. There really is no "I" in the classic African view of the world.

For Redmond and Dumas, there was joy in finding what they termed "skin folks" who were also intellectual kinfolks, wordsmiths, and rappers of both the streets and of metaphysics. Not since his days with Jay Wright had Henry found such harmony with a fellow black writer. Redmond's memory of Henry and the EHE community revolved around what he referred to in his introduction to Henry's posthumous poetry collection, *Knees of a Natural Man*, as "night-mooded conversations, testy warrior rap, beer lunches and sexual tease. 'Take off your clothes,' was the much-heard challenge around the EHE. I used the phrase frequently, as did Dumas and other members of our literary-activist cult. However, some faculty members and residents, gleaning only the surface-literal meaning, were uncomfortable with its use."[18] In Henry's poetry, the idea of taking off clothes, of doing away with artifice and pretense, is a major theme. This challenge to creatively disrobe spoke to both men's interest in uncovering the core of the black psyche, which, in their view, had been buried by American greed, violence, and assimilation. But it was also male-oriented and sexually charged.

The friendship of Henry and Redmond brought kindred spirits together. Redmond had the gold-plated credentials for black men in America in the 1960s: a bachelor's degree and a graduate degree. Despite Henry's lack of these academic credentials, Redmond and others on the racially integrated EHE faculty and staff considered Henry a first-rate writer and teacher. He was effective during his time in the EHE, always writing and typing poems, dedicating them to various people. It was standard for Henry to arrive at a bar, party, or on campus with poem in hand. In this largely black world, Henry's lack of credentials did not cause him or others to make allowances for him. He was judged as a writer and teacher, neither of which was necessarily predicated by a degree.

As a teacher, Henry became an overnight legend at the EHE. In a short period, he had fashioned a reputation as a deep thinker and committed mentor. Although Henry was not at his best emotionally or psychologically, he impressed students with his level of engagement. The premise behind the program, explained Sherman Fowler, one of Henry's former students and upon whom he had a major impact, was that "ordinary brothers and sisters" could be brought into the college setting and, with a viable support system, earn their degrees and transform their lives. "I was twenty-four," Fowler remembers, "a barber, and one day a brother asked me if I wanted to go to college."[19] It was that simple. There were no standardized tests or entrance exams; all the students had to do was commit to the EHE process and the largely Afrocentric curriculum. In Fowler's case, Henry and the EHE led to him becoming an administrator in the East St. Louis public schools as well as an expert in freelance photography.

Henry understood the challenges, for Fowler and other students, of pursuing a higher education, given his own tenuous path that had resulted in no degree. Finally, however, of the jobs he had held, the writer-in-residence position came closest to aligning with his skill set. Publishing his own work may have remained a priority, but he took seriously the opportunity and responsibility of influencing young people's lives.

His relationship with Sherman Fowler was indicative of Henry's commitment to the EHE program. They were not so much teacher and student as big brother and little brother. In the classroom, Henry was, in Fowler's words, "always fast, light years ahead, way out there, in classes as well as in private. He introduced his classes to the music of Sun Ra," whose experimentalist sensibility made John Coltrane seem moderately conservative. "At first," noted Fowler, "Sun Ra's music didn't make sense, but eventually it did." Fowler moved to another level of understanding, largely crediting Henry with providing the exposure to different ways of absorbing the black world in particular. Outside the classroom, Henry had an impact on Fowler's life as well. As Fowler explained it, "Henry also inspired me to go to Africa. Henry, Eugene, and Don Henderson organized a scholarship fund for me to spend my junior year in Africa."[20] Ironically, their primary source of fund-raising was the clubs where they chased women and got high. Raising money involved nothing formal, but Redmond, a major figure in the community, was trusted to gather the dollars and use them as he had promised.

The fact that Henry, even in the midst of hanging out in clubs and juke joints, would be focused on helping a student seems incongruous. But Henry was never one to separate literary or academic endeavors from the larger world. The people he encountered in sometimes volatile social settings, in his mind, had, consciously or not, maintained a cultural, linguistic, and psychological relationship to Africa. Why would they not support the young Fowler in his attempt to visit the ancestral continent? In these night spots in East Boogie, Henry was reunited with the black world, where the funky sounds and frenetic movements of James Brown and other musicians were viewed as signs of black cultural stability, where gospel and rhythm and blues could weave back and forth between the church and the club, where that longstanding fusion between the sacred and profane, and between what was African and African American, was a matter of fact rather than of debate.

In these spaces, in a short period of time, Henry and Eugene Redmond—as brothers will—saw some of the best and worst of each other. Redmond had not become ensconced in the drug culture that many of his friends, including Henry, had fallen into. He knew himself well enough to know that he could not realize his artistic ambitions if he was ginned up or searching out narcotics. In this sense, he and Henry were headed in different directions, but their mutual affection was evident early on. Redmond was honored when Henry dedicated two poems, "Epiphany" and "Ode to Otis," to him: "Epiphany is a fertility ritual of cultural reclamation, tribal regeneration, creative fecundity and human-natural kinship. It represented a master poet and griot saluting a brother-bard, a new friend to whom Henry frequently referred as a 'writin nigger,' which was something I had not experienced until then—that is, an accomplished black writer telling me that I could write well. And then to have two poems—'Ode to Otis' and 'Epiphany'—inspired by me! How much more can a so-help-me-John Henry-hope-to-die poet expect in one live-time?"[21]

In Redmond's mind, Henry's dedication of the poems was the ultimate compliment, and in their artistic and racial kinship, Henry had redefined the most negative term ascribed to blacks, calling his friend a "writin nigger." Along with Jay Wright, Redmond emerged as the other black writer with whom Henry developed an organic relationship that was based on a love of black poetic voice. Wright and Redmond of course practiced different aesthetics, but their point of convergence, for Henry, involved their commitment to the craft and to the black vernacular and intellectual tradition.

Enmeshed now in the black world of EHE, Henry made scant mention of Lois and Loretta in this new community, and although she had made the move across country just in time for the spring semester of 1968, Loretta seemed an appreciated but distant memory to Henry. She and the boys were now comfortably settled in their new home outside of East St. Louis. This was a convenient setup for Henry, since he had his place in town. Surely Loretta must have sensed that this arrangement was not the best for their family. But for a brief period, she tried to make it work. She continued as a kind of invisible spouse. Even at Hiram, noted Claude Steele, Henry's family had not been in the picture. "That side of his life—Mrs. Dumas—was completely out of the picture in the Hiram world. You know what—the eighteen months or almost two years that I knew him, pretty, you know, on a daily basis—his family never came into view."[22] In looking back on his EHE experience, Sherman Fowler held a similar view, remembering conversations with Henry that, in his words, "were about the black family in conceptual terms but never Henry's family."[23] He could talk about the black family in general or even someone else's family, but he strangely detached his own family from those conversations.

With his family safely out of view, Henry was looking for that one black superwoman who had it all—someone intellectually engaging and romantically daring—a creation of his imagination, it seems, who would meet his multiple needs as man and artist. He wanted to have a deep connection with a black woman, absent some of the social conservatism he could no longer embrace.[24] In this search for a soul-mate, Henry put too much pressure on himself and the women he encountered. In the end, no woman could meet his needs all the time, the difference between illusion and reality.

According to Redmond, in his presence Henry was repeatedly "being turned down by women. Henry was helpless."[25] In one instance, Henry fell for a black woman who was known, as Redmond and Fowler remember, as an "exploiter." She was after one of the things that had eluded Henry for most of his life— money—and had quickly determined that Henry was a waste of her time. He nevertheless insisted on pursuing her, and he took the rejection hard.

Even though he had returned to a world similar in culture to the Harlem of his youth, Henry did not impress the women he encountered in East Boogie. Such had been the case, for different reasons, during his time at Rutgers, as well. The women in East St. Louis that Henry gravitated toward were superficial or concerned only with material gain. Eventually, Redmond and Fowler convinced him to move on from this latest heartbreak, assuring him that he would find the black woman of his dreams. Although his family was there, Henry had not introduced them to this world. For all intents and purposes, Redmond and Fowler determined that, in form if not fact, Henry was living the life of a single man. But for Henry, rejection seemed to be waiting around the corner. Henry's search for literary and romantic recognition consumed him. Life on the periphery affords more freedom, but it also can distort one's expectations. Was Henry simply seeking too much on both fronts? Had he failed to understand the difference between the practical and the ideal? In reality, he, like all of us, needed to move back and forth between the two.

Before and after his family arrived, the buffer for Henry's social mishaps with black women and his drug use was the classroom. He was indeed a functioning addict. He found a way to measure up, but in other settings the impact of his drug use had whittled him down. In some ways, too, his search for this supreme love was a means of distraction; it had become a way for him to deflect attention from his more measured publishing success. When Henry had arrived in East St. Louis, his talent was apparent, as was his growing dependence on drugs. To be sure, drug use was part of the social milieu, but Henry's was excessive, even with already loose behavioral parameters. And of his friends in East Boogie, Redmond could see the results most clearly. In his mind, hashish, a stronger version of marijuana, was the most consistent culprit in Henry's descent. The other person who now saw and felt the irreversible impact of Henry's behavior was Loretta.

Henry certainly should not have relocated his family while harboring such negative feelings about his marriage. Despite the shifting cultural sands around marriage in the 1960s, Henry may have still been hounded by convention. Better to be unhappily married than divorced. His decision not to end things before he moved everyone out suggests that he simply did not want to deal with the consequences of this reality. In sum, Henry had long ago concluded that Loretta could no longer be the kind of wife he envisioned. He and Sherman Fowler had discussed the frustrations of marriage. Henry, as Fowler recalls these discussions, felt that he had been "young, married and stuck. Henry wanted what he wanted, a woman to fulfill his sexual fantasies. Some guys outgrow women. Loretta wasn't at harmony with him."[26] Henry also talked with Fowler about how he and Loretta had parted ways when it came to religion. She was not questioning the relevance of Christianity. At this point, with her marriage crumbling, Loretta's faith and commitment to the church remained steady. According to Fowler, Henry now viewed Christianity as a tool used for the oppression and emasculation of black men. Fowler framed the challenge for men like him and Henry embracing Christianity in this way: "Almost all black women are caught up in this Jesus thing. Where's the woman in the Trinity? Brothers have a hard time swallowing that shit. God must be homosexual. Where's the Son coming from? Don't walk into the wall blindfolded."[27]

Henry was raising questions about the gospel he had once felt compelled to preach. To Henry's friends in both East St. Louis and Ohio, the suggestion that he had once been devoutly religious, had even taught Sunday school for children, was an imaginative leap they were unable to make. Claude Steele, upon learning years later that Henry had previously been a devout Christian, exclaimed, "Oh, my God!" In his back-to-black phase, Henry's friends would be incredulous to learn that years ago he wooed his wife with his knowledge of classical music, which was now, in Henry's view, nothing more than a sophisticated musical ruse for white chauvinism and elitism. Henry, Redmond, and other black folks, in Redmond's words, "willfully withdrew from the white world, creating enclaves or special places where they could just be themselves."[28]

After the assassination of Martin Luther King Jr. on April 4, 1968, Henry, Redmond, and others prepared for an all-out attack on black communities. They went to a gun shop outside of East St. Louis to purchase weapons for what they thought was an imminent and inevitable confrontation with a white power structure bent on violence. It was a turbulent time. The image of a "pregnant white woman in line to purchase a pearl-handle 32" remains seared in Redmond's memory. For him and his associates—who ranged from artists, activists, and intellectuals to hooligans and drug dealers—the image of white women packing heat signified the racial apocalypse. Redmond and these men, many of whom had military experience, were not, in his words, "so much interested in a race war; they were arming themselves to protect their families and communities."[29] Martin Luther King Jr. was nonviolent, but that couldn't protect him from the violence of others. What were the masses of black Americans to think about their safety and well-being?

Not only was the purchase of guns a sign of things to come, but Henry's willingness now to carry a weapon represented a significant shift in his temperament. Henry had written a tribute to black America's Moses, "Our King Is Dead," and he read this poem in various social contexts around East St. Louis. Unrelenting in his critique of America, Henry declared that, for him, and by extension scores of other blacks, there would be no turning back:

> but in America to be a black king
> means you must learn how to die . . . for I have lived in hell all my life
> I have eaten fire and brimstone
> I too am a volcano . . . Let no cold hand knock at my door
> Let no wild dogs come for our kings
> ANYMORE.[30]

One of his final poems, this became a kind of dramatic and poetic anthem in its unapologetic articulation of what it cost to be a black prophet.

As Henry contemplated this imminent racial conflict, he penned a poetic retrospective of his life. "A New Proposal" is undated but placed in the section of *Knees of a Natural Man* called "Songthesis: East St. Louis Epiphanies." The poem, a relatively short reflection, looks back on the marriage that had at one time sustained the speaker:

(to my wife, after literal kef)[31]
i will go with you again to the field
to pick wild roses

and skip flatround stones off the lake
up and into the sky

(a rocked fanged hillside
driving us stumbling home thru the storm)

i will gather our roseseeds together with you
again and plant them in due sun

and handle their tender growth with careful fingers

This is because i see you coming lovely
as i crawl from my hangover after sleep.

Your pace—even and steady I am risen
to your coming form.

As we balance the road together,
don't stop running if you dont see me
ahead sometimes because,

i never forget the scent of wild roses
and i still see how we used to sail into the sky.[32]

Henry's male friends report that he no longer wanted to be with Loretta. In this poem, however, written in a period when Henry was pursuing an authentic black love, he reflected on what he and Loretta had shared before their fall. It was a simpler time when they met on a snowy evening in 1953. For both of them, however, much had changed since then. Somehow, even as he pursued a personal and artistic life far different from that established with Loretta, he appreciated where they had gone together, as we see in this line, "and i still see how we used to sail into the sky."

"A New Proposal" is a tribute to what Henry and Loretta once shared. In the final line, the past tense inherent in "used to" is essential. Henry acknowledges what they had accomplished, that, as he notes in the previous stanza, they did once "balance the road together." Despite this equilibrium they shared, he could not envision them together in the future. Although the date of the poem's composition is unknown, the poem is symbolic of the last encounter Henry and Loretta would share.

Her marriage was certainly at its nadir, but Loretta thought there was a small chance for reconciliation. In May 1968, she impressed upon Henry the fact that she could no longer accept a nominal marriage in which she was the lone participant. "I assured him," she explained, "that if we divorced he would have complete access to David and Michael. I even told him I'd continue to type his manuscripts." But even as she made her case, Loretta realized that Henry was not only living another life in East St. Louis, but that he had never intended to revive his family. As she saw it, she and the boys had come to Illinois for nothing. She now resolved to take her boys home. For her, the marriage was over. Until then, she had refused to comprehend what Henry would never say but what his behavior clearly indicated: that he no longer wanted to be with the family they had created.

A patient woman by nature, Loretta did what, for her, had been the unthinkable. "I burned the letters he had written during his time in the Arabian Peninsula. I started a mini-bonfire in the backyard. The envelope with the letters was too thick, so I had to take each piece of correspondence and burn it." In essence, Loretta burned Henry in effigy. Although she still loved him, it was time to move on. The other unsettling aspect of this situation for Loretta was that, at the time, neither her family nor Henry's knew the extent of their problems. Henry may have believed that Loretta would be better off without him; he had shared as much with Robert Pinsky during the Rutgers years. "Henry confided to me," Pinsky intimated, "that Loretta's father thought she had married below herself, and that he, Henry, tended to agree."[33]

For the first time in her marriage, Loretta accepted the fact that Henry was failing as a husband. As wife and mother, she was exasperated. Looking back on that moment years later, she regretted that she had not pushed Henry to consider treatment for his dependence on drugs. "That was not part of our culture back then. You didn't discuss such things. Henry needed help. Whether that would have saved our marriage, I don't know, but someone needed to intervene." In the absence of such help, Henry proved more vulnerable to himself and to others. But something good did come out of those few months that Loretta and the boys were in the Midwest: on March 15, 1968, still caught up in the vortex that was his life, Henry finally responded, eighteen months after he was notified, to the news that his story "The Lake" had been accepted for publication by *Trace* magazine. Had he responded sooner, Henry may have had his story published in May 1968, along with a piece by novelist Clarence Major. Instead, "The Lake" was published in May 1969.

•

I might pray

but don't fuck with me

cause I don't play.

—HENRY DUMAS,

"I Laugh Talk Joke"

CHAPTER NINE

From Sweet Home to Harlem

If hope and optimism ushered in the decade of the 1960s, death and social despair were right behind them. Hooligans in Mississippi tried to fight the freedom wave in 1963 by killing one of its native sons, Medgar Evers, on June 12. Three months later, on September 15, Cynthia Wesler, Carole Robertson, Addie Mae Collins, and Denise McNair—as they were learning about love and forgiveness in Sunday school—were killed by a Klan bomb at Birmingham's Sixteenth Street Baptist Church. Just before Thanksgiving, on November 22, a sniper snuffed out the life of President John F. Kennedy in Dallas, Texas. Just two years later, in 1965, Malcolm X, the thorn in the political flesh of gradualist-minded blacks and whites, was assassinated on February 21 in New York.

The decade approached its end with Martin Luther King Jr. fighting for the right of low-skilled laborers to petition for better pay and safer work conditions and criticizing U.S. engagement with Vietnam. For that, and his ability to shame America for its glaring moral hypocrisy, he took a bullet on a Memphis balcony in April 1968. With the deaths of these people and scores of others unknown to the U.S. public, death and violence became the imprimatur for this generation of youth.

In Harlem, each decade after the renaissance had contributed to a growth in the level of collective angst. By the 1960s, it no longer resembled the place of Henry's adolescent years, where kids played stickball in the streets and marbles on manhole covers. On Henry's arrival in 1944, optimism in Harlem had been on a slight uptick, thanks to the eventual Allied victory in World War II and the recognition of the heroic efforts of black troops in a segregated military. But change, even at a time when white America had incontrovertible proof of black patriotism, had not come fast enough. Black servicemen had hoped for a more equal playing field, but instead they encountered a postwar agenda that sought to reinstate prewar social barriers.

Now, twenty-five years later, the children of the war generation were rejecting what they considered the slow-footed, apologetic approach to racial equality. For many frustrated and disaffected black youth, Malcolm X's philosophy—though he had distanced himself from some of his own ideological cant before his death—had been condensed to four words: "By any means necessary." With mocking defiance, blacks who found themselves in urban crawl spaces dismissed the idea of incremental progress, insisting on freedom and decent living conditions now, not later.

Langston Hughes, as early as 1951, considered the state of Harlem in a poem of that title. "What happens to a dream deferred?," the speaker asks, "Does it dry up like a raisin in the sun?" A meditation on Harlem suffering, the poem offers a series of questions about the unofficial capital of black culture. For New York in the 1960s, the final question proved prophetic: "Or does it explode?"[1]

There were at least three moments in New York during the 1960s that provided unequivocal answers to Hughes's final question. In July 1964, a white police officer (at that time most officers in Harlem were white) shot and killed a fifteen-year-old black boy, unleashing a wave of violent responses by frustrated citizens who felt there was nowhere to turn for justice. Across the world, in Cairo, Egypt, Malcolm X said the unrest in Harlem was in response to "outright scare tactics" by the New York police.[2]

Three years later, in July 1967, a similar incident occurred, this time in the Puerto Rican enclave of East Harlem. A youth wielding a knife was fatally shot, igniting a powder keg of frustration with the police akin to that found in predominantly black central Harlem. Violence had become such a concern in Harlem that more police officers (some of whom were now black) had been hired. With crime on the rise and the social ferment of the 1960s, the Transit Authority Police more than doubled its ranks from eight hundred in 1965 to eighteen hundred in 1966. With one of the largest public transportation systems in the world, the creation and expansion of the transit police was a reflection of the city's growth.

But everyone knew it would take more than an expanded police operation to address the core problems in Harlem. In New York's *Amsterdam News* (the largest black weekly in the country), black leaders and opinion-makers expressed ambivalence about the political and social prospects of 1968. Whitney Young Jr., known for his advocacy for black equality in government and corporations, on January 6 cautioned that the "year could be either the most dangerous in decades or the most productive."[3] In the same edition, Jackie Robinson—who carried the weight of desegregating major league baseball in 1947—in his column urged Harlem and its leaders to rise to the challenges of the day. "Harlem should resolve to acquire for itself political representation which is not absentee," Robinson urged. "The old-line Negro leadership and the Negro church should make a concerted stand to stage a comeback in the esteem of angry, black, leaderless youth."[4] Robinson's concerns were well-founded; two weeks later, on January 20, the lead story in the *Amsterdam News* said it all: "Crime Takes Over Harlem." More times than not, and not just in Robinson's view, increases in crime were tied to the lack of opportunities for angry and disenfranchised youth.

Young people, in a word, were distrustful of institutions. College students and community activists were also critiquing suspect race policies at institutions of higher learning. On April 23, 1968, an interracial coalition of Columbia University students and Harlem community organizers occupied campus buildings to protest the "imperialist" war in Vietnam and the presence of the military on campus. A further cause of civil unrest in Harlem was the construction of a university gymnasium in nearby Morningside Park. Although Columbia presented the initiative as a public-private partnership that would benefit both the institution and neighborhood residents, community organizers were concerned that ultimately they would not enjoy the same access as Columbia students, faculty, and staff. After a week of protestors occupying various buildings and the gym site, police moved in, arresting 712 students.

As racial tension continued to escalate, on May 20, possibly the day Henry arrived in New York, H. Rap Brown, Amiri Baraka, and other black power leaders spoke at a benefit performance. The objective was to provide bail for Eldridge Cleaver and six other members of the Black Panther Party imprisoned in California. Just a few months earlier, Cleaver's book, *Soul on Ice*, had been published. A black power manifesto that argued for a more strident articulation of black masculinity, Cleaver's version of racial and sexual psychology was laughable to some but inspiring to others.

With prominent black men carrying the nationalist flag and disgruntled black citizens tired of a system of oppression, just weeks after King's death, black America was reaching an emotional crescendo. Harlem was at a boiling point and so, too, was its adopted son. Henry had come to town for the wedding of his friend Bill Seiboth, a talented drummer who had a reputation for hitting the bottle as much as the drums. Seiboth may have introduced Henry to the world of white jazz musicians, which in turn may have included those who were presumptuous in their cultural knowledge of African Americans. Indeed, three white jazz musicians who display cultural hubris—the misconception that since they know jazz, they therefore also know the black experience—show up in Henry's jazz parable, "Will the Circle Be Unbroken?"

Henry left no written record about his friendship with Seiboth, but it was clearly meaningful enough for Seiboth to ask him to stand as his best man. At this point, Henry had obviously wanted out of his own marriage, but his participation in the wedding may have served as an acknowledgment that Seiboth and his bride deserved the right to imagine matrimony on their own terms. Like so many people, however, Henry was still reeling from the nightmare of King's assassination when he arrived in New York, as he was from the turbulence of his own life. Just days before, Loretta had spelled out for him that their marriage was over, that she would be filing for divorce.

Troubled by the dissolution of his family, and on edge as a result of racial hostility in New York, Henry had traveled to New York with his pearl-handled .22 caliber pistol. His decision to carry a firearm, a choice he would not have made just a year earlier, reflected a change in his emotional framework. By itself, considering the volatility in pockets of Harlem and other urban centers, the decision made sense. But Henry's decision coincided with his more intense engagement with drugs. Now carrying a weapon, he became part of a growing subgroup of black men, Baraka included, willing to bear firearms. "Arm yourself," so the saying went, "or harm yourself": that is, not having a gun made you susceptible to harm by others. This was undoubtedly the reason Henry had obtained a weapon. His possession of a firearm was more a reflection of his willingness to consider self-defense. The time for nonviolent resistance had come and gone, and the idea of black men brandishing weapons gave rogue police yet another reason to shoot first and ask questions later. Blacks who carried weapons looked at it this way: either way, they were likely to be attacked. Some form of defense was better than nothing.

On Thursday, May 23, a cool rain fell in New York, as the mercury struggled to reach fifty-two degrees. With pistol on his person, Henry

was, like the city, searching for the warmth of spring. He would probably contact Aunt Mary and Uncle Jack, and he had called ahead of time to alert Lois
that he would be in the city. With his marriage over, Henry was probably feeling somber. Although freedom from marriage was what he had said he wanted
for some years, it nonetheless meant that Henry would lose his family as his
crutch. He could no longer lean on the excuse of his family weighing him down,
providing him cover from the idea that other factors resulted in his failure to
secure a contract for his novel.

In 1958, he had lit upon the Rutgers campus, and in the following ten years
he had shown moments of brilliance. With his crew of friends, both black and
white, he had been part of a stimulating cultural backdrop of that era. But also
during the latter part of that period, he had given up parts of himself to drugs
and alcohol. He did not engage in some of the most suspect behaviors often
associated with addiction, but his use of those substances played out in his life
in multiple ways. Now back in New York, he was reminded of some of his best
and most frustrating literary and personal moments. Sun Ra understood his
disjointed and conflicted feelings about his life, and it was to the jazz maestro
that Henry went now for counsel.

His friend and mentor offered insight as Henry confided his latest trials,
but Sun Ra was unsettled by Henry's decision to carry a pistol. As an artist, Sun
Ra realized the futility in the act. He also understood Henry's fragile condition and was acutely aware of the recent police violence in Harlem. With that
knowledge, Sun Ra convinced his protégé to leave the gun with him before he
left later that evening. Like a character in one of his stories, Henry was trying
to understand his present condition.

On the same day, a rookie member of the New York City Transit Authority
Police, Peter Bienkowski, prepared for his evening shift. On a typical night, officers worked from eight o'clock in the evening to four o'clock in the morning.
They had an assigned subway route, during which they walked the train from
one end to the other, looking for suspicious characters or people involved in
inappropriate or illicit behavior. In 1968, there were few late-night riders, which
made for mostly uneventful but spooky nights for the transit police.

On the evening of May 23, Bienkowski, according to his statement published in the *Amsterdam News*, observed Henry in a dangerous confrontation
with another man, whose race and identity were never determined, on the
subway platform at 125th Street and Lenox Avenue in Harlem. According to
the officer, Henry was belligerent, and he assaulted the officer when he tried
to intervene. In response, the officer fired his weapon and brought an end to

a life filled with both promise and frustration. A year earlier, on May 22, 1967, Harlem bid farewell to its most celebrated writer, Langston Hughes. A year and a day later, another writer was gone, but Harlem hardly knew this thirty-three-year-old man.

The process of figuring out what really happened that night has been complicated by time. Over forty years have now passed since Henry's death, during which time the accounts of his behavior and the officer's rationale for shooting him have passed into myth. The reason for the lack of a consistent narrative around Henry's death is that none of the people (or the individual) involved in the supposed altercation ever came forward as witnesses. Without a definitive story, over the years, alternative stories have emerged. And the criticism, understandably, has focused on the man who killed him. But absent from such perspectives is consideration of Henry's state of mind at the time. This, coupled with the fact that the police report and all transit records seem to have been destroyed when the Transit Police merged with the New York Police Department in 1995, makes for the perfect conditions around which myths can grow. Information on the shooting is now nowhere to be found in the civic institutions of New York.[5] With no police records, piecing together Henry's last moments today is an exercise in finding the most plausible explanation for the events that transpired. Over forty years later, Bienkowsi's account of the shooting remains the only one available.

With Loretta back in Illinois and no identification on Henry's person linking him to Aunt Mary and Uncle Jack, it took some time for arrangements to be made for family to identify his body. And because Henry had been out of the city for over a year and was not well-known there, many people responded to the reports of his death with a sense of distant sympathy; his death saddened them, but the deaths of black men were becoming common, and Henry was neither young nor famous.

The following day, Clem Fiori, Lois Silber, and Earl Thomas went to the morgue, the first friends or family to view Henry's body. Thomas's mother had heard about the shooting on the radio and told her son, and he probably contacted Fiori. In looking back on that surreal moment, when, as Thomas recollected, "we went in to identify Henry's body, the detective said to me, 'whatever possessed a guy of his background to do this?' Somebody knew that Henry was not your average street person or somebody from the neighborhood."[6] It is not clear what prompted the detective to comment on Henry's background. Was Henry carrying his notebook or other literary materials with him? Or was he dressed in a way that signaled a certain level of accomplishment and refinement that ran counter to what the detective usually encountered in cases such as this? We simply don't know. Clem Fiori felt overwhelmed by the moment: "I remember feeling so demoralized about the whole thing. I thought we should all be going in there asking questions. I didn't do anything. I still feel guilty about that."[7] Overcome by emotion, Lois could not bear to enter the morgue, even with Thomas and Fiori at her side.

Although she did not participate in the identification, Lois was the one to speak with officers at the morgue about the circumstances of Henry's violent death. She was aware of his visit to New York and, like Earl Thomas's mother, had heard the news on the radio. In correspondence to Jay Wright, penned the day after the shooting, Lois described the moment when she, Clem Fiori, and Earl Thomas came together:

> By this time it was raining. It was a miserable day. Earl and Clem got here one right after the other, about 2:15 [p.m.]. I left the office and walked over to the morgue on 30th and 1st Avenue. They were both very upset. I waited while they did the identifying. According to the police at the morgue, Henry had been harassing a group of from a dozen to two dozen people with a knife, the transit patrolman (twenty-three years old) tried to stop him, got slashed on the arm, fired the warning shot, got cut above the eye, and shot Henry twice.[8]

The people who had known Henry in his formative period as a writer were the first ones of his acquaintance to view him at the morgue. None of them had seen Henry recently, but Thomas and Fiori did talk with Henry periodically, and their respective friendships were solid. They knew of Henry's personal and artistic challenges in East St. Louis, but there was little Thomas and Fiori, in New Jersey, could do for their friend.

For Lois in particular, Henry's death was a moment of terrible ambivalence. She still held tremendous resentment for the violent moment that occurred at the end of their relationship almost eighteen months earlier. "I wonder," she wrote to Wright in another letter, "if he was drunk when it happened; I cannot believe he was sober. He was here for Bill and Sue's wedding, as best man."[9] Lois believed that Henry could not have been in possession of a sound mind—that is, sober, he would not have acted so recklessly.

When Loretta Dumas, from whom he was recently estranged, learned that Henry had been involved in a shooting, as she put it, she initially "assumed Henry had shot someone. Henry was in a bad place emotionally. It made sense that he would shoot someone."[10] Although Henry had never been physically

abusive toward her, Loretta believed his instability was conducive to violent behavior. "He had mood swings, a totally different mindset than when we married. It was the impact of drugs. He was simply a different person, now capable
of violence." Although no single person had a full understanding of Henry's
burgeoning instability, family members in both Arkansas and New York were
particularly oblivious to Henry's emotional disposition. In their minds, he was
successful on all fronts, with a college position in Illinois, his family, and of
course his writing. His death, in more ways than one, was the shot in the dark,
revealing a much different set of realities.

Henry's shooting occurred toward the end of a decade during which New
York police had been implicated in a number of questionable shootings. Redmond and other black men who knew Henry considered the shooting an all-
too-frequent price for being a black man, his death a classic case of white police misconduct. Showing the deeply felt mistrust of the authorities at the time,
when Redmond flew to New York for the memorial service—along with a suit-
case full of money collected for Loretta in East St. Louis—he brought guns.
Reading Henry's death as a blatant result of racism, Redmond and other men
in East St. Louis thought about chasing down Bienkowski. For them, the death
of their friend was clear evidence that, as Redmond put it, "the race war was
on. I had been in the marines. I knew about reconnaissance, so if I had to go
out, I was going out fightin'."[11] But after arriving in New York, Redmond turned
away from the impulse to seek vengeance, instead focusing on the task at hand:
that of laying his friend to rest.

Henry was killed in a place he had called home, and now his family had
to make funeral arrangements. Numbed by the state of their relationship and
now by Henry's death, Loretta signed off on the details of the service, allowing Henry's family to organize the memorial. Five days later, on a rainy May 28
(it had also rained on the day Henry was killed), family and friends gathered in
the Bronx at the McCall Funeral Home.

In a soulful piece written the day after the funeral, Redmond put in words
the feeling of loss experienced by many in attendance:

> The articulate preacher had not known the poet
> But the poet's mother.
> One could see that the circumstances of the killing
> Had undermined his faith
> He sought a way out: Equating the poet with "Mr. Lincoln."
> He also knew the poet wrote:

"This young man will survive
In his stories and poems," the bowed audience was reminded.
"He walked upright like a man . . .
There are mysteries; life is a mystery,
Death is a mystery."
The radiant black man of cloth
Was unpretentious; he broke with tradition—promising
No alternatives to death.
Seemingly unaware of heaven or hell, he suggested simply "a last
resting place."
Those in the chapel stared intently, bleakly
Into their own thoughts.
Outside the skies cried for the dead black bard.[12]

Redmond's account of the sermon reflects Henry's life and literary sensibility. Just as the preacher had promised no "alternative to death," Henry did not seek easy ways out of his difficult, and often self-created, personal, financial, and creative quandaries. Nor did he offer simplistic resolution in his fiction and poetry. There was nothing simple or clear about this moment. For Appliance Porter, the pain was unimaginable. She would live thirty-two more years, having buried both her sons, a tragic distinction that Loretta Dumas would sadly come to share.

Still fractured by ambivalence about Henry, Lois did not attend the service, although Loretta and the family knew nothing about her. Nonetheless, she received a thorough account of the service from Joanna Fiori, the wife of Henry's good friend Clem. After Henry was buried, Lois acknowledged her history with and love for him in the second-hand account of the funeral she wrote to Jay Wright, who was still in Mexico. The funeral "was all military," she wrote. "For poor Henry it is terribly ironic and sad. I think the worst part of it physically is that he was buried way out on Long Island (Farmingdale?) in a military cemetery. When Joanna told me about it I cried for the first time."[13]

The Hank that many people had come to know was far from the airman and Sunday-school teacher of his earlier years; he had ventured far from the discipline and focus of that life. His burial in the National Military Cemetery in Long Island troubled both Loretta and Lois for different reasons. Appliance, Aunt Mary, and Uncle Jack thought the cost of burial in the city exorbitant; and Loretta, still anesthetized to this new reality, was unable to take control. A military burial, his family decided, was the most economical option. But Henry probably would not have wanted to be buried in a place where all the headstones are white, and at least symbolically, standing at attention, so far from his Harlem home.

It would take years for those who knew Henry to process his death in both personal and literary terms. Part of that healing process would come in the form of multiple volumes of Henry's poetry and fiction finding their way to print by 1976. But in 1984, a student named William Halsey, who never knew Henry, undertook a study of his work for his senior thesis at the State University of New York (Westbury). After reading an article about him, Halsey, a poet, decided to call Officer Bienkowski. "I was surprised," wrote Halsey, "that he was willing to talk and [I] took quick note of the quietness in his voice. He remembered the incident. I found out later that he killed Henry Dumas as a rookie with the police and that it was the only incident of deadly force on his record of seventeen years." Not the rogue cop that Halsey, Redmond, and others had imagined, Bienkowski "confided that he knew nothing about Henry Dumas other than the particulars of that night. 'I never knew what he did,' he told me." Halsey, for his part, "felt compelled to tell him that Henry was a man of literary accomplishment, to tell as many people as I could what Dumas did."[14] Bienkowski detected nothing specific about Henry's background, whereas the detective, as Earl Thomas remembered, sensed that Henry had reached a certain level or station in life. Neither man knew Henry, but their contradictory responses are indicative of how people responded differently, depending on the side of Henry they came to know.

Halsey's interview with Bienkowski was yet another irony associated with Henry's fate. It appears that this was a tragic accident, not fueled by racial animosity or mistaken identity but perhaps by the survival instinct on the part of a rookie cop with a gun. From his vantage point, Halsey concluded that Bienkowski had simply been caught up in a feverish moment with only seconds to make a decision. Furthermore, William Joseph, a retired transit policeman who was stationed in Queens in 1968, opines that if black members of the police force had thought that Henry's shooting had been a cold act of racial hostility, they would have protested. Joseph remembers intense encounters between officers and disgruntled citizens in various enclaves of the city. It was a complicated time for Joseph, who, as a black officer, represented the institution that symbolized the abuse of power in most black communities. He and other black officers did what they could by keeping track of suspicious shootings of black citizens and of black policemen. When compelled by the evidence, they would petition the leadership to investigate. Joseph cannot recall hearing news of Dumas's shooting. Had there been an uproar in Harlem over Henry's case, Joseph feels certain he and other black officers would have known about it.[15] In death, as in life, Henry could not make it to center stage.

News of Henry's death did not make it to the obituary desk at the *New York Times*, but it was broadcast over the radio. In 1968, black radio stations and newspapers were the main source of information in African American communities, since white outlets largely ignored everyone else. In fact, the only story that appeared about Henry in print was in the *Amsterdam News* eight days after the incident. In the following excerpt, there are some factual miscues in the story, revealing how much Henry had distanced himself from his New York relatives:

> Dumas, who was employed with a government anti-poverty program [*sic*] at Southern Illinois University, was shot to death during a fight with Transit Authority Ptl. Peter Bienkowski, who was slashed on his face, according to police.
>
> Police said Dumas and an unidentified man were scuffling in the subway when the officer walked up to them and attempted to stop the fracas. Police said Dumas, resentful at the interference, slashed the officer who shot and killed him.
>
> Dumas is survived by his wife, Loretta; two sons, David, 10, and Michael, 8 [*sic*]; his mother, Mrs. Appliance Dumas [*sic*] Watson; his father, Henry Sr.; a cousin Jo Ann [*sic*] Canales; an uncle, George Knowles and his aunt, Mrs. Mary Gillens.
>
> Mrs. Gillens told the *Amsterdam News* that it's difficult for her to believe her nephew battled with a policeman. "He became a civil rights activist after serving in the Korean War [*sic*] with the Air Force, but it's hard for me to believe he would fight a cop," she said.[16]

Aunt Mary's reaction reflected her limited knowledge of Henry's recent troubles. Big Henry, hardly the authority figure, had his own struggles with alcohol. Appliance and other family members were always glad to hear from Henry, but their knowledge of him was fragmentary. When Henry called or visited his mother or Aunt Mary, they would lecture him for not keeping in better touch, which would not have been conducive to his having a heart-to-heart with them. Upon leaving Harlem, Henry had simply moved out into the world, preoccupied with, or not wanting to reveal to his childhood family, the chaos of his life. Since he had always loved and respected his family, there were probably aspects of his life that he felt were better left unknown.

And there were also facts that either the *Amsterdam News* or the family simply got wrong: Appliance's surname had never been Dumas, as she had never married Big Henry, but in 1942 she did marry Kennard Carey Watson; Henry was still thirty-three years old (his birthday was in July); and Michael was six, not eight. Other discrepancies revealed the family's lack of knowledge about Henry's life. The first involved his aunt's reference to him as a civil-rights activist (he was more of a sympathetic or engaged observer); the second point is the reference to him as a Korean War veteran (although both Henry and Billy served in the military, it was Billy who served during the war period); perhaps most telling was Aunt Mary's inability to imagine that Henry could act violently.

If his family had struggled to understand his life, it was even more difficult for them to make sense of his death. Ultimately, communication between Henry and his childhood family had grown so weak and vague over the years that his colleagues, classmates, and friends in New Jersey, Ohio, and Illinois knew more about his current life, a pattern that was not inconsistent in the migratory society then developing in the United States. In his case, Henry's family fell outside of the arc of communication. Until his shocking and violent death, these different, often competing, strands of information had not been brought together.

Henry was a deeply private person, selectively sharing information in his relationships. He respected his childhood family and perhaps did not want to be judged a failure. From the time he arrived at Rutgers and began following a trajectory that most of his family would have objected to, he refrained from revealing to them the dimensions of his life that would have challenged their spiritual and social views and revealed his own shortcomings.

Of the friends and family who mourned the loss of Henry, Sun Ra, as his biographer has noted, "became angrier than anyone had ever seen him before, and he raged on and on for days, cursing the city and its inhabitants, and reminding anyone that would listen that he had warned Dumas to be careful."[17] He had sensed that his artistic brother was restless, weary, and, most important, volatile. One of the last poems Henry wrote was called "black ohm," part of an unpublished piece titled "Getting Our Shit Together." The poem awakens us to Henry's state of mind toward the end of his life. Dated May 13, these words were written days before his death:

> Who has power in America?
> The white man
> How does he maintain his power?
> Through organization, bureaucracy, through
> A hierarchy of leaders and institutions.
> Why does he have his power so based?

Why does he structure his system this way?
Because it suits his nature, because it
Is the nature of the white anglo European man
The alabaster man to do it that way.[18]

More an outline of rhetorical questions and observations to which most people knew the answers, Henry's last creation did not measure with his earlier poetry and fiction, most of which explores the ambiguities of race and nation and the search for an organic black cultural identity.

The poem does, however, in its free verse and episodic form, recall Walt Whitman, whose poetry Henry embraced during his days at Rutgers. Henry's final resting place in Long Island is, in a final irony, Whitman's birthplace, where the American muse spent the early years of his life. Henry concluded his journey in the town that produced one of America's most celebrated poets and one of Henry's earliest poetic models. But unlike Whitman, Henry would receive his recognition as a writer posthumously.

Epilogue

In writing this biography, I faced a set of contradictory realities: a relatively small but enthusiastic band of literary scholars and writers who knew of Dumas's work, and a considerably larger number of people who did not. Although nominally aware of Dumas, I nonetheless fell into that latter category. As I started to read Dumas's work and the 1988 volume of *Black American Literature Forum* (now *African American Review*) devoted to his legacy, I wrestled with major questions: If scholars and creative writers had written so movingly about the Dumas legacy twenty years after his death, why had the biography not been done already? Had his life simply ended too early for a biography? Were there enough primary resources to support such a project?

At that point I knew I needed help from people who knew Dumas intimately. When I contacted Eugene B. Redmond and Loretta Dumas in 2002, they responded graciously to my interest in pursuing the biography but were understandably cautious. After all, previous attempts to tell Dumas's story had come to naught. As we developed a rapport, they eventually granted me access to the materials, some of which are held by Redmond in Illinois and some by Loretta Dumas in New Jersey. Visiting both places multiple times, I was impressed by what I

saw—college essays, drafts of stories, newspaper articles, and notes to creditors—a wealth and assortment of materials, indeed.

Even with such a fruitful cache of documents, the personal dimension of
Henry Dumas, the man behind the poems and stories, the knowledge essential to fashioning a full arc of Dumas's life, was missing. His college papers allowed me to figure out how well he understood *The Great Gatsby* during his
time at Rutgers, for example, but didn't shed light on Dumas's personal development. To address this conspicuous information gap, Loretta Dumas and
Redmond consented to numerous interviews with me and provided the names
of pivotal people to interview who ultimately provided what proved to be sur-
prising and enlightening backstories. Of all these sources, both Redmond and
Loretta Dumas identified one person whose papers would be essential in putting together the puzzle that was Dumas's life. That person was Lois Wright.
They did not know what information she had or what documents were in her
possession, but they knew she was in Dumas's life during a formative period
in his literary development.

Eventually I contacted Lois Wright and her husband, Jay Wright, who had
been a dear friend of Dumas's at Rutgers. Both could speak about him in ways
few others could. In the end, Jay Wright decided not to consent to a formal interview about his friend. Some things are better left unsaid, the poet reasoned,
not because they are necessarily bad, but because they are not meant for public
revelation. Jay Wright, however, often was helpful in confirming dates, places,
and names.

Fortunately for me, Lois Wright not only consented to be interviewed, but
she brought to life the cultural scene at Rutgers in the 1960s. We engaged in
numerous conversations about Dumas, their relationship, and her memory of
him as a writer. She also allowed me to view his correspondence to her. Without this unusual configuration of sources—Dumas's wife, his intimate companion, one of his best friends (now married to former companion), and his
closest friend in the last year of his life—this book would not have been possible. Loretta Dumas, Eugene B. Redmond, and Lois Wright knew Henry up
close. Indeed, they knew him well enough to know they could not know everything about him.

Writing the biography of a literary figure presents any num-
ber of challenges. To start with, Dumas's relatively short literary life meant
that the archive would be correspondingly slim. Dumas had certainly amassed
an impressive body of work, but not the equivalent in correspondence. And

most of his publications would occur posthumously. Critics tend to be kinder, even quixotic, when the writer is deceased. The other issue related to Dumas's papers centered on this question: despite an early death, did he produce enough lasting poetry and fiction to warrant a full-scale view of his short life?

On the literature side, the answer is a resounding "yes," with some qualifications. From the materials available, I had to reconcile myself with the fact that some of the most puzzling questions about Dumas's life would not be answered in his papers or in the numerous interviews I conducted. The larger historical record and my understanding of it in relation to Dumas's life would have to suffice.

On the more practical side, I now had to trace how Dumas's fiction and poetry had made their way to print. After her husband's death, Loretta Dumas did not view the publication of his work as her primary concern. More pressing questions of finances and justice were pounding at her door. On the first point, the couple had always been cash-strapped, and the expense of laying him to rest was a reminder of their money woes. With Dumas's family handling the funeral and burial details, and with her endeavoring to be a source of comfort for her sons, Loretta Dumas made it through this period, though she admits that she was in a fog.

As she emerged from this haze, attending to the business affairs related to Henry's death, Loretta Dumas approached the question of justice, consulting in turn four lawyers about filing a lawsuit against the New York City Transit Police. All four, one of whom was an African American and former policeman, advised her to dismiss that idea. There was no evidence upon which a case could be based. No witnesses to the shooting stepped forward, and there was no organized protest to challenge the official account of what had happened. Had Dumas been a household name in black literary circles, had his reputation as a writer been established, there likely would have been more of a collective response to the tragedy. Moreover, black communities in particular were still confronting the pain wrought by the assassination of MLK. Absent the internet and the ubiquitous media outlets of today, news of his violent death on a subway platform was not widely publicized, and neither was the story of his inimitable life widely known or circulated.

More than that, Loretta knew that Henry, especially during the last year of his life, had grown emotionally volatile. She could not assert, in other words, that her husband's alleged behavior that night on the subway platform was an anomaly. She also needed to consider the impact of a protracted legal case on her sons. How would they respond to having the less savory aspects of their father's life become part of the public record? Loretta could not shield them from this information as they grew older. Her plan was to address certain parts of their father's complicated life in her own time, on a need-to-know basis. But for now, protecting them and maintaining steady employment for herself was her priority, and this formula was part of the reason behind her decision to hand off to Eugene B. Redmond the oversight of Dumas's literary legacy.

After getting David and Michael situated back East, Loretta returned to Illinois, with the help of one of her brothers, to pack the remainder of her family's belongings. The largest item was Henry's car. He had left it at Sherman Fowler's house before flying to New York for Bill Seiboth's wedding. Sherman Fowler knew Loretta only through Henry's observations. In his mind, she was a nice woman who had not met the intellectual and romantic needs of his friend. Fowler was one of the first signs, for Loretta, of the world Henry had created without her in Illinois and New Jersey. She would learn far more about him—the beautiful and the ugly—after his death. Her visit to Fowler's house, as he remembers it, was brief and uneventful.[1]

As Loretta set out to reconstruct her life back home in New Jersey, she took many of Henry's papers back with her. But she also left a number of papers behind with a neighbor whose name she cannot recall. This woman agreed to hold the materials until Loretta told her to do otherwise, but Loretta never contacted her.

Serendipitously, sometime later in 1968, Edward Crosby, the man who had brought Henry, Shelby Steele, and others to the EHE in East St. Louis, attended a dinner party at the home of the woman with whom Loretta had left the boxes. But Crosby, who during my interviews with him also could not remember her name, recalled that Henry's name was mentioned in conversation as the evening unfolded. The host commented that she was holding a number of boxes containing documents and manuscripts for Loretta Dumas. At that moment, the stage was set for Dumas's literary debut. Armed with the best intentions, Crosby, with the permission of this unnamed hostess, seized the documents. Not long after, he approached Redmond and Hale Chatfield about publishing Dumas's work. He knew Chatfield had a longer history with Dumas, and that Redmond, in less than a year, had nevertheless come to know Dumas intimately.

Soon Redmond and Chatfield were on their way to New Jersey to visit Loretta Dumas and assess the feasibility of publishing her husband's work posthumously. Initially, Dumas's friends in New Jersey assumed Earl Thomas would serve as the point person in the process. Chatfield's involvement made sense, and they knew enough about the politics of publishing to know that a black person would need to have a hand in the project. If not Thomas, so his friends from

Rutgers thought, the only other logical choice would have been Jay Wright. But neither man was sought out during this process.

News of Redmond's role stunned Dumas's East Coast friends. They concluded wrongly that the East St. Louis poet had manipulated Loretta into granting him the privilege of serving as executor. Loretta was certainly still dealing with the aftermath of Henry's death, but her rationale for selecting Redmond was practical, based on sound logic and her information at the time. Redmond had spent an extraordinary amount of time with Henry in a truncated but intense period, becoming a confidante during the last year of his life. Moreover, because Henry had never brought Loretta into his literary world, her knowledge of his Rutgers friends, and their knowledge of her, was cursory or fragmentary. In fact, she knew Earl Thomas as well as she knew Redmond: hardly at all. She would not even have a conversation with Thomas until a decade after Dumas's death, when he moved to the Highland Park community where she had returned after Illinois. From what she would later learn about Earl Thomas (she only learned about most of Henry's Rutgers friends years after his death), she may have approached him, but Thomas's background was in education and social work, not literary history and creative writing.

The task of getting Henry's work published, coincided with the feverish politics of race and publishing in the 1960s and 1970s. From Phillis Wheatley to Malcolm X, a white person had almost always signed off on, reviewed, or approved black texts. Some of the writers who identified with the Black Arts Movement, however, were less interested in white responses to or approval of their work. For those whites who had supported and in some instances contributed to efforts at black cultural autonomy, they had to consider something counterintuitive: although they had supported the freedom struggle, some African Americans felt the need to chart out their ultimate destiny by themselves, a subject of exploration in Dumas's fictional meditation on black cultural authenticity, "Will the Circle Be Unbroken?" Some black writers published with smaller black presses, among them Broadside, Third World, Jihad Productions, and Black River Writers Press, the last cofounded by Redmond and inspired by Dumas, in East St. Louis in 1967. But the reality for most black writers was that they needed to establish relationships with white publishers, although at times these relationships became antagonistic. Black writers needed the white apparatus without the input.

In his study of black writers and white publishers, John K. Young points out the way that some of these writers operated in tenuous publishing waters.[2] In the 1969 paperback reprint of the *Black Fire Anthology* (which included Dumas's supernatural tale, "Fon"), Young notes that editors LeRoi Jones and Larry Neal closed ranks against publisher William Morrow for not allowing them to add writers to the new edition. Jones and Neal felt this decision a white power play and said as much in their editors' note: "Various accidents kept this work from appearing in the 1st edition. We hoped it wd be in the paperback, but these devils claim it costs too much to reprint. Hopefully, the 2nd edition of the paperback will have all the people we cd think of. The frustration of working through all these bull-shit white people should be obvious."[3] In this provocative gesture, Young observes, "Jones and Neal mark themselves as independent agents from the publisher, even as they are economically dependent on these same devils."[4]

Another writer who tried to revise, if not rectify, the hierarchy of race in publishing was Ishmael Reed. In the first edition of his 1972 novel, *Mumbo Jumbo*, Reed, evidently with Doubleday's permission, if not blessing, created a second, black copyright page, with white text. "By remaking the copyright page as black," Young contends, "Reed in his collaboration with Doubleday insists on marking the text as 'his' even as he transfers it economically and legally to a publishing system in which he may function as a racial token."[5]

Into this briar patch of race and publishing, Redmond and Chatfield fell. They were certainly aware of the potential problems and possibilities their relationship could symbolize. Early on, their relationship seemed cordial. Chatfield handled the editing and Redmond focused more on the thematic and conceptual concerns in Dumas's work. Through Edward Crosby's overture to Southern Illinois University Press, they coedited *Ark of Bones and Other Stories* and *Poetry for My People*, both of which the press published in 1970.[6] In *Ark of Bones*, Chatfield and Redmond wrote the preface and introduction, respectively. In *Poetry*, they agreed to have Imamu Ameer Baraka (as Amiri Baraka then spelled his name) write the preface and Jay Wright the introduction. To this point, Chatfield and Redmond had maintained an effective relationship, if for no other reason than their kindred desire to bring their friend's work into print. But this cordiality concealed a growing tension beneath the surface.

Black literature—after civil rights and black power, Martin and Malcolm, Rosa Parks and Angela Davis—was on the threshold of significant change. Toni Morrison was one of the principal publishing forces behind this transformation. In 1968, when she assumed her position as senior editor after having worked for years in the scholastic division of Random House, Morrison facilitated the literary debuts of numerous writers, black women in particular. Gayl

Jones, Toni Cade Bambara, and Angela Davis, among others, are some of the most well-known authors whose work Morrison championed.

These writers, including Morrison herself in her debut novel, *The Bluest Eye*, were interested in telling black stories that were not made to conform to narrow aesthetic standards, either black or white. Indeed, Morrison would embrace Henry Dumas based purely on this more expansive concept of black aesthetics. As Redmond recounts the story, during Morrison's time at Random House, she sometimes called on the poet Quincy Troupe to babysit her son. One day, she arrived to pick him up and spotted the Southern Illinois University Press editions of Dumas's poetry and fiction. Troupe gave her some background on Dumas, and she simply sat and read late into the night. Soon after, Redmond remembered, "she called wanting to know if I had more writings by Henry."[7] From that point she was part of what she would term the "cult" of Henry Dumas.[8]

Morrison's dive into Dumas's imaginative worlds prompted her to approach Redmond about publishing Henry's work. But Redmond, who was charting his own distinguished path as poet, scholar, and activist, was reluctant. "I had my own things to do," he explained to her, "but I also was committed to letting people know about the Dumas legacy."[9] In Loretta Dumas's mind, however, Redmond's role at that point was purely organic: "Eugene and I never discussed him becoming literary executor. He never initiated anything like that. In fact, we really have never approached publishers about his work; they've contacted us. People might not believe this, but Eugene only became, from a legal standpoint, literary executor in April 2012." Indeed, the other presses that would publish Dumas's work, Thunder's Mouth and Coffee House, approached Redmond and Loretta Dumas about publishing Dumas's work.

"I am grateful to Eugene for bringing Henry's work to my attention," Morrison remarked years later. His work was "beautiful, different from contemporary black writers; it had a different geography, a wider plateau. It had a quality of timelessness. You sensed these budding identity questions."[10] In Morrison's view, some black writers were leaning on racial subject matter and political perspectives that did not address the complexity of the subjects they were writing about. In these cases, the definitions of blackness were too narrow, too limiting in scope, to produce the most challenging and engaging forms of black storytelling. Some black writers had been conditioned to think of blackness in only monolithic and social realist terms, which in turn created, for Morrison, another kind of black literary ghetto.[11]

In Dumas's creative world, Morrison felt she had found a voice aware of

tradition but equally comfortable expanding or departing from it when necessary. Since Random House had articulated a commitment to publishing minority writers, she embraced the opportunity to place Dumas in the publishing
pipeline. As senior editor, Morrison published lines of his poetry in *The Black
Book* (1974), a compendium of African Americana in words, photographs, letters, songs, and other testaments to the black presence in the United States.
With its celebration of black experience, paying homage to black people of letters, of the soil, and all the black folks in between, *The Black Book* was the perfect venue for Dumas's verse.

Morrison's ultimate homage to Dumas, beyond that of publishing his work,
may actually be in something she claims not to have done. She contends there
is no correlation between the Sweet Home plantation that plays a role in *Beloved* and Dumas's boyhood home, Sweet Home, Arkansas. Wittingly or not,
Morrison's evocation of Dumas's birthplace is at least symbolic of literary kinship, though by her account fully serendipitous.[12]

After his death, Dumas would join the list of writers whose efforts Morrison supported. But as she embraced Dumas and Redmond, the politics of race,
specifically the role of whites in the publishing of black books, made for high
drama in the Dumas publishing story. As editor, Morrison had to figure out
the best way of marketing the Random House editions of Dumas's poetry and
short stories previously published by Southern Illinois University Press. The
press had decided not to undertake further print runs, and Morrison wanted
Dumas's work to remain in print.

From the perspective of the publisher, reprints and new editions of previously published books involve less time and investment, because they have already been edited and usually designed, compared with brand-new, unedited
manuscripts. So, reprinting Henry's work was an easy and inexpensive way for
Morrison to build her list, and for Random House to add another black name
to the roster. Nonetheless, Redmond found himself dealing with a publisher
that had no advertising budget.

Acknowledging the marketing and literary challenges of publishing a deceased writer's unfinished body of work, Morrison and Redmond ushered Random House editions of *Ark of Bones* and *Play Ebony Play Ivory* into print in 1974.
To his astonishment, Hale Chatfield had been dropped from this literary equation, his name removed from the volumes. In hindsight, Redmond acknowledged that doing so was a tough decision, made under the weight of interracial
struggle and conflict.

To celebrate and create excitement over the Random House editions in 1974,
Morrison organized a book party to be held at the Center for Inter-American

Relations in New York City. The invitation laid out her mission: "It is very difficult to do publicity for an unknown writer and much more difficult to do publicity for an unknown and no longer living writer. But we are determined to bring to the large community of Black artists and Black people in general this man's work."[13]

Morrison's letter sounded like an invitation to a black literary and artistic homecoming. The list of invitees was not racially exclusive, but the people Morrison referenced who had already committed to the book party were African American. Hale Chatfield was extended an invitation. But fuming over what he perceived to be Morrison and Redmond's slight, he declined. He thought the invitation to Park Avenue an empty gesture, part of a larger racial insult, feelings he revealed to Jay and Lois Wright.

In a letter to the couple, Chatfield spelled out how he was blindsided not by the publication of Dumas's books but by the removal of his name from the volumes. "It was wonderful to receive Jay's letter," he began, "though I wish the circumstances were less raunchy. The Random House thing's a complete rip-off from my point of view, and I'm delighted to learn (as I'd hoped) that Jay was not involved."[14]

What had begun as a collegial effort to bring Dumas's work to print had become, in Chatfield's mind, the ultimate con game. Loretta Dumas, in response to Chatfield's allegations, informed him by letter that she had "talked to Gene Redmond about the co-editorship of the work, and it will be handled justly. There are several ideas, and we will be in touch with you on it."[15] The most obvious solution was to restore Chatfield's name to future printings, but despite Morrison and Redmond's efforts, Dumas's work would not sell well enough for subsequent printings.

The removal of Chatfield's name was a calculated publishing decision informed heavily by the politics of racial identity, cultural autonomy, and the time and logistical demands of a major publisher. In a world where blackness, no matter the problems associated with its social construction, was in vogue, putting a white editor out front in the marketing of a black book would quite simply have turned off some black readers. Redmond and Morrison decided this was not the project to trumpet the virtues of racial collaboration. There were already enough challenges associated with publishing Dumas's books.

Beyond that, Redmond and Morrison felt territorial about Henry. He was, after all, a black writer killed by a white cop, and black writers, so the emotions of the period would dictate, should introduce him to the world. Redmond, of course, was not privy to all the discussions about marketing at Random House. But he and Morrison may have concluded that the success of Dumas's books would depend largely on their ability to market him as a black writer to black people. Morrison stated as much in her invitation to the Dumas book celebration. Chatfield's race, at best, would have been a distraction and, at worst, a detriment to book sales.

But the Henry Dumas of Chatfield's memory would have insisted on fairness and truth, even if it did not conform to the racial romanticism of black cultural nationalists. Then again, the Henry Dumas that Redmond knew had veered away from the white world—even his love of classical music was chaff in the wind. This was also another compelling piece of evidence for Loretta. Although toward the end of his life he and Loretta had few substantive conversations, Henry had updated her on his new cultural aesthetics. "He told me," she remarked years later, "at some point in the final year of his life, that he could no longer suffer the sounds of Bach, Brahms, and Beethoven." Henry had grown skeptical about the possibility of racial progress in literature and beyond.

By the time Henry arrived in East St. Louis, he was ensconced in the black world, although he had not forsaken white people categorically. After all, he was the best man in the wedding of a white friend in New York before he was killed. And he still called Lois on occasion, the last time just prior to his final trip to New York. But even with these examples of romance and friendship across racial borders, Henry was drawn even closer to his roots, to cultural lodestones that Chatfield probably would not have known. He had to straddle, by necessity, two worlds, a negotiation, as Redmond put it, "common to our generation." "Hale may have known Henry," Redmond once quipped, "but how well did he understand him?" In other words, Chatfield would not necessarily have been in the position to have the relevant cultural knowledge for properly contextualizing Dumas's work. For instance, in the preface to *Ark of Bones*, as Redmond observes, Chatfield wrote that Henry loved "overcooked beef," but Redmond pointed out something that Chatfield may not have understood: "that most black people like their beef well done."[16] And on that hook Redmond hung his rationale for assuming responsibility for Dumas's literary materials.

The irony in all of this is that, despite Morrison and Redmond's best efforts, Dumas's books (including subsequent editions by other publishers) have not generated the kind of attention they merit to date. More people know about him, but Dumas still has not become a household name. Nonetheless, he lived with creative tenacity, and what he created continues to bring a steady stream of admirers to his literary ark. In retrospect, as we consider the role Redmond has played in the Dumas publishing tree, it seems that he was indeed the person to do it. Both Earl Thomas and Jay Wright have reached significant heights in their respective careers, but neither followed the kind of creative writer–scholar–activist path of Redmond. In other words, Redmond's creative arc has come closest to what Henry's creative arc most likely would have been.

Indeed, for Redmond and Dumas, things traveled full circle. Dumas labored, unsuccessfully, to have his work published by a major publishing house. Even after his death, with the backing of Southern Illinois University Press and later Random House and the longstanding efforts of Redmond and Loretta Dumas, his work is not where it deserves to be in the African American literary canon. In *The Norton Anthology of African American Literature*, which some consider to be the definitive anthology of African American literature, Dumas is invisible, yet visible. He is excluded from the lineup of writers, also in the second edition, but acknowledged as a literary forerunner in an essay on the Black Arts Movement. "His work resonated with the overt attention to Africa found in the poetical rhythms and nationalist politics of the Black Arts movement," writes Houston A. Baker Jr. "Yet Dumas's stories were often roughly polished polemics."[17]

Not all, or even most, scholars necessarily agree with Baker's reading, but Dumas's exclusion from the anthology certainly limits the degree to which Dumas will be revealed to the next generation of students. As Reggie Scott Young explains, "Dumas's exclusion is important because no other anthology is as influential as the *Norton*, and exclusion of a writer means her or his works are less likely to be taught and that unfamiliar readers will not receive exposure to that writer for future reference."[18]

Even with this disadvantage, Dumas's work, thanks to Loretta Dumas, Redmond, and company, has experienced something of a renaissance, most notably in the 2003 Coffee House edition of his collected fiction, *Echo Tree*. Additionally, perhaps as a sign of the rising interest in Dumas's work, Norton plans to include in its 2014 *Anthology of African American Literature* two of Dumas's poems, "Black Star Line" and "The Zebra Goes Wild Where the Sidewalk Ends," and one short story, his haunting jazz tale "Will the Circle Be Unbroken?" Yet another sign of the critical tide turning in Dumas's favor is the inclusion of eight Dumas poems in the 2014 edition of *The Oxford Anthology of Modern and Contemporary American Poetry*.

In the introduction, I likened Henry Dumas to Countee Cullen, the poet of Harlem Renaissance fame. Cullen is most remembered for his searing insight into the difficulty of being a black artist, of finding a way, despite publishing and cultural obstacles, to simply sing. Henry Dumas would offer a visual metaphor in his life as a writer, that of visibility, riffing on Ralph Ellison's signature novel, *Invisible Man*. Throughout Dumas's work, characters and poetic personae sing and see things that others do not understand. In a white world that often refuses to acknowledge what blacks feel, see, and think, characters in Dumas's creative world assume their view of the world to be valid and valuable. In literary terms, Dumas hardly wrote for the moment. His was a creative vision that transcended time and place. In this sense, the mainstream literary world is finally catching up with this most visible man.

Notes

A NOTE ON PERSONAL SOURCES

All references to Loretta Dumas, Eugene B. Redmond, and Lois Wright are based on numerous interviews with them from June 2004 to January 2012. Only particularly revealing interviews are dated in the notes. At the time of my research for this book, the papers and manuscripts of Henry Dumas (HDP) were privately held. The same is true for the Lois Wright papers (LWP).

PROLOGUE

1. Toni Morrison, "On Behalf of Henry Dumas," *Black American Literature Forum* 22, no. 2 (summer 1988): 310.

2. Quincy Troupe, "For the Griot from Sweet Home, Henry Dumas: A Tribute to His Genius," *Black American Literature Forum* 22, no. 2 (summer 1988): 379.

3. Arnold Rampersad, "Henry Dumas's World of Fiction," *Black American Literature Forum* 22, no. 2 (summer 1988): 329.

4. Eugene B. Redmond, foreword to *Echo Tree: The Collected Short Fiction of Henry Dumas*, by Henry Dumas (Minneapolis, Minn.: Coffee House Press, 2003), xlvi.

5. Countee Cullen, *My Soul's High Song: Collected Writings of Countee Cullen*, ed. Gerald Early (New York: Doubleday, 1991), 104.

CHAPTER ONE. ARKANSAS BOYHOOD

1. Judith Kilpatrick, "(Extra)Ordinary Men: African American Lawyers and Civil Rights in Arkansas before 1950," *Arkansas Law Review* 53 (2000): 346.

2. Gene Vizant, "Mirage and Reality: Economic Conditions in Black Little Rock in the 1920s," *Arkansas Historical Quarterly* 63, no. 3 (autumn 2004), 268–69, 278.

3. Michael B. Dougan, *Arkansas Odyssey: The Saga of Arkansas from Prehistoric Times to Present: A History* (Little Rock, Ark.: Rose Publishing, 1995), 438.

4. Adella Porter Hale, interview with author, digital recording, 4 December 2004. I conducted two person-to-person and several phone interviews with Hale between 2004 and 2010.

5. James N. Gregory, "The Dust Bowl Migration," in *Poverty in the United States: An Encyclopedia of History, Politics, and Policy,* eds. Gwendolyn Mink and Alice O'Connor (Santa Barbara, Calif.: ABC-Clio, 2004): 244.

6. James N. Gregory, *American Exodus: The Dust Bowl Migration and Okie Culture* (New York: Oxford University Press, 1989), 20.

7. Dougan, *Arkansas Odyssey*, 431.

8. Isabel Wilkerson, *The Warmth of Other Suns* (New York: Random House, 2010), 10–11.

9. Donald Holley, "Leaving the Land of Opportunity: Arkansas and the Great Migration," *Arkansas Historical Quarterly* 64, no. 3 (autumn 2005): 249, 252.

10. Hale interview.

11. Dougan, *Arkansas Odyssey*, 438.

12. There are discrepancies regarding Lynn—or Minnie—Porter's legal name. Some family members nicknamed her "Nin." According to the Porter family oral history, when she was interviewed for the 1930 census, the interviewer heard someone refer to her by her nickname, but they misheard the nickname. As a result, she is listed as Lynn Porter. Her grandchildren called her Grandma Lynn, but her death certificate reads Minnie Porter. Throughout the book, I refer to her as Grandma Lynn Porter.

13. William H. Metzler, "Population Movement in Arkansas," *Arkansas Gazette Sunday Magazine,* 21 April 1940. Quoted in Holley, "Leaving the Land of Opportunity," 247.

14. Hale interview.

15. Ibid.

16. Dougan, *Arkansas Odyssey*, 439.

17. Amara Bachu, "Timing of First Births: 1930–34 to 1990–94," Working Paper No. 25, Population Division, U.S. Bureau of the Census, presented at the Annual Meeting of the Population Association of America, Chicago, Ill., April 1998.

18. Henry thought of Billy as his brother, rather than as his half-brother.

19. Zella Hargrove Gaither, *Arkansas Confederate Home* (Little Rock, Ark.: New Era Press, 1920), 7.

20. Ibid., 5.

21. Hayes interview.

22. Ibid.

23. Hale interview.

24. Ibid.

25. Ibid.

26. He only earned one A that year, in homework, and all the other grades were Bs and B pluses.

27. Jennifer Ritterhouse, *Growing Up Jim Crow: The Racial Socialization of Black and*

White Southern Children, 1890–1940 (Chapel Hill: University of North Carolina Press, 2006) 183.

28. Hayes interview.

29. The statistics are from Holley, "Leaving the Land of Opportunity," 252, 255.

30. Joanne Canales, phone interview by author, 10 December 2004.

31. If he had remained in Sweet Home and completed high school, Henry might have been able, despite the financial challenges, to consider attending one of the black colleges throughout the South, three of which were near home: Shorter College, Arkansas Baptist College, Philander Smith, and the University of Arkansas, Pine Bluff. But he and his family wanted his options to be governed by his interests, not by the demands of Jim Crow.

32. Henry Dumas, *Echo Tree: The Collected Short Fiction of Henry Dumas* (Minneapolis, Minn.: Coffee House Press), 56.

CHAPTER TWO. SKYSCRAPERS, SUBWAYS, AND CAMELS

1. Isabel Wilkerson, *The Warmth of Other Suns* (New York: Random House, 2010), 249.

2. Lawrence P. Jackson, *The Indignant Generation: A Narrative History of African American Writers and Critics, 1934–1960* (Princeton, N.J.: Princeton University Press, 2011): 179.

3. Arnold Rampersad, *Ralph Ellison: A Biography* (New York: Knopf, 2007), 174.

4. Ibid.

5. Jackson, *Indignant Generation*, 185–86.

6. Ibid., 186.

7. Ibid., 262.

8. Thomas Sugrue, *Sweet Land of Liberty: The Forgotten Struggle for Civil Rights in the North* (New York: Random House, 2008), 188.

9. Thomas Sowell, "The Education of Minority Children," http://www.tsowell.com /speducat.html#N11, accessed 10 October 2011.

10. Aunt Mary's father and Joanne's father, Oscar Nalls, were brothers.

11. Joanne Canales, phone interview by author, 10 December 2004.

12. Ibid.

13. Ibid.

14. Sondra K. Wilson, *Meet Me at the Theresa* (New York: Atria Books, 2004), 86.

15. George H. Locke, "The High School of Commerce New York City," *School Review: A Journal of Secondary Education* 11, no. 7 (September 1903): 555–62.

16. The irony is that William Grant Still, considered the dean of black classical composers, was born in Mississippi in 1895, but he spent most of his early years in Little Rock, Arkansas. There is, however, no evidence to suggest that Henry was aware of his work.

17. Canales, interview.

18. He wrote about this moment years later in a course at Rutgers University. Henry Dumas, "The Brief History of One Man," 1960, HDP.

19. Milton A. Gordon, "An Analysis of Enrollment Data for Black Students in Institu-

tions of Higher Education, from 1940–1972," *Journal of Negro Education* 45, no. 2 (spring 1976): 118.

20. James J. Heckman and Paul A. LaFontaine, "The American High School Graduation Rate, Trends and Levels," National Bureau of Economic Research Working Paper 13670 (Dec. 2007), figure 9.

21. Henry Dumas, handwritten MS, HDP.

22. Loretta Dumas's letters to her husband have never been located, and she destroyed his letters to her in 1968.

CHAPTER THREE. LEARNING TO READ, WRITE, AND THINK

1. Loretta Dumas, interview by author, 1 June 2005.

2. Ibid. Loretta still has at least one audiotape of Henry performing a one-man character skit in the 1960s.

3. Loretta Dumas interview, 1 June 2005

4. Ibid.

5. Robert Pinsky, email interview by author, 21 January 2009. He served as U.S. poet laureate 1997–2000, during the Clinton administration.

6. Henry Dumas, "Morality in the Luck of Roaring Camp," 18 November 1958, course paper, HDP.

7. J. David Stevens, "'She War a Woman': Family Roles, Gender, and Sexuality in Bret Harte's Western Fiction," *American Literature: A Journal of Literary History, Criticism, and Bibliography* 69, no. 3 (1997): 571.

8. Henry Dumas, "A Study of American Manners," 20 December 1958, 1, 3, course paper, HDP.

9. Paul Fussell had served in the U.S. Army Infantry during World War II, afterward distinguishing himself as a scholar in eighteenth-century British Literature. He also developed a serious interest in depictions of war in literature and film.

10. Gloria Smith, phone interview by author, 4 April 2009.

11. Alan Cheuse, phone interview by author, 17 July 2006. Cheuse is a noted book reviewer for National Public Radio and acclaimed writer of fiction and memoir.

12. Amiri Baraka, *The Autobiography of LeRoi Jones* (Chicago, Ill.: Lawrence Hill Books, 1997), 230.

13. Ibid.

14. Ramiro de Maeztu, "Hamlet and Quijote," trans. Jake Bair, *Anthologist* 33, no. 2 (1961–1962).

15. Jake Bair, phone interview by author, 11 April 2010.

16. Ibid.

17. Ibid.

18. Pinsky interview.

19. Lindsey later had an illustrious career in the federal government as regional director of the Equal Employment Opportunity Office.

20. Laura Lindsey, interview by author, 6 June 2005.

21. Ibid.

22. Robinson went on to a remarkable career in math and computer programming.

He helped to program the 747 jet computer systems, wrote a book on the program, and was responsible for teaching pilots the system. He also programmed satellites survey-ing Russia during the cold war.

23. "Probe into Social Club Slaying Set for July 22," *Chicago Defender* (Daily Edition), 15 July 1959, A6.

24. Henry Dumas, *Echo Tree: The Collected Short Fiction of Henry Dumas* (Minneapolis, Minn.: Coffee House Press, 2003), 23. The title of Dumas's collected fiction comes from the story, first published in the *Anthologist* 33, no. 4 (1961): 15–21.

25. Dumas, *Echo Tree*, 28.

26. Ibid.

27. Henry Dumas, "What Is an American?," undated course paper, HDP.

28. Ibid.

29. Henry Dumas, "A City Game," *Anthologist* 32, no. 3 (1961): 3. Dumas later renamed it "A Harlem Game."

30. Henry Dumas, "A Harlem Game," in *Echo Tree*, 98.

31. Ibid., 98.

32. Ibid., 102.

33. Loretta Dumas, interview by author, digital recording, 4 December 2006.

34. William Wynkoop, marginalia in Henry Dumas, "The Shaft of Light: Com-ments on and Experiences of Emerson's "Self Reliance," 27 October 1960, course pa-per, HDP.

35. Baraka, *Autobiography*, 234.

36. Dumas, "Essay on Walt Whitman," course paper, HDP.

37. Ibid., 14.

38. Ibid., 7.

39. Duncan Osborne, "Portrait of a Retiree: William Magee Wynkoop," *PlanSponsor Magazine/Digital*, May 1996, http://www.plansponsor.com/MagazineArticle.aspx?id= 6442461917&magazine=6442461794, accessed 15 March 2013. PlanSponsor is a leading authority on retirement and benefits programs for employers. The article focuses on Wynkoop's forty-six-year relationship with Roy Strickland, highlighting the fact that Wynkoop "will not be able to leave any benefits to his life partner." Wynkoop and Strickland were also featured in a 1996 Associated Press article about same-sex mar-riages in New York City. At eighty and seventy-eight years of age, respectively, the men were wed in a civil ceremony. See "2 Dozen Same-Sex Marriages in Midtown," *New York Times*, 17 June 1996, http://www.nytimes.com/1996/06/17/nyregion/2-dozen-same-sex -marriages-in-midtown.html, accessed 15 March 2013.

CHAPTER FOUR. ANOTHER CONVERSION

1. "Fund Use Hit in Segregation," *New Brunswick Home News*, 17 January 1961, 5.

2. "Meet to Aid Sharecroppers," *New Brunswick Home News*, 17 January 1961, 5. There is no record of Henry having attended this meeting, but that he kept this article about the meeting suggests he was interested in what was discussed.

3. Richard L. Saunders, "What Happened? 'Tent City,' Tennessee," http://www.utm .edu/organizations/civilrights/tent_city_history.html, accessed 15 March 2013.

4. Henry Dumas, *Echo Tree: The Collected Short Fiction of Henry Dumas* (Minneapolis, Minn.: Coffee House Press, 2003), 57.

5. Henry Dumas, *Jonoah and the Green Stone* (New York: Random House, 1976), 104.

6. Charlie Butts, interview by author, digital recording, 28 May 2006.

7. With Henry's firsthand knowledge of the struggle for fair treatment in western Tennessee, another case and point that spring were the Freedom Rides that occurred later that May and on into November. Interracial groups of college students (and later, older adults) trained by the Congress of Racial Equality (CORE) challenged Jim Crow by traveling together on buses and trains through the Deep South, in peaceful defiance of state laws prohibiting such acts. Although they performed their civil disobedience to perfection, they were greeted with bats, pipes, explosives, and some of the worst words of the American idiom in Alabama and Mississippi. See Raymond Arsenault, *Freedom Riders: 1961 and the Struggle for Racial Justice* (New York: Oxford University Press), 2.

8. Hemingway's story was also collected in *Men without Women* (New York: Scribner), 1927.

9. Ralph Waldo Emerson, *The American Scholar, Self Reliance, Compensation* (New York: American Book Company, 1893), 97.

10. Henry Dumas, "In Dry September the Killers Came," 9 January, 1961, course paper, HDP.

11. Ibid.

12. "Take This River!" was published in the *Anthologist* in 1961 and reprinted in *Echo Tree*, the posthumous volume of his collected fiction.

13. Henry Dumas, "Take This River!," in *Echo Tree*, 1.

14. Ibid.

15. Manning Marable, *Malcolm X: A Life of Reinvention* (New York: Viking, 2011), 162.

16. Ibid., 185.

17. Novene Pasha to Henry Dumas, letter 14 September 1961, HDP.

18. Earl Thomas, interview by author, Willingboro, N.J., digital recording, 4 June 2005.

19. Ibid.

20. Marable, *Malcolm X*, 178.

21. Henry Dumas to *Rutgers Daily Targum*, unpublished letter, n.d., 1961, HDP.

22. In 1962 Henry would publish in the *Anthologist* a moving story about the dead and the living, titled "Echo Tree," for which his byline was "X Dumas." Perhaps Henry was trying to needle the white readership at Rutgers by evoking Malcolm X in his signature. Whatever his motivation, his use of the symbolic X was significant and symbolic, and the only known instance of him doing so.

23. Tom Dent, "Umbra Days," *Black American Literature Forum* 14, no. 3 (autumn 1980): 106–7.

24. Arnold Rampersad, *Ralph Ellison: A Biography* (New York: Knopf: 2007), 391.

25. Ibid., 487. Rampersad recounts how Morrison approached Ellison to write a short foreword for Leon Forrest's first novel, *There Is a Tree More Ancient than Eden*, published in 1973. Ellison complied, though begrudgingly.

26. Alan Cheuse, phone interview by author, 17 July 2006.

27. Jay Wright, introduction to *Play Ebony Play Ivory*, by Henry Dumas (New York: Random House, 1974), xvii. Here it should be noted that Jay and Lois Wright have recovered all rights to the introduction.

CHAPTER FIVE. PROGRESS, SETBACKS, AND ROMANCE

1. Paul M. Cubeta to Henry Dumas, letter 7 June 1963, HDP.

2. Robert Frost attended nearly every Bread Loaf Conference over forty-two years. He was absent from the bucolic surroundings of Middlebury in the summer of 1963; the iconic poet, who had read at President Kennedy's inauguration in 1961, had died in January 1963.

3. Edward M. Cifelli, *John Ciardi: A Biography* (Fayetteville: University of Arkansas Press, 1997), 243.

4. Alan Cheuse, *Listening to the Page* (New York: Columbia University Press, 2001), 3.

5. Dumas must have met Gloria Oden at some point. In his personal phone book, her contact information at the American Institute of Physics was listed. Her wide-ranging interests in literature and science were no doubt intriguing to a man with disparate interests himself.

6. Lennox Raphael, email to author, 22 September 2011.

7. Earl Thomas, interview by author, Willingborough, N.J., digital recording, 4 June 2005.

8. Stephanie Coontz, *Marriage: A History* (New York: Viking, 2005), 250.

9. Lois Wright, interview by author, Bradford, Vt., 2 August 2007.

10. Thomas interview; Clem Fiori, interview by author, Willingboro, N.J., digital recording, 4 June 2005.

11. Wright interview, 2 August 2007.

12. Henry Dumas, "A Boll of Roses," in *Echo Tree: The Collected Short Fiction of Henry Dumas* (Minneapolis, Minn.: Coffee House Press, 2003), 83.

13. Henry Dumas to Lois Silber, letter 4 October 1963, LWP.

14. Henry Dumas to Lois Silber, letter 29 October 1963, LWP.

15. Henry Dumas to Lois Silber, letter 25 November 1963, LWP.

16. Henry Dumas to Lois Silber, undated letter [1963], LWP.

17. Wright interview, 2 August 2007.

18. Henry Dumas to Lois Silber, undated letter [1963], LWP.

19. Henry Dumas to Lois Silber, letter 3 December 1963, LWP.

20. Henry Dumas to Lois Silber, letter 9 December 1963, LWP. In his final remark, Henry confirmed his significant friendship with Jake Bair, while assuring Lois that she should not be jealous of Jake or any man with whom he was close.

21. As a senior in 1961, Bair was selected for the Henry Rutgers Scholars Program.

22. Henry Dumas to Lois Silber, letter 12 December 1963, LWP.

23. Henry Dumas to Lois Silber, letter 16 December 1963, LWP.

24. David Garrow, *Bearing the Cross: Martin Luther King, Jr., and the Southern Christian Leadership Conference* (New York: William Morrow, 1986), 638 n26, 40–41.

25. Henry Dumas to Lois Silber, letter 19 December 1963, LWP.

26. Manning Marable, *Malcolm X: A Life of Reinvention* (New York: Penguin, 2011), 111.

27. Amiri Baraka, *Autobiography of LeRoi Jones* (Chicago, Ill.: Lawrence Hill Books, 1997), 248–49.

28. Henry Dumas to Lois Silber, letter 2 January 1964, LWP.

CHAPTER SIX. CHASING CHANGE

1. Henry Dumas to Lois Silber, letter 2 January 1964, LWP.

2. Henry Dumas to Lois Silber, letter 16 January 1964, LWP.

3. Herman Hesse, *Siddhartha* (New York: Bantam Books, 1957), 60.

4. Ibid., 14.

5. Ibid., 66.

6. *Hillary's Class*, 60 min., PBS Frontline Documentary, Boston, 1994.

7. Henry Dumas to Lois Silber, letter circa 1964, LWP.

8. Henry Dumas to Lois Silber, undated letter 1964, LWP.

9. Ibid., LWP.

10. Hettie Jones, *How I Became Hettie Jones* (New York: Grove Press, 1990), 51–52.

11. Henry Dumas to Lois Silber, undated letter 1964, LWP.

12. Clem Fiori and Earl Thomas, interview by author, Willingborough, N.J., digital recording, 4 June 2005.

13. Henry Dumas to Lois Silber, undated letter 1964, LWP.

14. Henry Dumas, *Knees of a Natural Man: The Selected Poetry of Henry Dumas* (New York: Thunder's Mouth Press, 1989), 63.

15. Henry Dumas to Lois Silber, letter 18 March 1964, LWP.

16. Ibid.

17. Wright interview, 2 August 2007.

18. Henry and Loretta Dumas to Creditors, letter 27 June 1964, HDP. Henry wrote the letter after consulting a lawyer, Joseph Stevens, of New Brunswick, N.J.

19. Henry Dumas to Lois Silber, letter 28 September 1964, LWP.

CHAPTER SEVEN. PAGES WITHOUT A PUBLISHER

1. Middleton A. Harris, comp., *The Black Book* (New York: Random House, 1974). As a senior editor at Random House, Toni Morrison was instrumental in bringing this book to life and in planting lines from Henry's poetry in the collection.

2. Henry Dumas to William Sloane, letter 13 March 1965, HDP.

3. Henry Dumas to Helen Hurd, letter 8 April 1965, HDP.

4. Ibid.

5. Henry Dumas to Lois Silber, undated letter [1965].

6. Henry Dumas to Viking Press, letter 14 April 1965, HDP.

7. Henry Dumas, *Jonoah and the Stone* (New York: Random House, 1976), 15–16.

8. Ibid., 104.

9. Harold Cruse, *Crisis of the Negro Intellectual* (New York: Apollo, 1967), 500, 505.

10. Lois Wright, interview by author, Bradford, Vt., 2 August 2007.

11. Ibid.

12. Lawrence P. Jackson, *The Indignant Generation: A Narrative History of Black Writers and Critics, 1934–1960* (Princeton, N.J.: Princeton University Press, 2011), 7.

13. Lois Wright, phone interview by author, 6 January 2009.

14. Henry Dumas to W. L. Rothenberg, letter 1965, HDP.

15. Dumas wrote this poem in the 1960s, dedicating it to his friend and fellow poet Jay Wright.

16. Henry Dumas, "The Playground Is My Home," in *Play Ebony Play Ivory* (New York: Random House, 1974).

17. Ibid.

18. Wright interview, 6 January 2009.

19. Wright interview, 2 August 2007.

20. John F. Szwed, *Space Is the Place: The Lives and Times of Sun Ra* (New York: Pantheon, 1997), 238.

21. Vertamae Smart-Grosvenor, phone interview by author, 7 July 2011.

22. Szwed, *Space Is the Place*, 222.

23. Henry Dumas, "Ark of Bones," in *Echo Tree: The Collected Short Fiction of Henry Dumas* (Minneapolis, Minn.: Coffee House Press, 2003), 18.

24. Ibid., 19.

25. Szwed, *Space Is the Place*, 223. Also, Szwed employs the term *folksay*.

26. Henry Dumas, "Outer Space Blues," in *Play Ebony Play Ivory*, 72–73.

27. Szwed, *Space Is the Place*, 5.

28. *The Ark and the Ankh, Sun Ra/Henry Dumas in Conversation 1966*, Slug's Saloon, New York City, Ikef, B00006AL8J, compact disc.

29. Nat Hentoff, "The New Jazz—Black, Angry and Hard to Understand," *New York Times Magazine*, 25 December 1966, 37. Clipping in HDP.

30. Henry Dumas, "Will the Circle Be Unbroken?," in *Echo Tree*, 107.

31. Larry P. Neal, "Henry Dumas: Literary Landmark," in *Henry Dumas Issue*, special issue, *Black American Literature Forum* 22, no. 2 (summer 1988): 313–15.

32. Norman Mailer, *Advertisements for Myself* (Cambridge, Mass.: Harvard University Press, 1992), 341.

33. Amiri Baraka, *The Autobiography of LeRoi Jones* (Chicago, Ill.: Lawrence Hill Books, 1994), 294.

CHAPTER EIGHT. HEADED TO EAST BOOGIE

1. Amiri Baraka, *The Autobiography of LeRoi Jones* (Chicago, Ill: Lawrence Hill Books, 1994), 198.

2. Hettie Jones, *How I Became Hettie Jones* (New York: Grove Press, 1990), 158.

3. Clem Fiori, interview by author, digital recording, 4 June 2005.

4. Lois Silber to Jay Wright, letter 24 May 1968, LWP.

5. Lois Silber to Jay Wright, letter 3 June 1968, LWP.

6. Earl Thomas, interview by author, 4 June 2005.

7. Claude Steele, now dean of the School of Education at Stanford University, has distinguished himself through his research on what he refers to as "stereotype threat"

in racial and gender groups in higher education. In *Young, Gifted, and Black*, he and other scholars explore the way in which, for example, women or racial minorities are affected by racial and gender stereotypes in academic testing. Their conclusion: if a minority group is presented with information about stereotypes associated with its members before taking a standardized test, the discussion of these stereotypes results in lower scores. If stereotypes are not mentioned, their scores are higher.

8. Claude Steele, phone interview by author, 2 August 2006.

9. Ibid.

10. Ibid.

11. Ibid.

12. Ibid.

13. Ibid.

14. At Steele's request, the people involved are not named to preserve their privacy.

15. Steele interview.

16. Ibid.

17. Thomas interview.

18. Eugene B. Redmond, introduction to *Knees of a Natural Man*, by Henry Dumas (New York: Thunder's Mouth Press, 1989), 4.

19. Sherman Fowler, interview by author, East St. Louis, Ill., 12 May 2005.

20. Ibid.

21. Redmond, introduction, 5.

22. Steele interview.

23. Fowler interview.

24. Ibid.

25. Eugene B. Redmond, interview by author, East St. Louis, Ill., 13 May 2005.

26. Fowler interview.

27. Ibid.

28. Redmond, phone interview by author, 22 February 2013.

29. Ibid.

30. Henry Dumas, "Our King Is Dead," *Black American Literature Forum* 22, no. 2 (summer 1988): 245.

31. Kef, a drowsy state of contentment, is usually associated with cannabis. Along with some of their friends in East St. Louis, Henry and Eugene B. Redmond associated the term with the ultimate kind of artistic or intellectual plane.

32. Henry Dumas, "A New Proposal," in *Knees of a Natural Man*, 150–51.

33. Robert Pinsky, emails with author, 21 January 2009.

CHAPTER NINE. FROM SWEET HOME TO HARLEM

1. Langston Hughes, *The Collected Poems of Langston Hughes* (New York: Knopf, 1996), 426.

2. "Malcolm X Lays Harlem Riots to 'Scare Tactics' of Police," *New York Times*, 21 July 1964, 22.

3. Whitney Young, "The New Year: Hopes and Doubts," *Amsterdam News*, 6 January 1968.

4. Jackie Robinson, Home Plate, "The New Year: Hopes and Doubts," *Amsterdam News*, 6 January 1968.

5. In response to my queries about the Dumas shooting, Leonora Gidlund, of the New York City Department of Records, emailed me stating "We do not have any police records." I also contacted Maira Liriano of the New York Public Library, and while she provided me with possible avenues to information, none proved fruitful.

6. Clem Fiori and Earl Thomas, interview by author, Willingborough, N.J., digital recording, 4 June 2005.

7. Fiori interview.

8. Lois Silber to Jay Wright, letter 24 May 1968, LWP.

9. Lois Silber to Jay Wright, letter 23 May 1968, LWP.

10. Loretta Dumas, interview by author, digital recording, 4 December 2006.

11. Eugene B. Redmond, interview by author, East St. Louis, Ill., 13 May 2005.

12. Eugene B. Redmond, "Poetic Reflections Enroute to, and during, the Funeral and Burial of Henry Dumas, Poet (May 29, 1968)," *Black American Literature Forum* 22, no. 2 (summer 1988): 334–35.

13. Lois Silber to Jay Wright, letter 1 June 1968, LWP.

14. William Halsey, "What We Are Doing with Our Precious Tradition," senior thesis, SUNY Westbury, 1984, 2.

15. William Joseph, phone interview by author, 17 March 2010.

16. "'Bury Man Killed in Subway Fracas," *Amsterdam News*, 1 June 1968, 13.

17. John F. Szwed, *Space Is the Place: The Lives and Times of Sun Ra* (New York: Pantheon, 1997), 223.

18. Henry Dumas, "Getting Your Shit Together," 13 May 1968, HDP.

EPILOGUE

1. Sherman Fowler, interview by author, East St. Louis, Ill., 12 May 2005.

2. John K. Young, *Black Writers, White Publishers* (Jackson: University Press of Mississippi, 2006).

3. LeRoi Jones and Larry Neal, eds., *Black Fire Anthology*, 2nd ed. (New York: William and Morrow, 1969), xvi.

4. Young, *Black Writers, White Publishers*, 67.

5. Ibid., 87.

6. In the later Random House edition of *Poetry for My People*, Redmond changed the title to "Play Ebony Play Ivory." The former title was too similar to Margaret Walker's 1942 poem or praise song for African Americans, "For My People."

7. Eugene B. Redmond, phone interview by author, 23 February 2013.

8. Toni Morrison, "On Behalf of Henry Dumas," *Black American Literature Forum* 22, no. 2 (summer 1988): 310.

9. Eugene Redmond quoted in ibid.

10. Toni Morrison, phone interview by author, 20 April 2006.

11. Morrison's most elaborate fictional critique of this racial ideology emerges in *Paradise*, her 1997 novel.

12. Trudier Harris also suggests that Dumas influenced Morrison's literary develop-

ment, including the Sweet Home Plantation in *Beloved*, in *South of Tradition: Essays on African American Literature* (Athens: University of Georgia Press, 2002), 140–47.

13. Morrison, "On Behalf of Henry Dumas."

14. Hale Chatfield to Jay and Lois Wright, letter 22 October 1974, possession of Lois Wright.

15. Loretta Dumas to Hale Chatfield, letter 25 October 1974, possession of Loretta Dumas.

16. Eugene B. Redmond, interview by author, East St. Louis, Ill., 13 May 2005.

17. Houston A. Baker, "The Black Arts Movement and Fiction," *Norton Anthology of African American Literature*, 2nd ed., gen ed. Henry Louis Gates Jr. and Nellie Y. McKay (New York: Norton), 2004.

18. Reggie Scott Young, "Theoretical Influences and Experimental Resemblances: Ernest J. Gaines and Recent Critical Approaches to the Study of African American Fiction," in *Contemporary African American Fiction: New Critical Essays*, ed. Dana A. Williams (Columbus: Ohio State University Press, 2009), 14–15.

Selected Bibliography

BOOKS BY HENRY DUMAS

Poetry for My People. Edited by Hale Chatfield and Eugene Redmond. Carbondale: Southern Illinois University Press, 1970.

Ark of Bones and Other Stories. Edited by Hale Chatfield and Eugene Redmond. Carbondale: Southern Illinois University, 1971.

Play Ebony Play Ivory. Edited by Eugene B. Redmond. New York: Random House, 1974.

Ark of Bones and Other Stories. Edited by Hale Chatfield and Eugene Redmond. New York: Random House, 1974, reprint.

Jonoah and the Green Stone. Arranged by Eugene B. Redmond. New York: Random House, 1976.

Rope of Wind and Other Stories. Edited and introduced by Eugene B. Redmond. New York: Random House, 1979.

Goodbye, Sweetwater: New and Selected Stories. Edited and with an introduction by Eugene B. Redmond. New York: Thunder's Mouth Press, 1988.

Knees of a Natural Man: The Selected Poetry of Henry Dumas. Edited and introduced by Eugene B. Redmond. New York: Thunder's Mouth Press, 1989.

Echo Tree: The Collected Short Fiction of Henry Dumas. Edited and introduced by Eugene B. Redmond, critical introduction by John S. Wright. Minneapolis, Minn.: Coffee House Press, 2003.

WORKS BY OTHER AUTHORS

Als, Hilton. "Ghosts in the House." *New Yorker Magazine,* 27 October 2003, 64–75.

Arsenault, Raymond. *Freedom Riders: 1961 and the Struggle for Racial Justice.* New York: Oxford University Press, 2006.

Bachu, Amara. "Timing of First Births: 1930–34 to 1990–94." Working Paper No. 25, Population Division, U.S. Bureau of the Census, presented at the Annual Meeting of the Population Association of America, Chicago, Ill., April 1998.

Baldwin, James. *Go Tell It on the Mountain*. New York: Dial, 2000.

Baraka, Amiri. *Preface to a Twenty Volume Suicide Note*. New York: Totem/Corinth, 1961.

———. *The LeRoi Jones/Amiri Baraka Reader*. Edited by William J. Harris. New York: Thunder's Mouth Press, 1991.

———. *The Autobiography of LeRoi Jones*. Chicago, Ill.: Lawrence Hill Books, 1994.

Boyd, Valerie. *Wrapped in Rainbows: The Life of Zora Neale Hurston*. New York: Scribner, 2003.

Branch, Taylor. *Parting the Waters: America in the King Years, 1954–63*. New York: Simon and Schuster, 1988.

Brodkin, Karen. *How Jews Became White Folks*. New Brunswick, N.J.: Rutgers University Press, 1998.

Brokaw, Tom. *Boom! Voices of the Sixties*. New York: Random House, 2007.

Brown, Claude. *Manchild in the Promised Land*. New York: Macmillan, 1965.

Brown, Lloyd W. *Amiri Baraka*. Boston: Twayne, 1980.

Carson, Rachel. *Silent Spring*. New York: Mariner, 2002.

Cheuse, Alan. *Listening to the Page*. New York: Columbia University Press, 2001.

Cifelli, Edward M. *John Ciardi: A Biography*. Fayetteville: University of Arkansas Press, 1997.

Coontz, Stephanie. *Marriage: A History*. New York: Viking, 2005.

De Crèvecour, J. Hector St. John. *Letters from an American Farmer; and, Sketches of Eighteenth-century America*. New York: Penguin, 1981.

De Jongh, James. *Vicious Modernism: Black Harlem and the Literary Imagination*. New York: Cambridge, 1990.

Dent, Tom. "Umbra Days." *Black American Literature Forum* (now *African American Review*) 14, no. 3 (autumn 1980): 105–8.

Dillard, Tom. "Madness with a Past: An Overview of Race Violence in Arkansas History." *Arkansas Review* 32, no. 2 (August 2001): 93–100.

Di Prima, Diane. *Recollections of My Life as a Woman*. New York: Viking, 2001.

Dougan, Michael B. *Arkansas Odyssey: The Saga of Arkansas from Prehistoric Times to Present: A History*. Little Rock, Ark.: Rose Publishing, 1995.

Dray, Philip. *At the Hands of Persons Unknown*. New York: Random House, 2002.

Dyson, Michael Eric. *Mercy, Mercy Me: The Art, Loves, and Demons of Marvin Gaye*. New York: Basic Civitas, 2004.

———. *April 4, 1968, Martin Luther King Jr.'s Death and How It Changed America*. New York: Basic Civitas, 2008.

Early, Gerald L. *This Is Where I Came In: Black America in the 1960s*. Lincoln: University of Nebraska Press, 2003.

Ellison, Ralph. *Invisible Man*. New York: Vintage, 1952.

———. *The Collected Essays of Ralph Ellison*. New York: Modern Library, 2003.

Emerson, Ralph Waldo. *The American Scholar, Self Reliance, Compensation.* New York: American Book Company, 1893.

Fabre, Michel. *The Unfinished Quest of Richard Wright.* Urbana and Chicago: University of Illinois Press, 1993.

Faulkner, William. *The Faulkner Reader.* New York: Random House, 1954.

Fitzgerald, F. Scott. *Great Gatsby.* New York: Columbia University Press, 1999.

Foster, Edward Halsey. *Understanding the Beats.* Columbia: University of South Carolina Press, 1992.

Franklin, John Hope. *Mirror to America: The Autobiography of John Hope Franklin.* New York: Farrar, Straus and Giroux, 2005.

Gaither, Zella Hargrove. *Arkansas Confederate Home.* Little Rock, Ark.: New Era Press, 1920.

Garrow, David. *Bearing the Cross: Martin Luther King, Jr., and the Southern Christian Leadership Conference.* New York: William Morrow, 1986.

Gibbens, Byrd. "Some Men of Sweet Home." *Pulaski County Historical Review* 47, no. 3 (1999): 46–54.

Gilyard, Keith. *John Oliver Killens: A Life of Literary Activism.* Athens: University of Georgia Press, 2010.

Gitlin, Todd. *The Sixties: Years of Hope, Days of Rage.* New York: Bantam, 1987.

Gordon, Milton A. "An Analysis of Enrollment Data for Black Students in Institutions of Higher Education, from 1940–1972." *Journal of Negro Education* 45, no. 2 (spring 1976): 117–21.

Gregory, James N. *American Exodus: The Dust Bowl Migration and Okie Culture.* New York: Oxford University Press, 1989.

Griffin, Farah Jasmine. *"Who Set You Flowin?" The African American Migration Narrative.* New York: Oxford University Press, 1995.

Harris, Middleton, comp. *The Black Book.* New York: Random House, 1974.

Heckman, James J., and Paul A. LaFontaine. "The American High School Graduation Rate, Trends and Levels." National Bureau of Economic Research Working Paper 13670 (Dec. 2007).

Hemingway, Ernest. *Men without Women.* New York: Charles Scribner's Sons, 1927, reprint 1997.

Hentoff, Nat. "The New Jazz—Black, Angry and Hard to Understand." *New York Times Magazine,* 25 December 1966.

Hesse, Herman. *Siddhartha.* Translated by Hilda Rosner. New York: Bantam Books, 1957.

Hodes Martha, ed. *Sex, Love, Race: Crossing Boundaries in North American History.* New York: New York University Press, 1999.

Holley, Donald. "Leaving the Land of Opportunity: Arkansas and the Great Migration." *Arkansas Historical Quarterly* 64, no. 3 (autumn 2005): 245–61.

Hughes, Langston. *The Collected Poems of Langston Hughes.* New York: Knopf, 1996.

Jackson, Lawrence P. *The Indignant Generation, A Narrative History of Black Writers and Critics, 1934–1960.* Princeton, N.J.: Princeton University Press, 2011.

Jahn, Janheinz. *Muntu; An Outline of the New African Culture.* Translated by Marjorie Grene. New York: Grove Press, 1961.

Johnson, Abby. *Propaganda and Aesthetics: The Literary Politics of Afro-American Magazines in the Twentieth Century.* Amherst: University of Massachusetts Press, 1979.

Johnson, Ben F., III. *Arkansas in Modern America, 1930–1999.* Fayetteville: University of Arkansas Press, 2002.

Johnson, Robert A. *Lying with the Heavenly Woman.* San Francisco: HarperCollins, 1994.

Jones, Hettie. *How I Became Hettie Jones.* New York: Grove Press, 1990.

Jones, LeRoi. *Blues People.* New York: Morrow/Quill, 1963.

Joseph, Peniel E. *Waiting 'Til the Midnight Hour: A Narrative History of Black Power in America.* New York: Henry Holt, 2006.

Kilpatrick, Judith. "(Extra)Ordinary Men: African American Lawyers and Civil Rights in Arkansas before 1950." *Arkansas Law Review* 53 (2000): 345–76.

King, Martin Luther Jr., *A Testament of Hope, The Essential Writings and Speeches of Martin Luther King Jr.* San Francisco: HarperCollins, 1986.

Klinger, David. *Into the Kill Zone: A Cop's Eye View of Deadly Force.* New York: Jossey-Bass, 2004.

Levinson, Daniel J. *The Seasons of a Man's Life.* New York: Ballantine, 1979.

Levy, Peter B. *Civil War on Race Street: The Civil Rights Movement in Cambridge, Maryland.* Gainesville: University of Florida Press, 2003.

Lockwood, Lee. *Conversations with Eldridge Cleaver.* New York: Dell, 1970.

Madhubuti, Haki R. *Yellow Black: The First Twenty-one Years of a Poet's Life: A Memoir.* Chicago, Ill.: Third World Press, 2005.

Malcolm X, with Alex Haley. *Autobiography of Malcolm X.* New York: Ballantine, 1965.

Marable, Manning. *Malcolm X: A Life of Reinvention.* New York: Viking, 2011.

Marter, Joan. *Off Limits: Rutgers University and the Avant-Garde, 1957–63.* New Brunswick, N.J.: Rutgers University Press and the Newark Museum, 1999.

Marwick, Arthur. *The Sixties: Cultural Revolution in Britain, France, Italy and the United States c. 1958–c. 1974.* New York: Oxford, 1998.

Metzler, William H. "Population Movement in Arkansas." *Arkansas Gazette Sunday Magazine,* 21 April 1940. Quoted in Donald Holley, "Leaving the Land of Opportunity: Arkansas and the Great Migration," *Arkansas Historical Quarterly* 64, no. 3 (autumn 2005): 247.

Morrison, Toni. *The Bluest Eye.* New York: Plume, 1970.

———. *Song of Solomon.* New York: Plume, 1977.

———. *Beloved.* New York: Plume, 1987.

———. "On Behalf of Henry Dumas." *Black American Literature Forum* 22, no. 2 (summer 1988): 310–12.

Neal, Larry. *Visions of a Liberated Future: Black Arts Movement Writings.* Edited by Michael Schwartz. New York: Thunder's Mouth Press, 1989.

Perry, Theresa, Claude Steele, and Asa G. Hilliard III. *Young, Gifted and Black: Promoting High Achievement among African-American Students.* Boston: Beacon Press, 2004.

Petry, Ann. *The Street.* New York: Mariner, 1998.

Phelps, Christopher. "The Prophet Reconsidered." *Chronicle Review*, 18 January 2008.

Pollack, Josh. "Saudi Arabia and the United States, 1931–2003." *Middle East Review of International Affairs* 6, no. 3 (September 2002): 3.

Rampersad, Arnold. "Henry Dumas's World of Fiction." *Black American Literature Forum* 22, no. 2 (summer 1988): 329–32.

———. *Ralph Ellison: A Biography.* New York: Knopf, 2007.

Redmond, Eugene B. *Drum Voices: The Mission of Afro American Poetry.* New York: Anchor, 1976.

———. Introduction to *Jonoah and the Green Stone*, by Henry Dumas. New York: Random House, 1976.

———. "Poetic Reflections Enroute to, and during, the Funeral and Burial of Henry Dumas, Poet (May 29, 1968)." *Black American Literature Forum* 22, no. 2 (summer 1988): 334–35.

———. Introduction to *Knees of a Natural Man*, by Henry Dumas. New York: Thunder's Mouth Press, 1989.

Reilly, Charlie. *Conversations with Amiri Baraka.* Jackson: University Press of Mississippi, 1994.

Ritterhouse, Jennifer. *Growing Up Jim Crow: The Racial Socialization of Black and White Southern Children, 1890–1940.* Chapel Hill: University of North Carolina Press, 2006.

Romano, Renee C. *Race Mixing: Black-White Marriage in Postwar America.* Cambridge, Mass.: Harvard University Press, 2003.

Salzman, Jack. *Bridges and Boundaries, African Americans and American Jews.* New York: George Braziller, 1992.

Saul, Scott. "The Devil and Henry Dumas." *Boston Review*, October/November 2004: 45–46.

———. *Freedom Is, Freedom Ain't: Jazz and the Making of the Sixties.* Cambridge, Mass.: Harvard University Press, 2003.

Schultz, Debra L. *Going South: Jewish Women in the Civil Rights Movement.* New York: New York University, 2001.

Smethurst, James. *The Black Arts Movement: Literary Nationalism in the 1960s and 1970s.* Chapel Hill: University of North Carolina Press, 2005.

Sollors, Werner. *Amiri Baraka/LeRoi Jones: The Quest for a "Populist Modernism."* New York: Columbia University Press, 1978.

Sowell, Thomas "The Education of Minority Children." http://www.tsowell.com /speducat.html#N11, accessed 10 October 2011.

Stein, Gertrude. *Stein: Writings, 1903–1932.* Vol. 1. New York: Library of America, 1998.

Stevens, J. David. "'She War a Woman': Family Roles, Gender, and Sexuality in Bret Harte's Western Fiction." *American Literature: A Journal of Literary History, Criticism, and Bibliography* 69, no. 3 (1997): 571–93.

Stockley, Grif. *Blood in Their Eyes: The Elaine Massacres of 1919.* Fayetteville: University of Arkansas Press, 2004.

Szwed, John F. *Space Is the Place: The Lives and Times of Sun Ra.* New York: Pantheon, 1997.

Talalay, Kathryn. *Composition in Black and White: The Life of Philippa Schuyler.* New York: Oxford University Press.

Whitman, Walt. *Leaves of Grass.* New York: Doubleday, 1940.

Wilkerson, Isabel. *The Warmth of Other Suns.* New York: Random House, 2010.

Wilson, Christopher. *Cop Knowledge.* Chicago, Ill.: University of Chicago Press, 2000.

Wilson, Sondra K. *Meet Me at the Theresa.* New York: Atria Books, 2004.

Wright, Jay. Introduction to *Play Ebony Play Ivory*, by Henry Dumas. New York: Random House, 1974.

Wright, Richard. *Black Boy (American Hunger).* New York: Library of America, 1991.

———. *Native Son.* New York: HarperPerennial, 1993.

Young, John K. *Black Writers, White Publishers.* Jackson: University of Mississippi Press, 2006.

Index

Ponton, Ashley, 31, 34, 36, 40, 140
Ponton, Laura, 36
Ponton, Loretta (Loretta Dumas) (LPD). *See*
  Dumas, Loretta (née Ponton) (LPD)
Porter, Adella (Adella Hale), 5, 14–15, 18–19
Porter, Appliance (Appliance Watson), 4–5,
  13–16, 21–22, 55, 150, 152–53
Porter, George, 14, 15
Porter, George "Sonny," 16
Porter, Lawrence, 52
Porter, Lynn "Minnie," 14, 17, 18, 168n12
Porter, Warrant, 52
posthumous publications of HLD, 2–3, 53, 62,
  101, 106, 116, 133, 154, 156–64, 172n12, 177n6.
  See also legacy of HLD; publishers and
  publication of HLD's writings
Powell, Geneva, 20
P.S. 5 elementary school, and HLD, 25–26
psychology, of white supremacy, 63–65, 172n22
publishers and publication of HLD's writings:
  overview of, 2, 110; "Ark of Bones," 102,
  116; *Ark of Bones and Other Stories*, 116–17,
  160, 162, 164; in *The Black Book* anthology,
  101, 162, 174n1; "black ohm," 153–54; black
  publishers and, 159; "Black Star Line,"
  165; black writers in white world and,
  73–75, 109, 113–14, 159–60, 162–65; "A Boll
  of Roses," 61, 79, 93, 102; *The Camel* and,
  33; "A City Game" ("A Harlem Game"),
  53–55, 93; "The Crossing," 4; "East Saint
  Hell," 122; *Echo Tree*, 165, 170n24; "Echo
  Tree," 51–52, 93, 170n24, 171n24, 172n22;
  "Epiphany," 135; Farrar, Straus and
  Giroux and, 108–9; financial needs of
  HLD and, 110; "Fon," 159–60; "Getting
  Our Shit Together," 153–54; "Goodbye,
  Sweetwater," 22, 81–82; "Harlem," 102, 111;
  "I Laugh Talk Joke," 142; intenseness of
  HLD and, 108–9; interracial relationships
  in context of, 103–8; *Jonoah and the Green
  Stone*, 36, 62, 99, 102, 106–7; "Kef 33," 38;
  "Kef 35," 89; *Knees of a Natural Man*, 133;
  "Knees of a Natural Man," 112, 175n15;
  "Lake, The," 7–8, 123–24, 141; "Listen
  to the Sound of My Horn," 93; literary
  affirmation for HLD and, 110; "Love Song,"
  73; LPD and, 157; LSW's assistance and,
  108, 110; "Machines Can Do It Too (IBM
  Blues)," 96; "The Metagenesis of Sun
  Ra," 117; "A New Proposal," 138–40; *Norton*
  and, 165; "Oceanic," 93; "Ode to Otis," 135;
  "Our King is Dead," 138; "Outer Space

Blues," 117; in *Oxford Anthology . . .* , 165;
  "The Playground Is My Home," 175n15;
  Poetry for My People / Play Ebony Play Ivory,
  160, 162, 177n6; posthumous publications,
  2–3, 53, 62, 101, 106, 116, 133, 154, 156–64,
  172n12, 177n6; "Rain God," 4; Random
  House and, 160–63, 165, 177n6; research
  on, 157; "Riot or Revolt," 102, 111–12;
  "Son of Msippi," 10; "Strike and Fade,"
  111–12; "Take This River!," 63–65, 172n22;
  "Thalia," 7–8; Viking Press and, 105–10;
  "Will the Circle Be Unbroken?," 4, 102,
  119–21, 145, 159, 165; "Zebra Goes Wild
  Where the Sidewalk Ends," 165. *See also*
  black writers; literary aspirations and
  setbacks, for HLD; *and specific writers*
publishers and publishing, and employment
  for LSW, 110, 111. *See also specific publishers
  and publishing companies*

race consciousness: overview of, 6; African
  diaspora community and, 128; black
  writers and, 75–76; interracial relationships
  in context of, 85, 87, 120–21; LSW and, 80;
  universal consciousness versus, 6, 100,
  113–19, 146; whites and, 6, 103–4; in writings
  by HLD, 101–2. *See also* Dumas, Henry Lee
  (HLD)
racial equality (civil rights). *See* civil rights
  (racial equality)
racial practices and violence: blacks' response
  to, 127–28, 138, 143, 145–46, 149; civil rights
  and, 142–43; in Harlem, 2–3, 143, 146–49,
  151–52, 177n15; Jim Crow and, 11, 16–18,
  20–21, 20–22; segregation and, 11, 16, 20–22,
  26, 60; in the South, 142. *See also* civil
  rights (racial equality); integration, and
  education; whites
racial separatism, 65–69, 78, 86, 172n22
Rampersad, Arnold, 7, 24, 71
Random House, 101, 109, 160–63, 165, 174n1,
  177n6
Raphael, Lennox, 6, 75–76, 102–4
Raphael, Maryanne, 75
Redmond, Eugene B.: biographical
  information about, 132–33; *Black American
  Literature Forum* and, 7; on blacks'
  response to racial violence, 138; black
  writers in white world and, 162–65; EHE
  program and, 132–33; friendship between
  HLD and, 132–33, 135; funeral for HLD
  and, 149–50; legacy and posthumous